ibiza & formentera

Gastronomy and Cuisine

Photography Oriol Aleu
Cuisine and stylism Ana Torróntegui
Texts Marga Font
Graphic design Joseta Torróntegui

TRIANGLE BOOKS

Cuisine_**ibiza&formentera**

Coordination and editing of the project: Oriol Aleu
Cuisine, stylism: Ana Torróntegui
Adaptation and revision of the recipes: Toni Moné
Texts: Marga Font
Graphic design and layout: Joseta Torróntegui
Kitchen assistant: Maria Torróntegui
Photographic pre-production: Oriol Casanoves
Photography: Oriol Aleu
Translation: Steve Cedar

ISBN: 978-84-8478-389-3
Registration number: B-11972-2009

Printed in Barcelona
7-2018

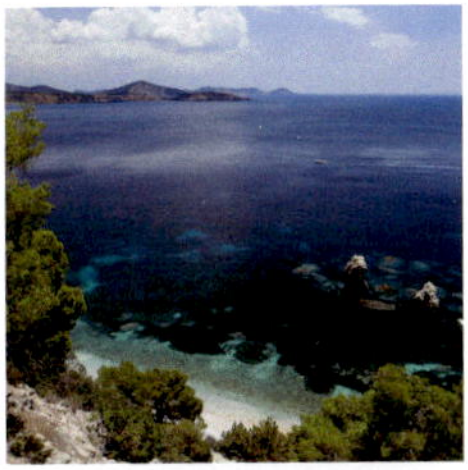
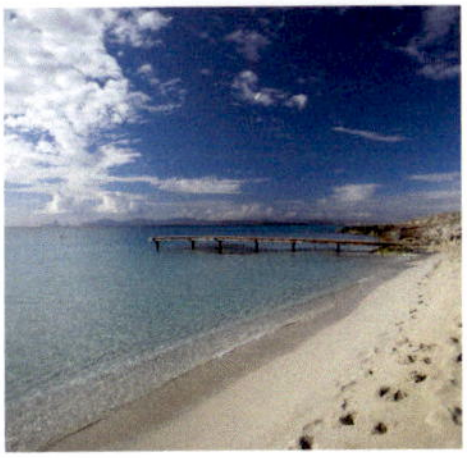
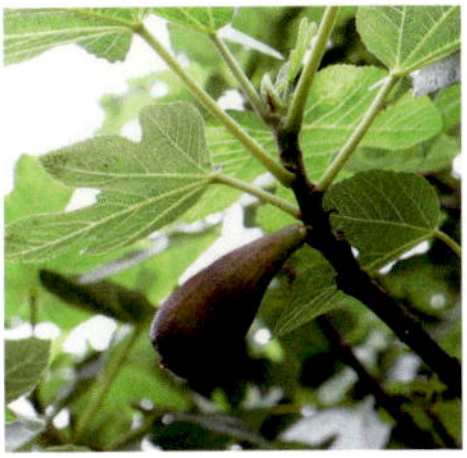
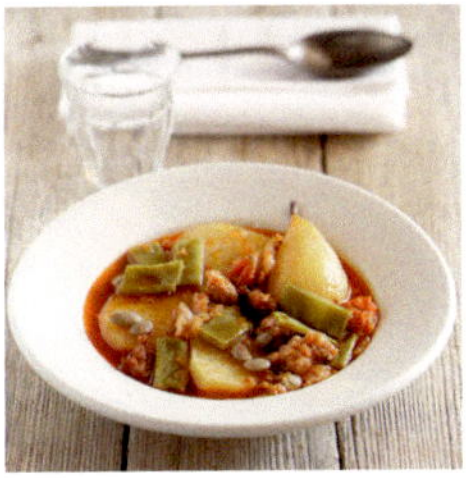

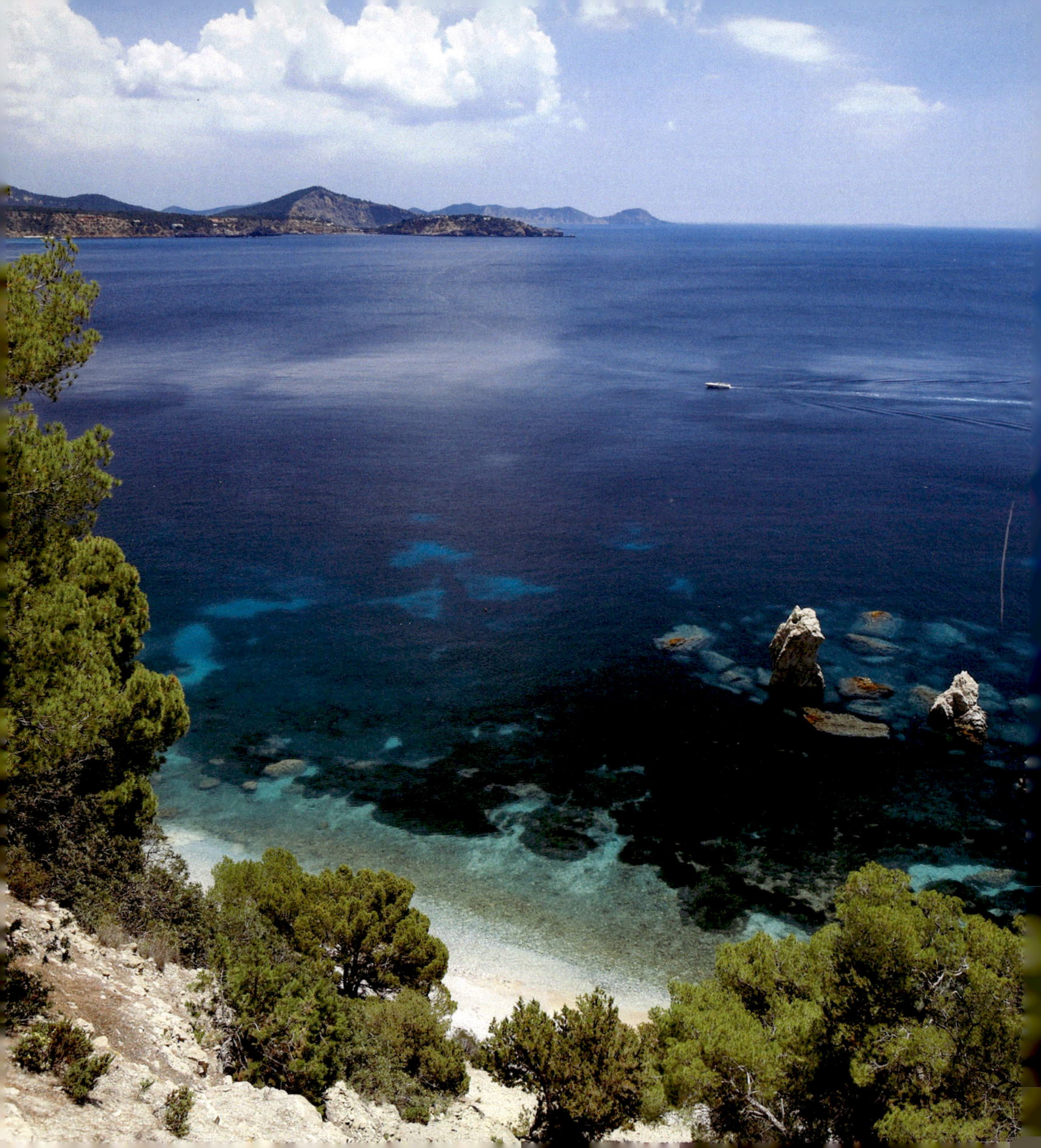

The North American writer Truman Capote was right when he referred to the islands: "Setting foot on one is like going along the walkway of a boat: the very suspension possesses you, it seems that nothing bad or vulgar can happen to you". This is indeed the sensation one has when reaching Ibiza and Formentera, authentic paradises even today in the 21st century despite the spread of tourism. They preserve their traditions and a beautiful, overwhelming landscape, combined with an air of freedom that sharpens up the senses.

Nevertheless, living on what is a small island in the middle of the Mediterranean —with very dry summers and very little rain— requires a great deal of imagination and ingenuity when preparing a recipe book. The land and the sea are generous, but an infinite number of hours and days of exhausting work must be put in to obtain their fruits. From them come the basic products —vegetables, fruit, meat and fish— which later art and necessity, with the passing of time, turn into gastronomic delights.

This is how it has been on Ibiza (Eivissa in Catalan) and Formentera, for centuries truly isolated islands, where a cuisine was formed made with seasonal products and based on the Mediterranean trilogy: wheat, wine and olive oil. Traditional, indeed, passed on by word of mouth from generation to generation, prepared with local products, and which luckily still conserves in its essence, its own gastronomic philosophy. A true item of World Heritage, as all the local cuisines of the world should be declared.

Mediterranean legacy and tradition

The invaders that passed through these islands left a culinary trail that can still be tasted today. Thus, in Formentera they still salt fish, as the Phoenicians probably did to preserve it for a long time. It is an ancestral technique that also produces unique landscapes: clean and salted, the fish is left to dry in the sun, often hung from the branches of a dry savin, giving the impression to the foreigner that on this island the fish grow from trees.

Although the Greeks did not settle on the Pine Islands, their gastronomic influences did reach here, extended across the Mediterranean: wheat bread, fish fried with olive oil or stews perfumed with aromatic herbs. The Romans probably remained on the islands between the 1st and 5th centuries, and refined the cuisine with sauces for meats and fish and the use of vinegar, a great food preserver.

The Arabs also enriched the island menu: specialists in the subtle combination of herbs and spices they introduced the use of saffron, sugar and cinnamon, sweetening above all confectionery. Perhaps, however, their most important legacy was the systems of irrigation and full use of water, which enabled them to introduce new vegetables, garden produce and fruits. This is what occurred, for example, in Ses Feixes, a small humid area close to the city of Eivissa and the Beach of Talamanca, which the Arabs channelled and where they established irrigation by capillarity. For centuries this was a very productive area that provided the city with garden produce and vegetables.

The Catalan conquest and repopulation of the 13th century brought new tastes, such as the use of lard, today on the decline in favour of the healthier olive oil. Also the *sofrit* —a sauce

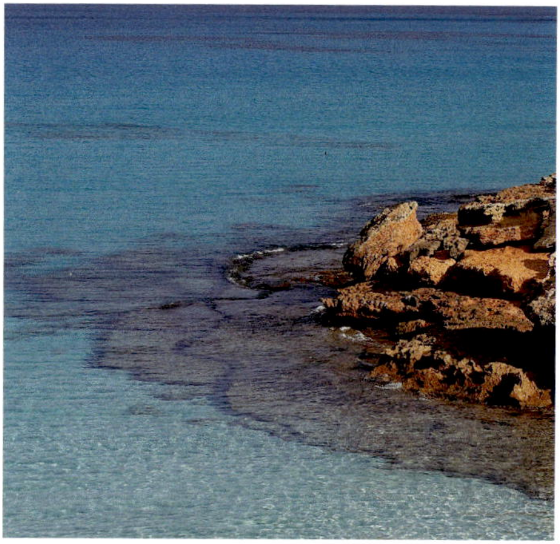

The rural landscape of Ibiza and Formentera is made up of isolated houses that traditionally have formed part of a self-sufficient life.

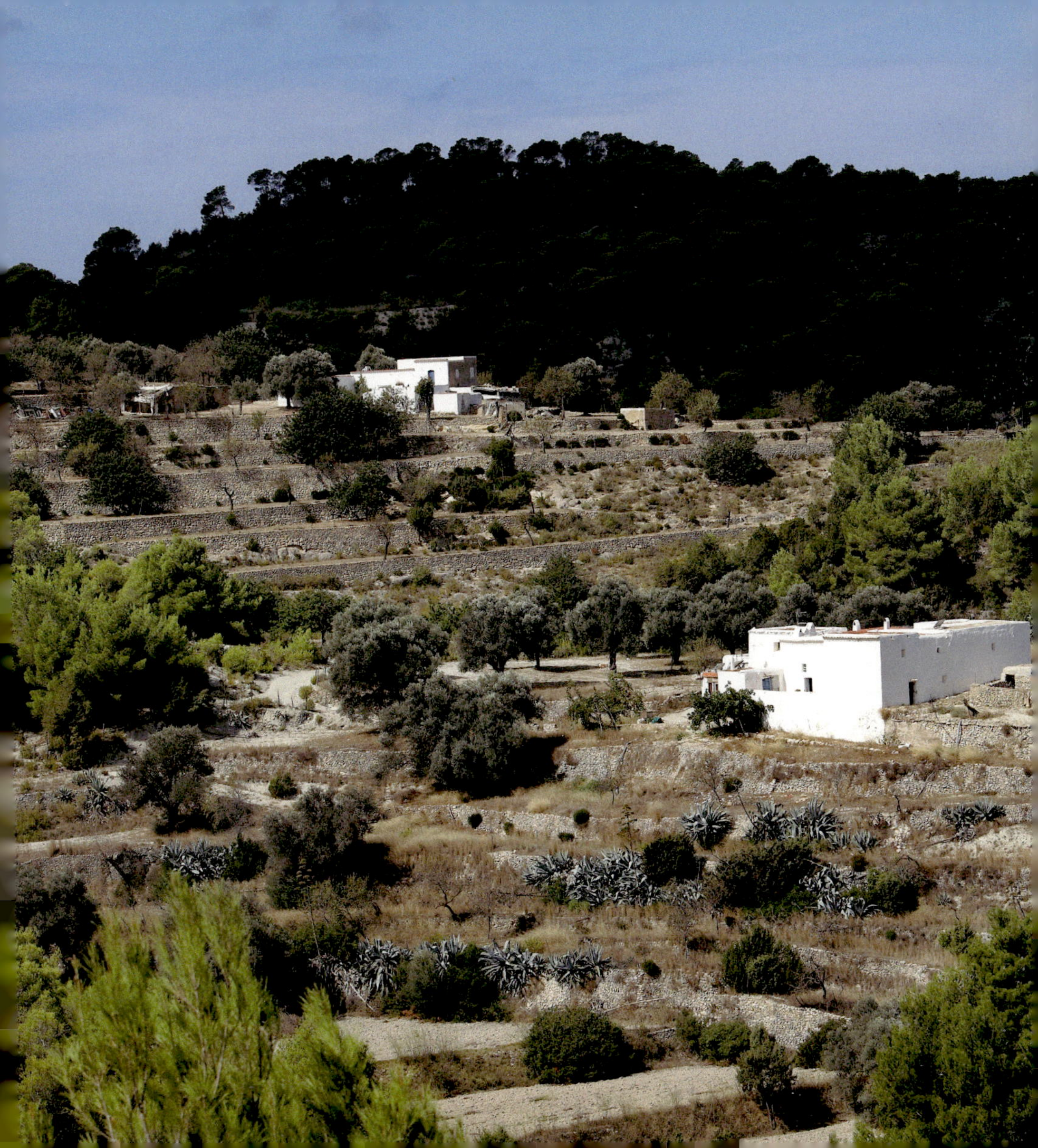

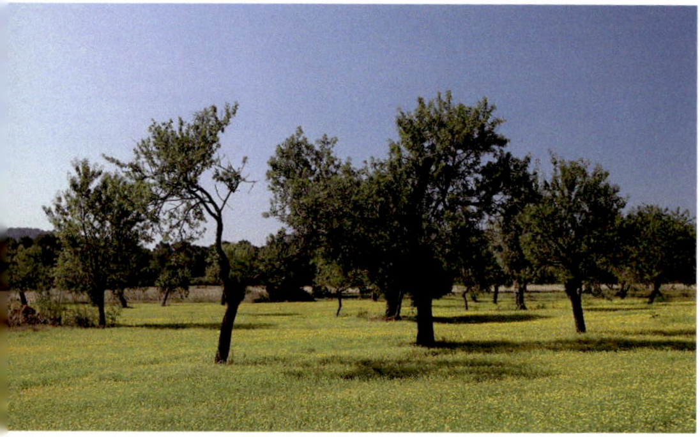

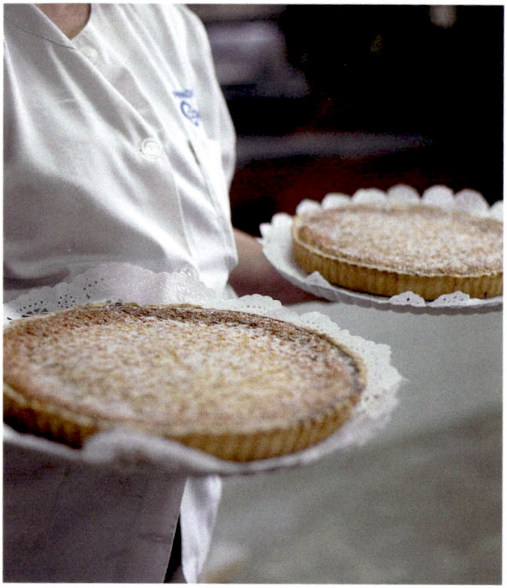

Fruit, almond and carob trees scatter the Pine Islands' fields. The *flaó*, below, is the star of confectionery.

base of olive oil, onion, tomato and garlic, with numerous variants—, and the *picada* or spicy sauce —the final touch to round off meat or fish stews, made from basil, parsley, *ñora* red pepper, saffron, almonds and toasted bread. The variety of *sofrits* and *picades* is infinite, of an extreme, highly personal and hereditary creativity.

In the 16th century came products from America that are today as Mediterranean as the potato, tomato and pepper, which enriched the diet and the recipe book. Two centuries later salted cod had the same effect: boats from Newfoundland and Iceland disembarked in Ibiza, while loading their holds with salt from the local salt flats for their new high sea campaigns. As in a large part of Europe, cod was triumphant in the Pine Islands, led above all by the typical dishes of Lent.

Traditional dishes and specialities. The cuisine prepared today in homes and restaurants on the Pine Islands synthesises the eating habits of their inhabitants over the last centuries. The traditional recipe book was compiled in a detailed way in the excellent and meticulous book *Bon profit! El llibre de la cuina eivissenca*, by Joan Castelló Guasch, which features everyday, seasonal and speciality dishes from Ibiza and Formentera.

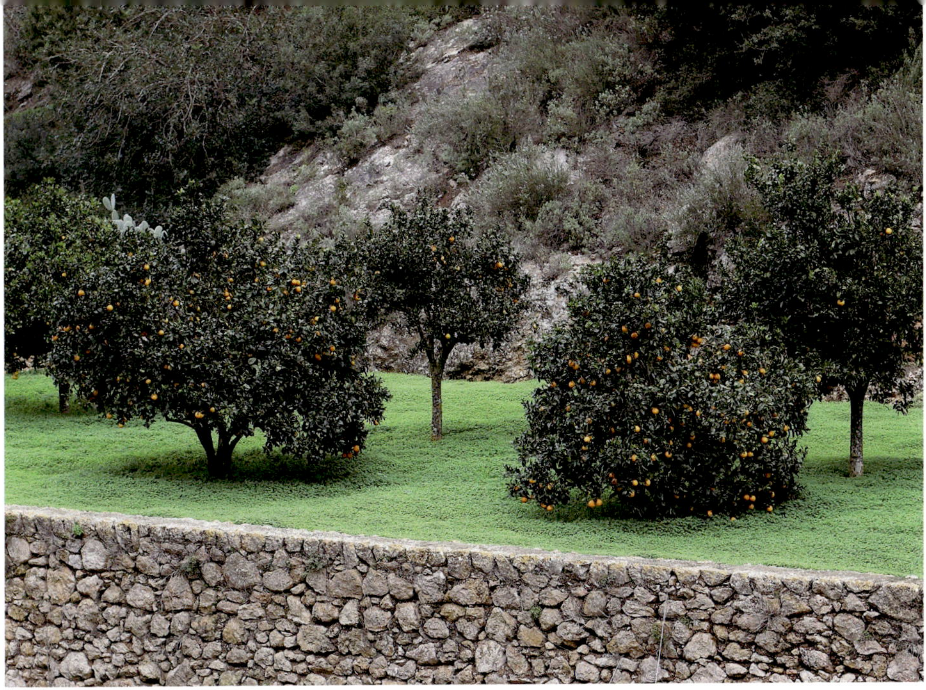

Salads and soups are prepared with vegetables and pulses. Among the former feature the traditional ones with green pepper, tomato and onion, as well as with dried fish in Formentera. Of the soups we should mention, because of its austere wisdom, the *pancuit*, made with garlic, parsley, dry bread and egg; the *sopa i bullit* —a stew with mixed meats, chickpeas, potatoes, cabbage, celery, onion and tomato—, and the vegetable purée.

Wheat pasta is also an important food, the main or accompanying ingredient of some dishes. In the past they prepared *formigons*, small balls made from wheat with a little water passed through a sieve, and later baked. They also made noodles, and semolina accompanied some dishes, such as the very modest semolina with wild mushrooms. They still eat today, as in yesteryear, short noodles with rabbit. And the spiral strips or *burbaies* appear in savoury recipes or, curious-

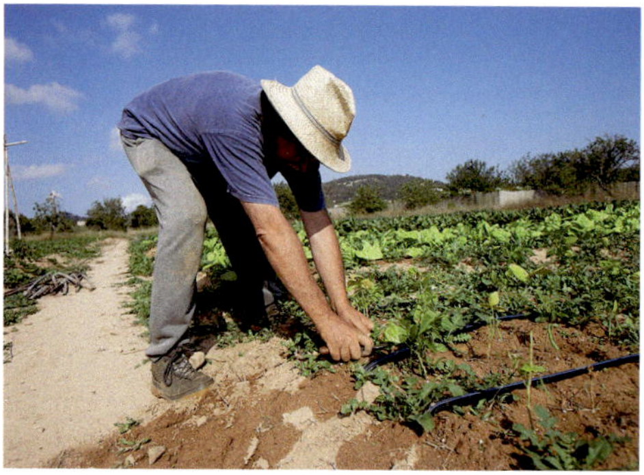

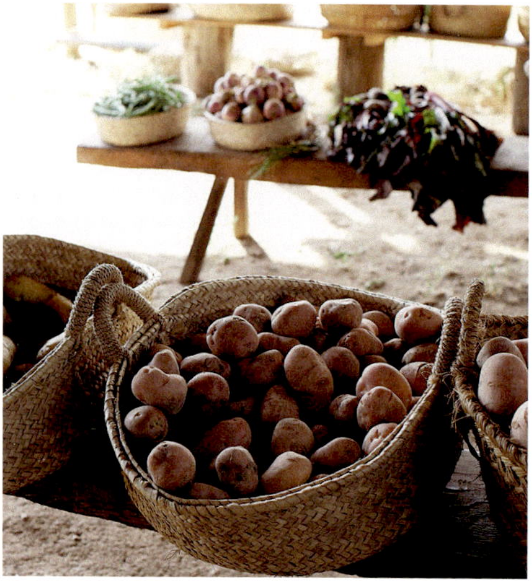

The Pla de Corona, in the district of Sant Antoni de Portmany, is one of the most fertile areas of the island of Ibiza.

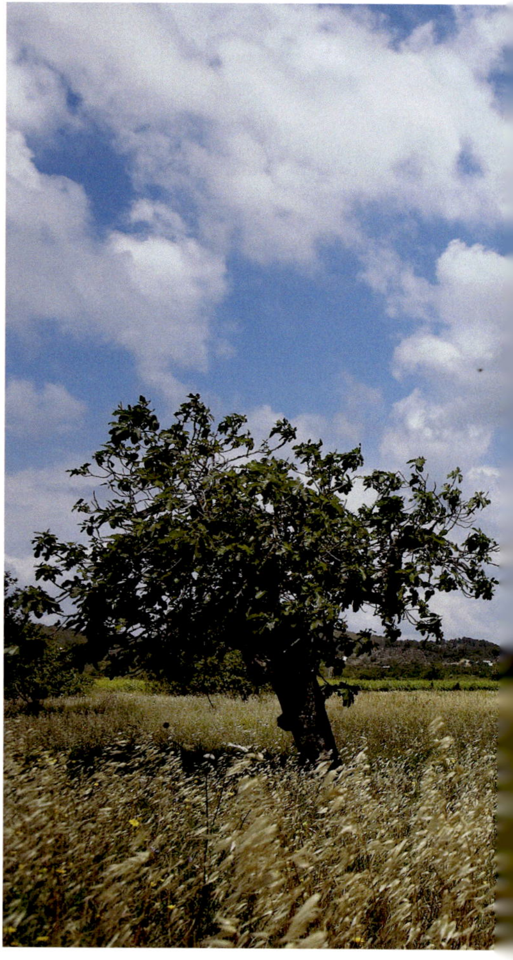

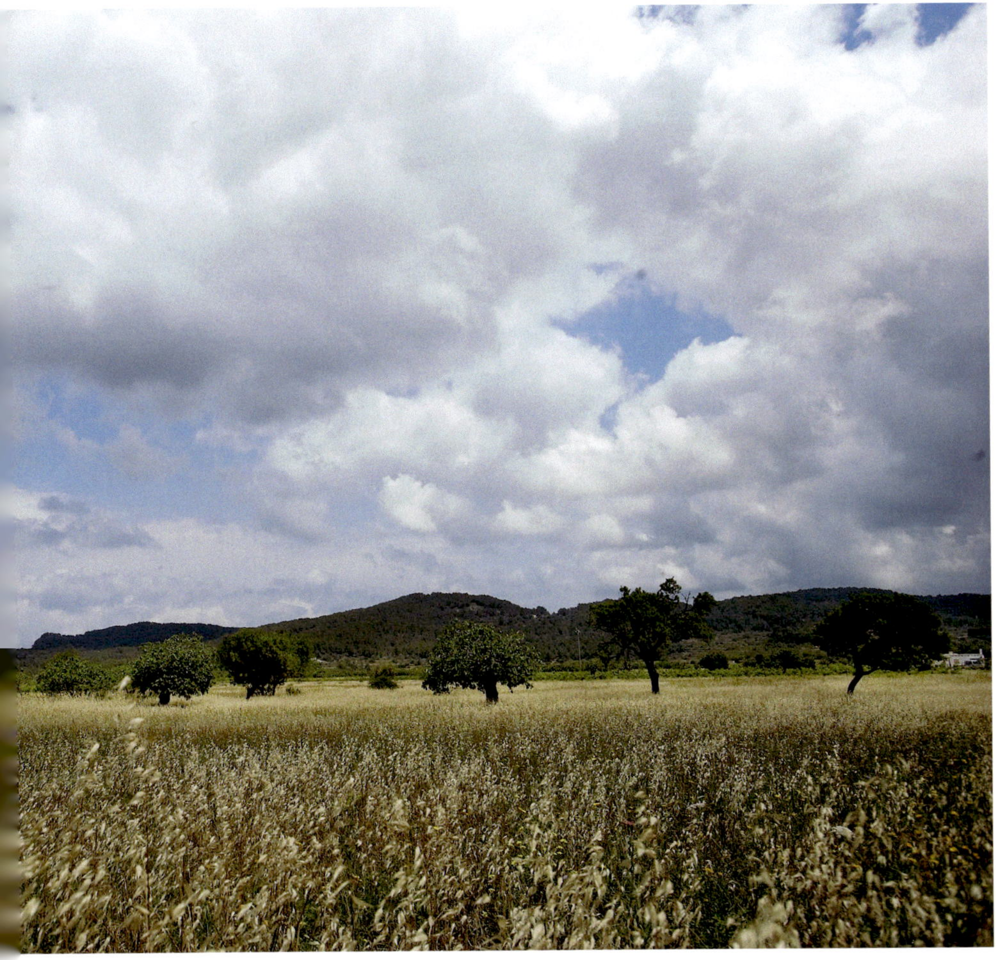

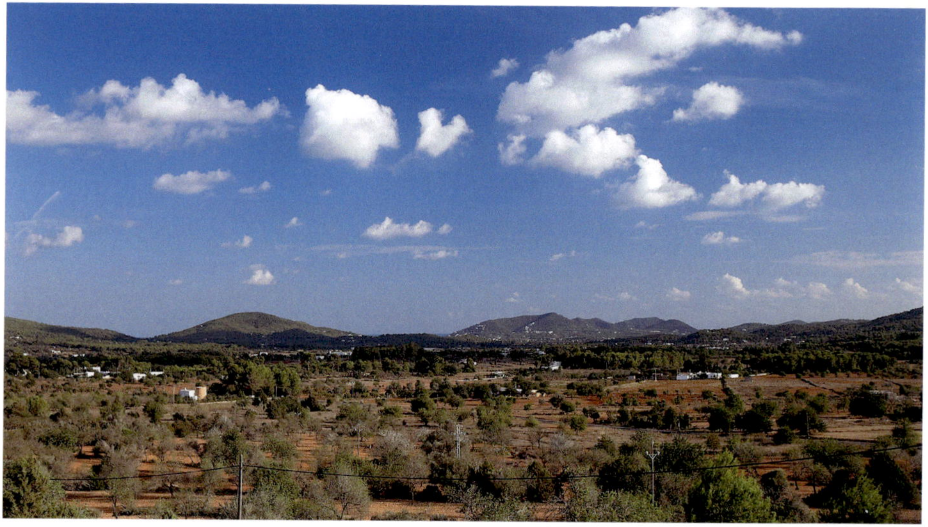

ly, sweets: in the Sant Joan macaronis they are boiled in milk with sugar, cinnamon and lemon, and served as a dessert, covered with sugar, cheese and cinnamon.

Many of the star dishes feature rice, such as the unforgettable fisherwoman's rice, in which first you eat the fish and seafood with which the stock has been prepared, and while the rice is being cooked, which is served as a second course; rice with dog-fish (*gató*), with beans or cabbage, *a la bruta* —with squid in its ink... A gastronomic world in itself. The stews and hotpots combine different meats and vegetables, always enriched with aromatic herbs: rabbit with peas or onion, meatball stew, peasant *sofrit* or fry-mix —*sobrassada* (Mallorcan sausage), sausage and *botifarró* (black pudding) with potatoes, all well stewed and spiced—, the hotpot (broad beans and peas with sausage and *sobrassada*) and the sublime, for simplicity, roast suckling pig.

Traditional rural life is still alive, above all in the inland areas of Ibiza and Formentera.

Nevertheless, there is no doubt that fish and seafood are the overwhelmingly more important ingredients, for their variety and wise preparation that enhances all their qualities, whether we are cooking some simple fried *raors (Xyrichthys novacula,* cleaver wrasse*)*, any grilled fresh fish, or more elaborate dishes, such as stuffed squid or octopus with peppers or onion. We should not forget one of the star recipes: the *borrida de rajada*, pickled skate, boiled and stewed with a sauce made with garlic, toasted bread, parsley, almonds and egg.

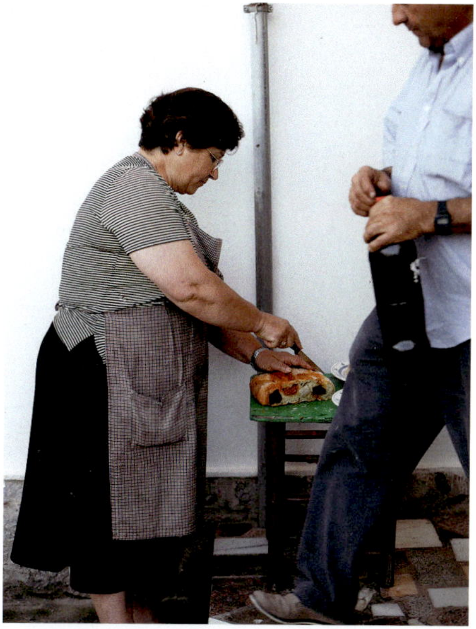

In the past some dishes were only prepared on specific dates. During Lent the *cuinat* was prepared from vegetables and pulses. The omnipresent today flaó —a unique cake made with mint and fresh cheese—, used to be made only at Easter, when the best cheeses were produced. There are, however, exceptions to the rule: the Christmas sauce, made from stock and almonds, which today as in yesteryear is only made during this seasonal period. It is a recipe typical of the Pine Islands, the *Pitiusas*, that arouses local passions. It is made in large quantities so that it lasts from Christmas through to Kings' Day on January 6th, and is eaten as a dip for the Christmas cake.

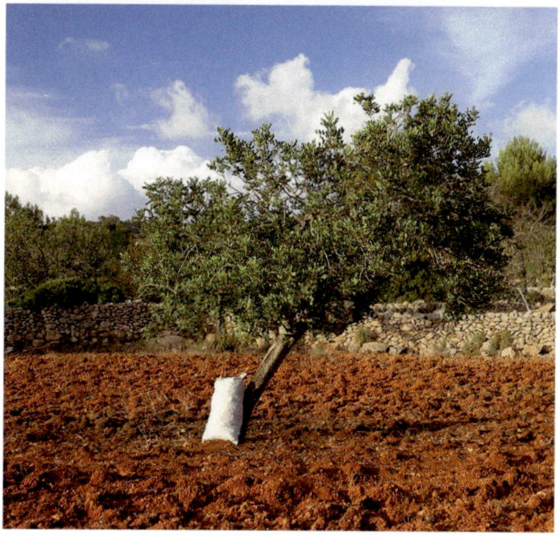

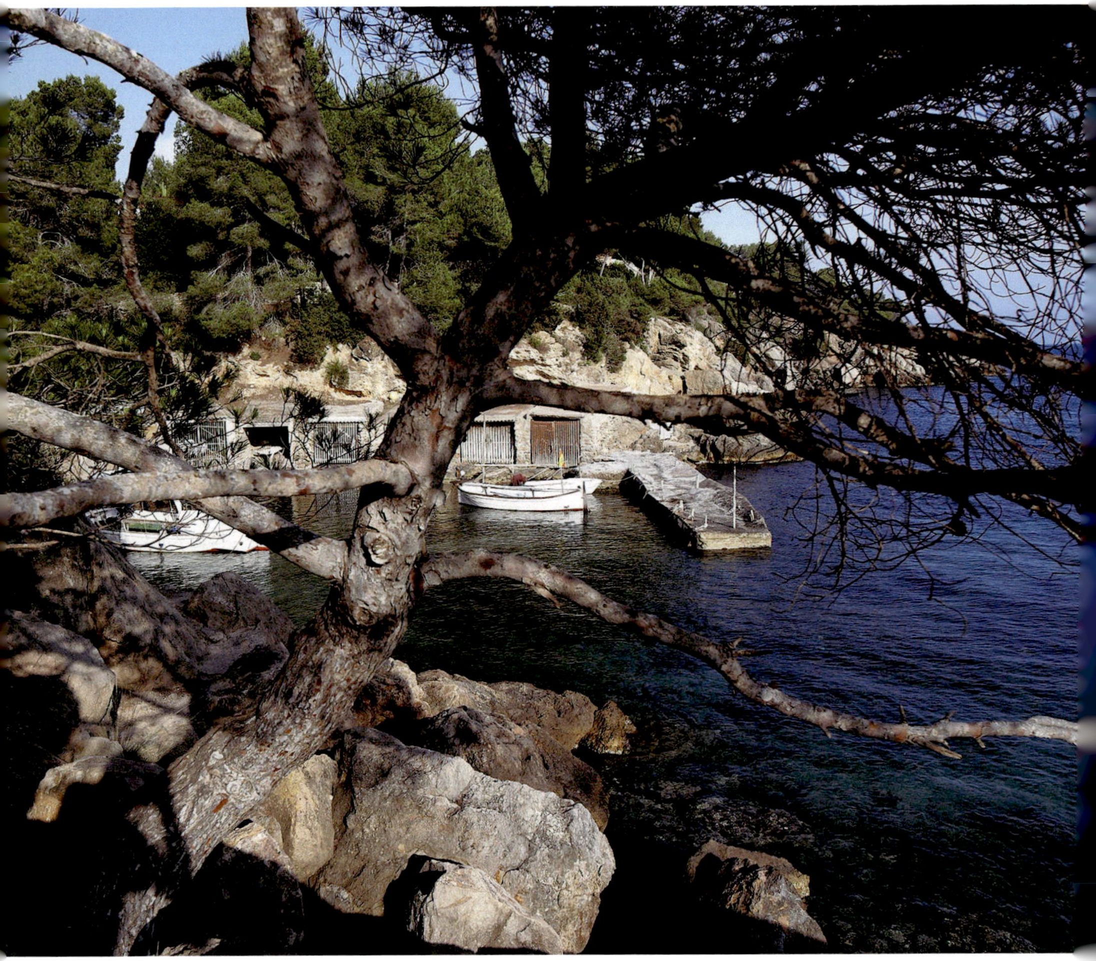

There are dishes that require two stages of preparation (called *menjar aparellat*, paired meal) and which are eaten together. This is the case of the *bullit de Nadal* (Christmas stew), which is prepared with salt pork (*xulla*) and poultry meat and bacon, the stock of which is used for the Christmas sauce; or the *bullit de peix*, the stock of which is eaten in soup before eating the fish.

Some specialities are the result of the inventiveness of using other preparations, such as the *sofrit* of potatoes and meat, which is made by sautéing the remains of the stock in oil with garlic or parsley. Others have disappeared along with their ingredients: the sea urchins —a delicious meat, but today in diminishing numbers and protected— appeared in some stews and rice dishes. This is also the case of the Balearic tern (*virot*, a species endemic to the Balearics in danger of extinction) and the turtle, which were the stars of typical dishes in Formentera.

The bars in the towns are the best places for tasting the local delights, such as a tapa of fried octopus. And, naturally, a glass of islands' spirits, the *frígola* or the aromatic and digestive herb liquors.

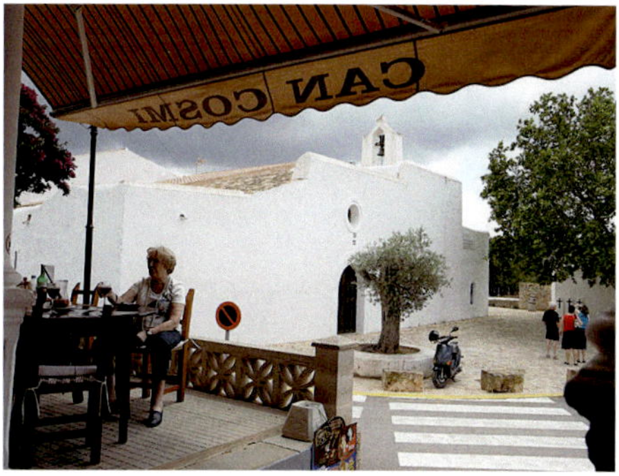

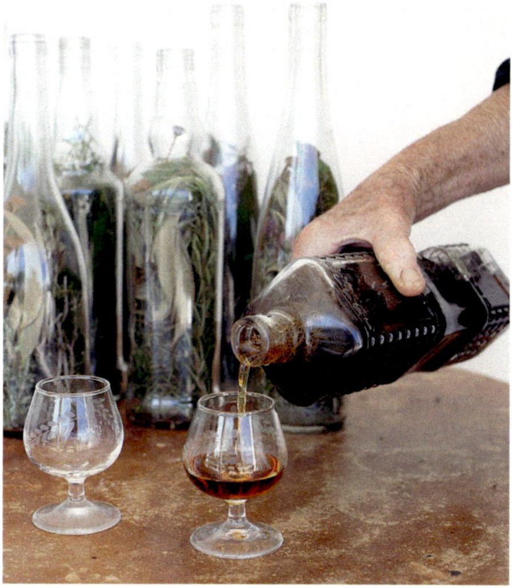

Above, the famous Can Cosmi bar, in Santa Agnès de Corona, an ideal spot to try the herbs, the local medicinal liquor.

The landscape

Ibiza, Formentera and the many adjoining islets are the westernmost islands of the Balearic archipelago, and make up a whole that is known as the *Pitiusas*, or Pine Islands. Due to their situation facing the eastern coastline of the Iberian Peninsula and close to that of North Africa, they have often had a strategic importance that has favoured trade relations with other peoples. However, as they are small islands, they have also experienced periods of absolute isolation.

Although today little more than three per cent of the local population dedicate their time to agriculture and livestock, in the past these activities —along with fishing and forestry— were primordial. For centuries production was for survival and conditioned by the frequent pirate attacks, which decreased towards the end of the 17th century.

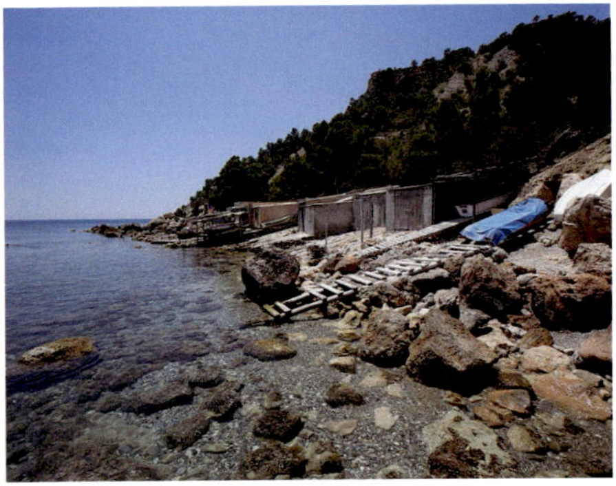

The landscape of the Pine Islands —such as the seductive island of Es Vedrà, on the right— still attracts visitors from all over the world.

At the end of the 18th century an Improvement Plan was carried out to modernise the agriculture and export some products: new estates were created, forestry was introduced and a network of paths was opened that linked the countryside with the city. Even though these improvements were not that efficiently applied, it did represent the change of agricultural production.

However, as from the tourist boom of the 1960s, the workers began to abandon the country to work in tourism-related activities, today the only economic driving force of Ibiza and Formentera. Today the most important crops are forages, barley, wheat, pulses, potatoes and garden produce.

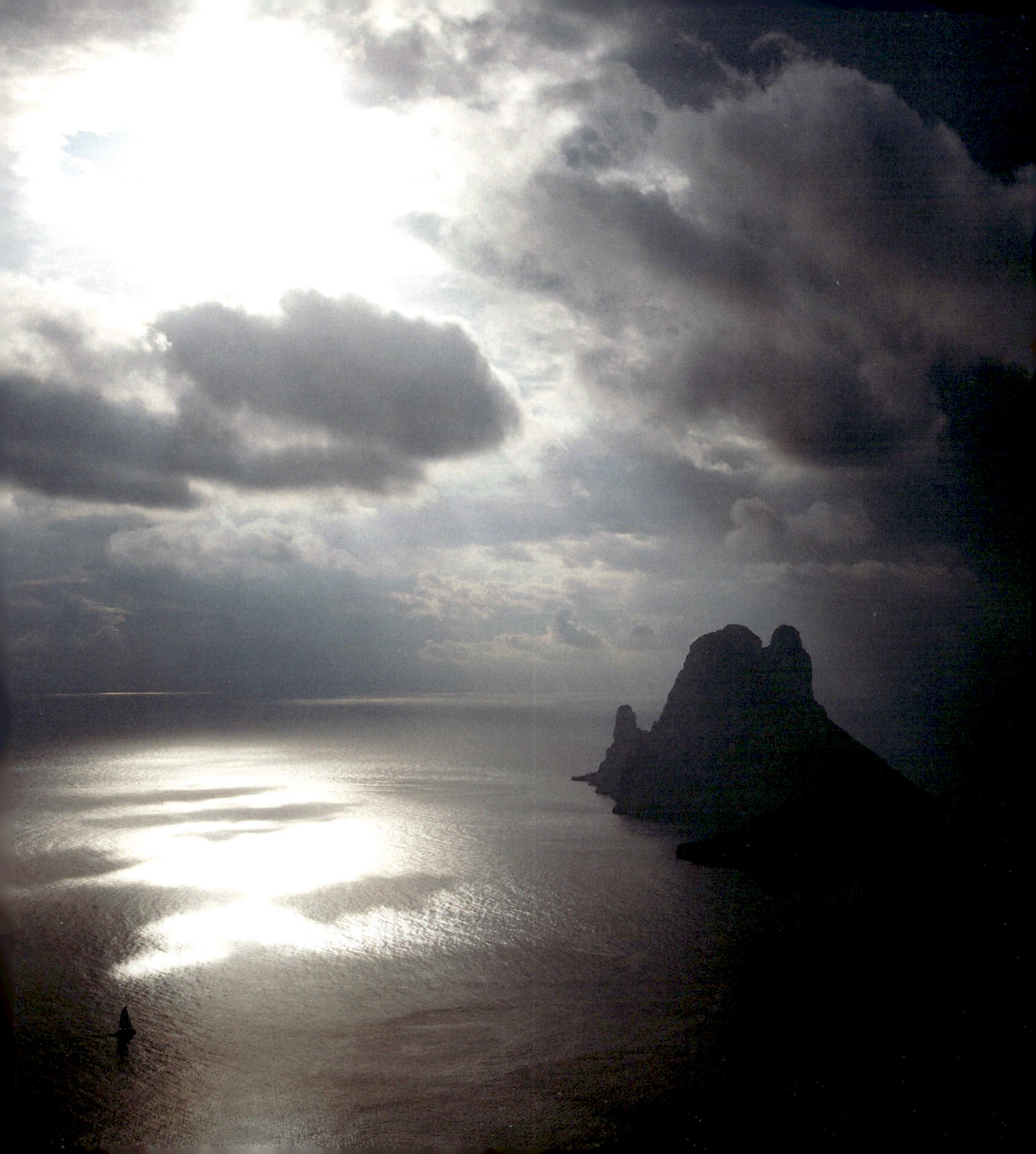

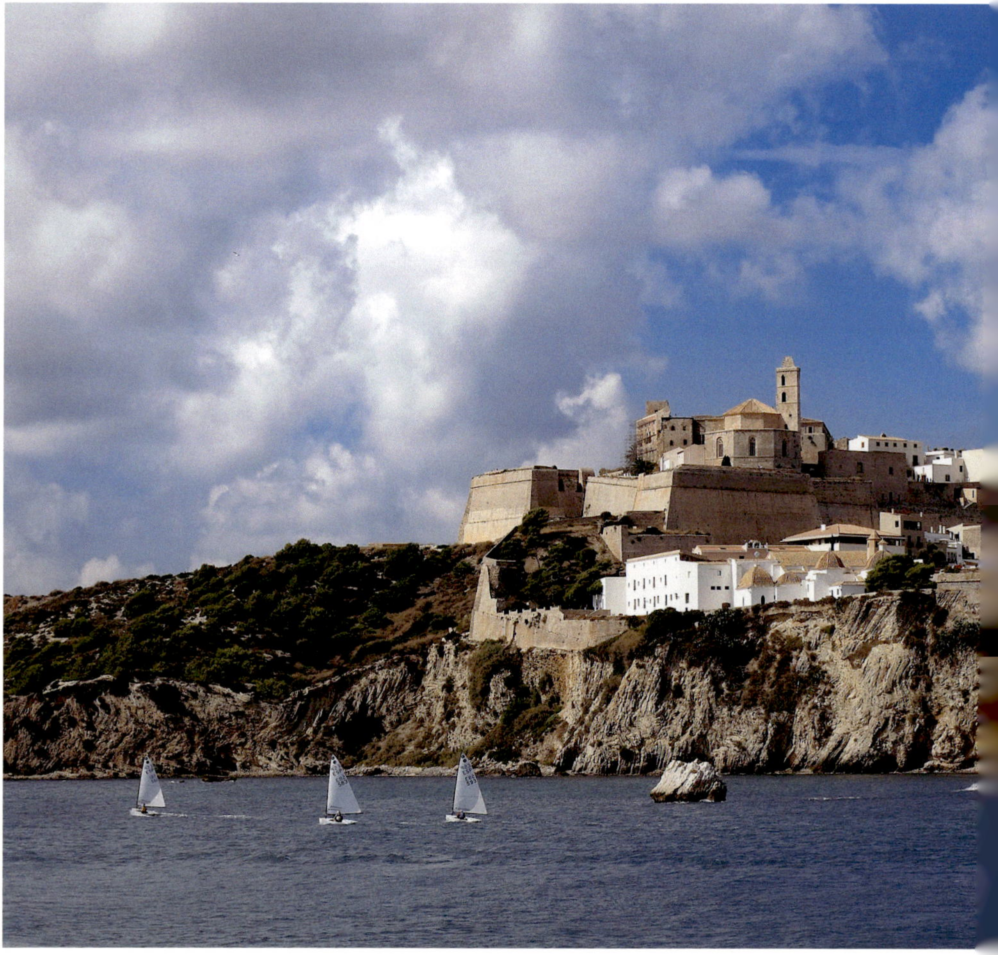

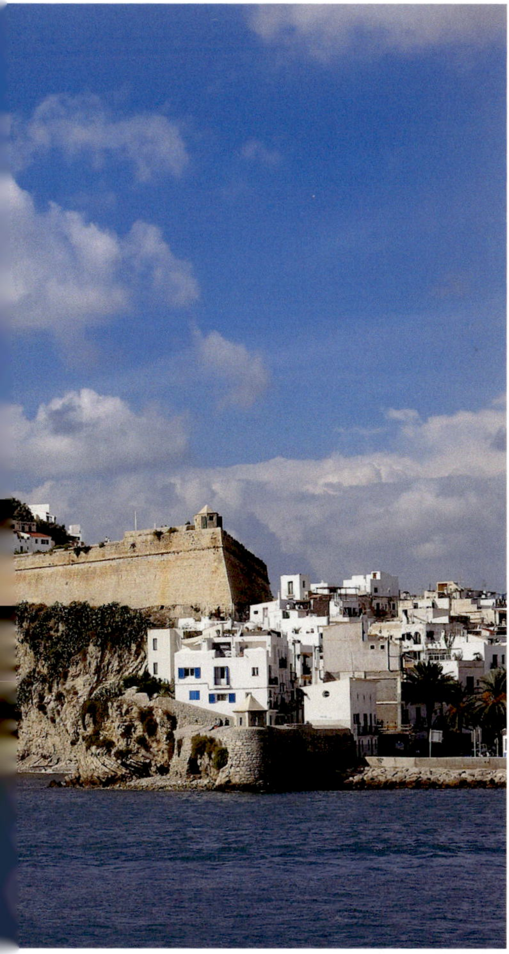

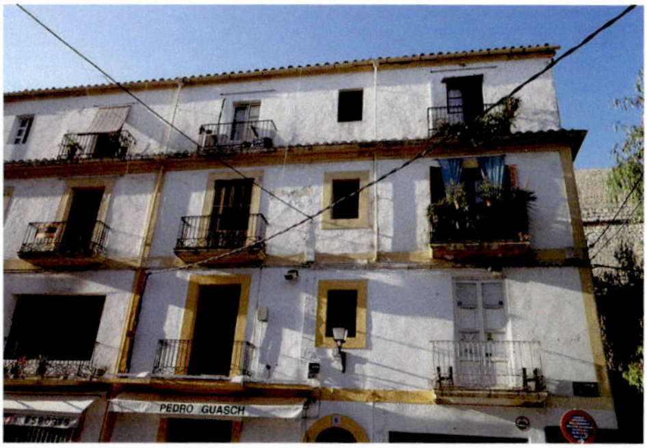

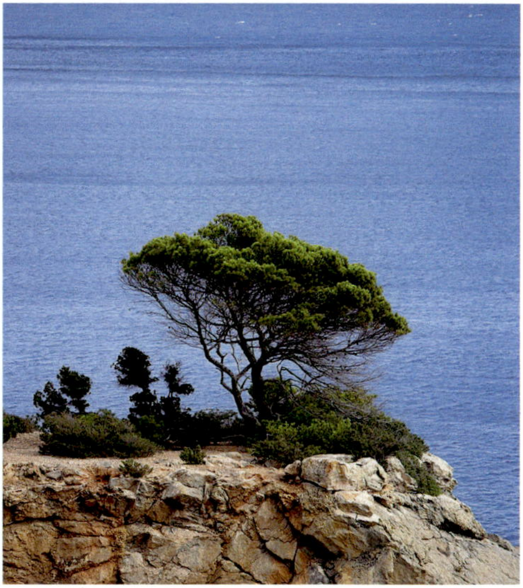

The walled city of Dalt Vila, on the left, was declared a World Heritage Site by UNESCO in 1999.

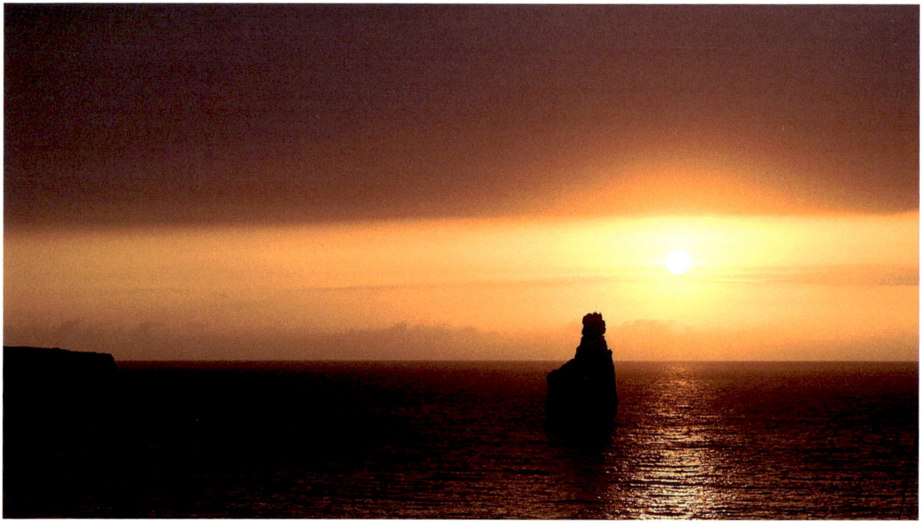

The attraction of Ibiza

In the mid-20th century, the landscape and idiosyncrasy of Ibiza attracted a massive contingent of artists and creators, above all from Europe, who found on this island a kind of lost paradise. The old continent had just come through the Second World War, and the isolation and beauty of the white island, as well as its mild climate, seduced creative minds such as Walter Benjamin, Tristan Tzara or Émile M. Cioran, to name just a few. A snippet by the writer Albert Camus, who was in Ibiza in 1935, reflects what this at the time remote island represented for these travellers:

"In Ibiza every day I went and sat down in the cafes that mark out the port. (...) I then sat there swaying by the sunlight, full of white churches and clayey walls, dry stretches of cultivated land and bristly olive trees. I drank a sweet tiger nut milk, took in the curve of the hills that were fac-

Sunset behind the Cap Bernat or Cavall Bernat, from the beach of Benirràs. On the right, detail of Ibiza architecture.

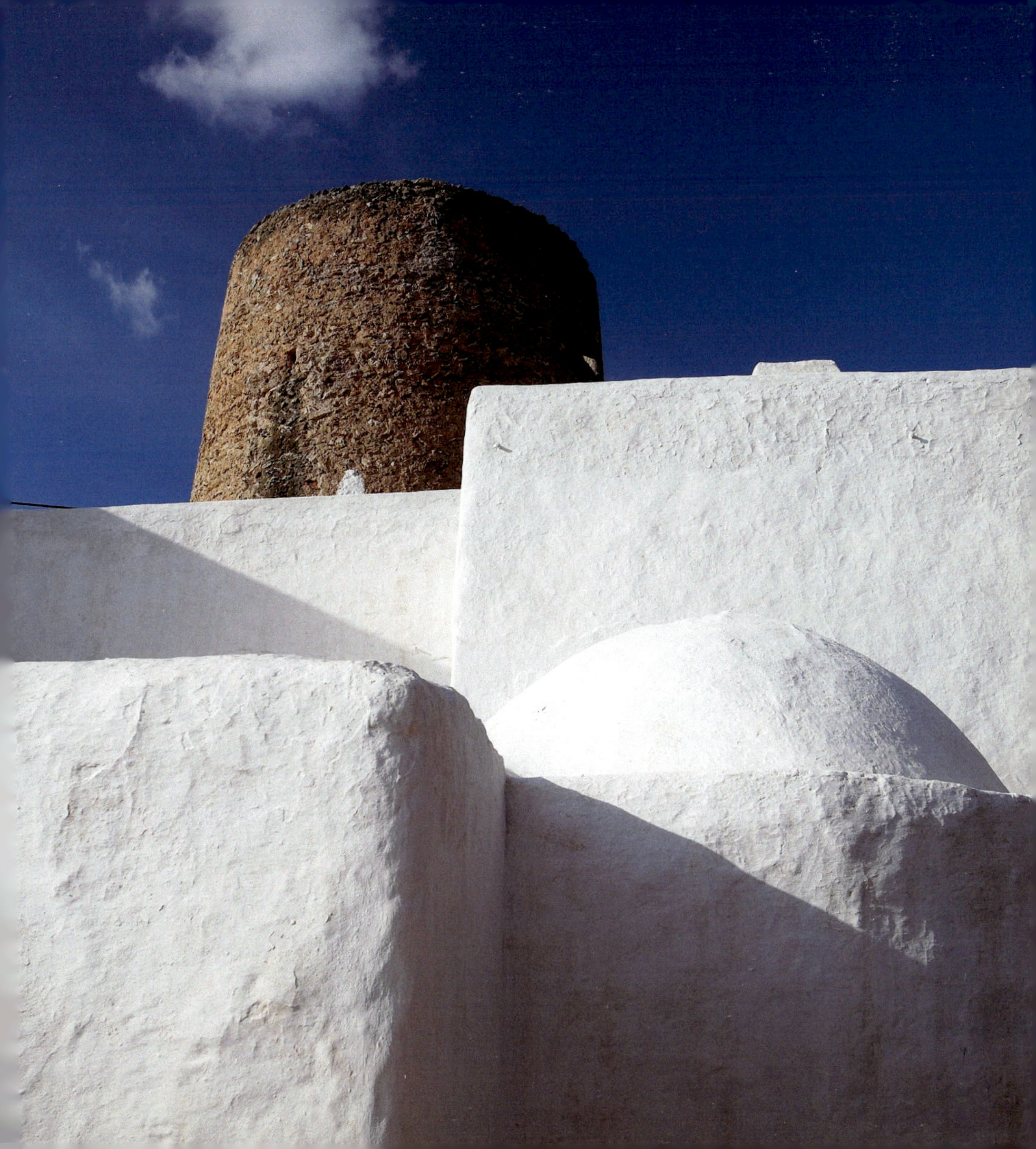

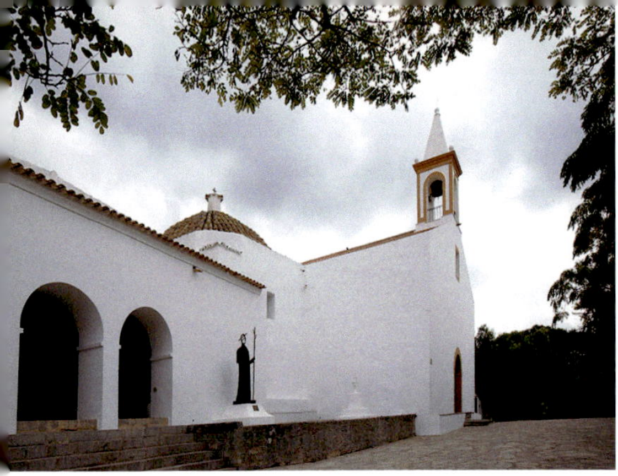
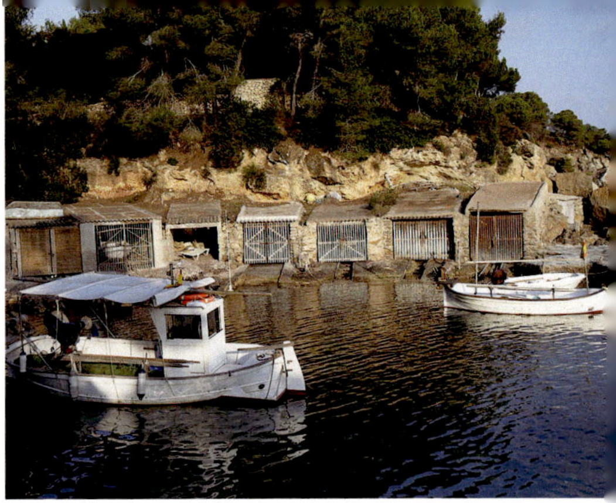
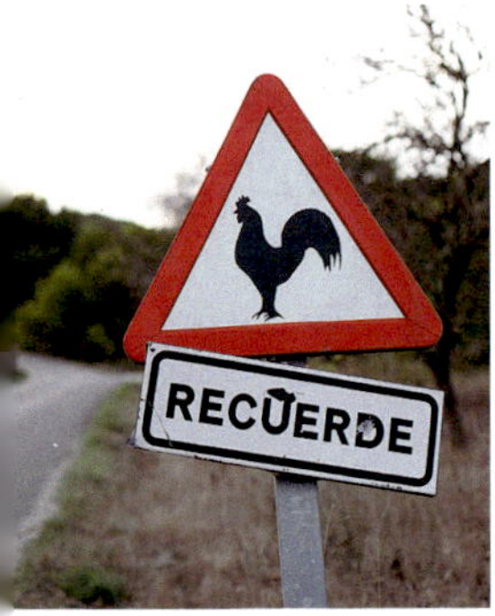
RECUERDE
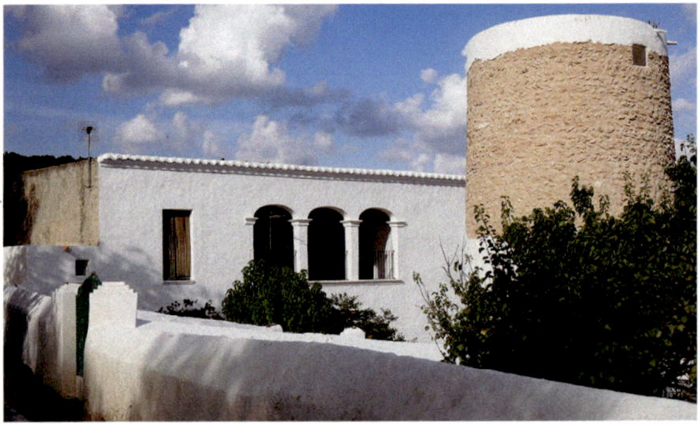
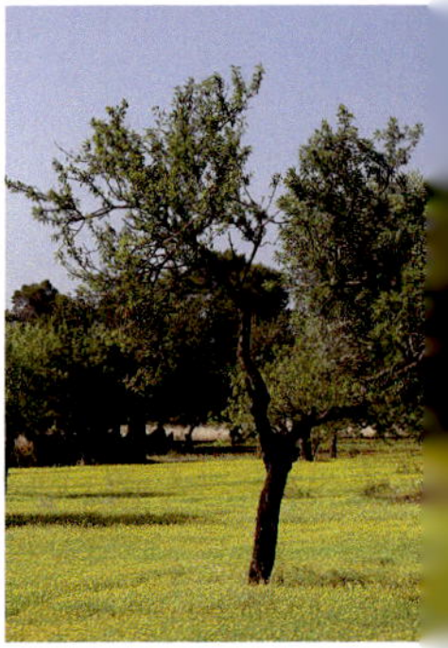
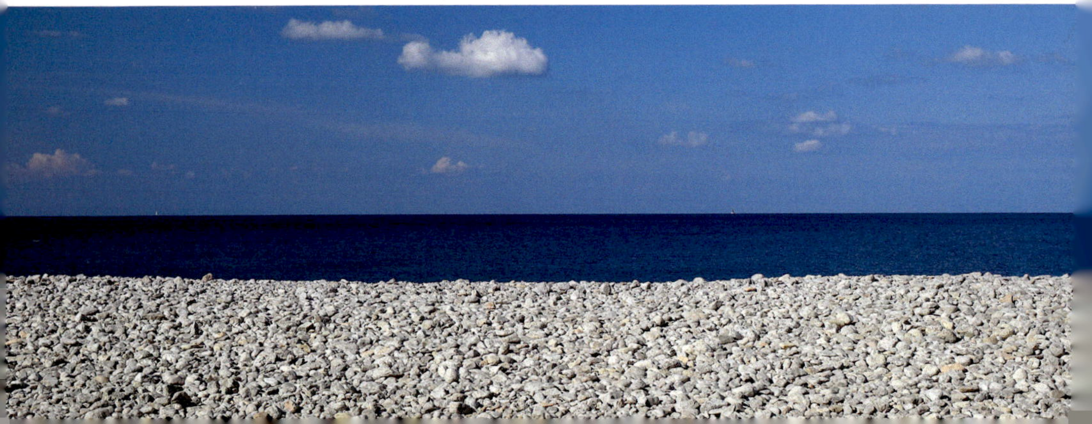

ing me; they dropped gently towards the sea. At dusk it was greenish. On the highest hill, the last breeze made the sails of a windmill turn (...) In this brief instant of dusk something fleeting and melancholy reigned, sensitive not to just one man but to a whole people. Myself, I wanted to love as if wanting to cry. It seemed to me that each hour of sleep would be robbed in advance of life..., in other words, at the time of desire without object" (from the book *The Wrong side and the Right Side*, 1937).

Today Ibiza continues to attract travellers and tourists from all over the world. For some reason beyond human understanding, on the island one takes in an avant-garde, eclectic and free air that coexists alongside its white churches and old traditions, above all in the rural districts: Sant Josep, Sant Antoni, Santa Eulària and Sant Joan.

Sant Josep de Sa Talaia. It is the largest district, in the south. Its 80 kilometres of coastline are made up of beautiful coves and beaches. It also houses the natural parks of Cala d'Hort and Ses Salines. Here there are archaeological sites as important as the Punic-Roman settlement of Ses Païses, from the 5th Century BC, used until the 8th century AD, and where the Carthaginians lived for more than 1,200 years. The remains have reconstructed a way of life based on fishing, grain cultivation, oil and wine production, and the rearing of sheep, goats and pigs.

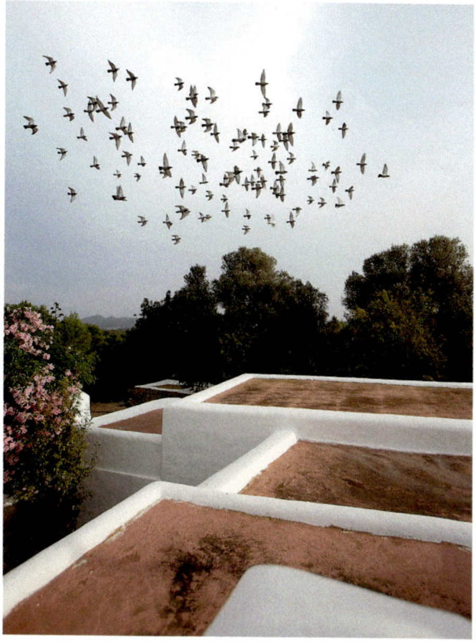

Despite mass tourism, Ibiza and Formentera have been able to conserve their character and tradition. As well as the beautiful scenery.

Sant Antoni de Portmany. It is the most touristic district, with beaches, coves and spectacular cliffs. The inland towns —such as Santa Agnès de Corona, Sant Mateu d'Aubarca and Sant Rafel— are small towns surrounded by a countryside scattered with vines, cereals, fruit

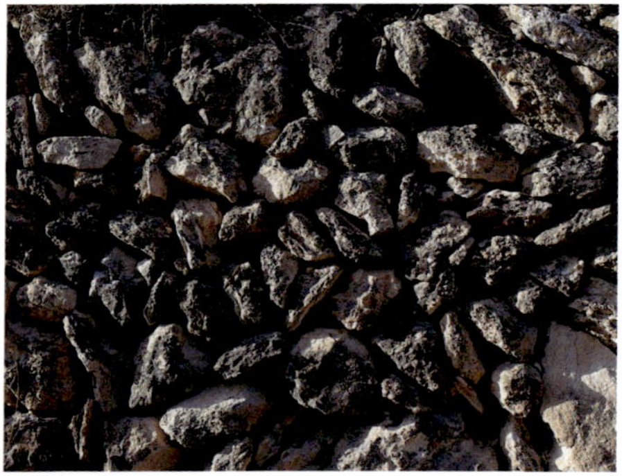

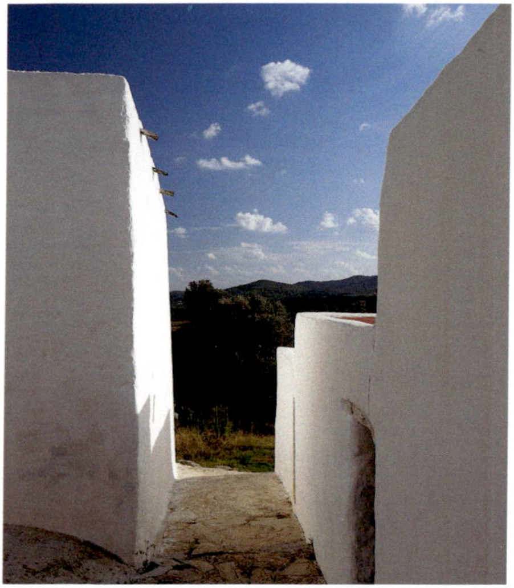

On the right, the lighthouse of Portinatx, in the north of Ibiza. Despite some tourist centres, it is the area that conserves the wildest coastline.

trees and almond trees. The bay of Sant Antoni is the largest natural harbour in Ibiza, baptised by the Romans as *Portus Magnus*. One of the most interesting places in this bay is Sa Punta des Molí, where one can visit an old flour mill, a waterwheel, an old oil mill (*trull*) and a peasant's cottage, which allows us to imagine what rural life was like before the emergence of tourism.

Santa Eulària des Riu. After the city of Ibiza this is the most populated district. The main town is Santa Eulària, crowned by the Puig de Missa, where the church is sited. Before entering the town one can see the remains of a Roman bridge, the Pont Vell, and the only river on the island. Santa Eulària was once very important, precisely because of this river, which made the millstones of the mill turn. The bridge, a constant crossing point of peasants, was, along with the saltworks, a continuous target of pirate attacks.

Other towns in the district are Sant Carles de Peralta, where in the 1950s many intellectuals made their homes there.

Sant Joan de Labritja. It is the least populated area, in the north of the island. Sant Joan was traditionally known for being the place with most freshwater springs. In the rural Ibiza of the

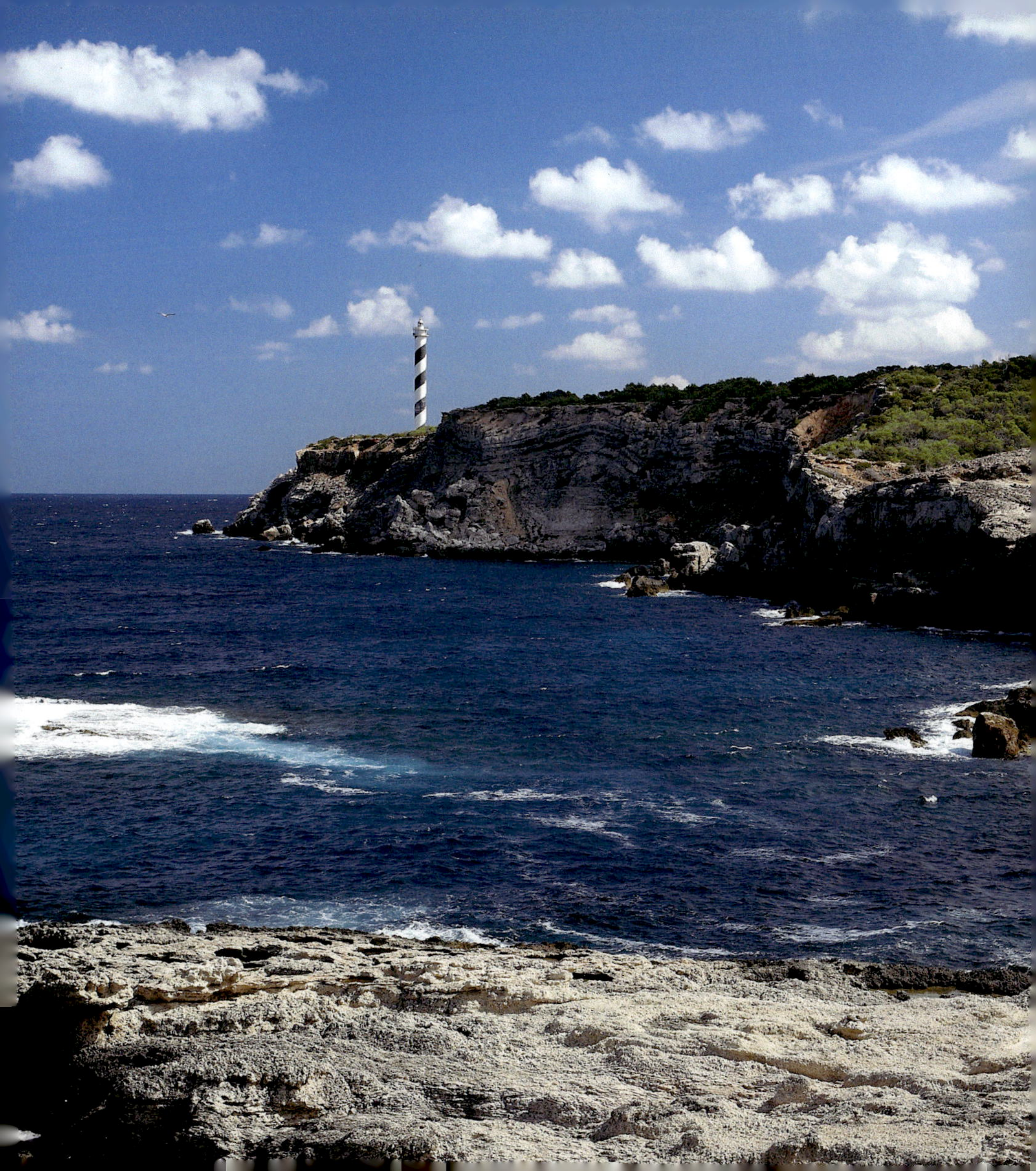

past, the estates with enough water for their houses and crops were the most fortunate. Alongside wells and springs traditional summer dances were held (*ballades*), a custom that has been recovered in the district.

Formentera or paradise

The origin of the name of the smallest Pine Island causes controversy. Some state that it comes from the Latin word *frumentaria* (or "island of wheat"), while others claim it is from the Latin word *promontoria* ("island of capes"), due to its silhouette dominated by the capes of Barbaria and La Mola. The former etymology has been the most widely accepted, and on the coat of arms of the island there is a defence tower with a sheaf of wheat.

From the Catalan conquest of 1235, Formentera did not have a stable population until the 18th century. For centuries it was an unpopulated area that the people from Ibiza used for cultivating, maintaining flocks of sheep or for obtaining forest resources, such as wood.

The land on the island has always been rather unproductive, due to the system of very small

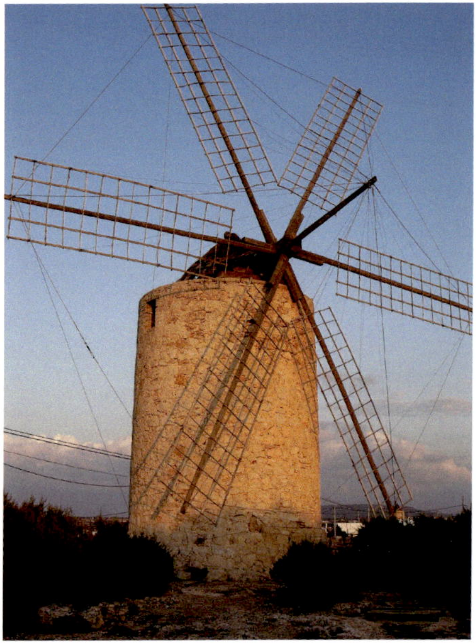

holdings, lack of rain and low quality soil. All this has conditioned production to self-consumption. Today cultivation includes, above all, wheat, barley, garden produce, pulses, potatoes, vines, almonds and figs. Livestock is a complement to agriculture, and sheep and goats, pigs, poultry and rabbits are bred.

The most important towns on the island are La Savina, Sant Francesc Xavier, Sant Ferran de Ses Roques, Es Pujols and Pilar de la Mola.

The beaches of Formentera, such as those of Illetes, are pure beauty. The scenery and nature are the island's most valuable heritage.

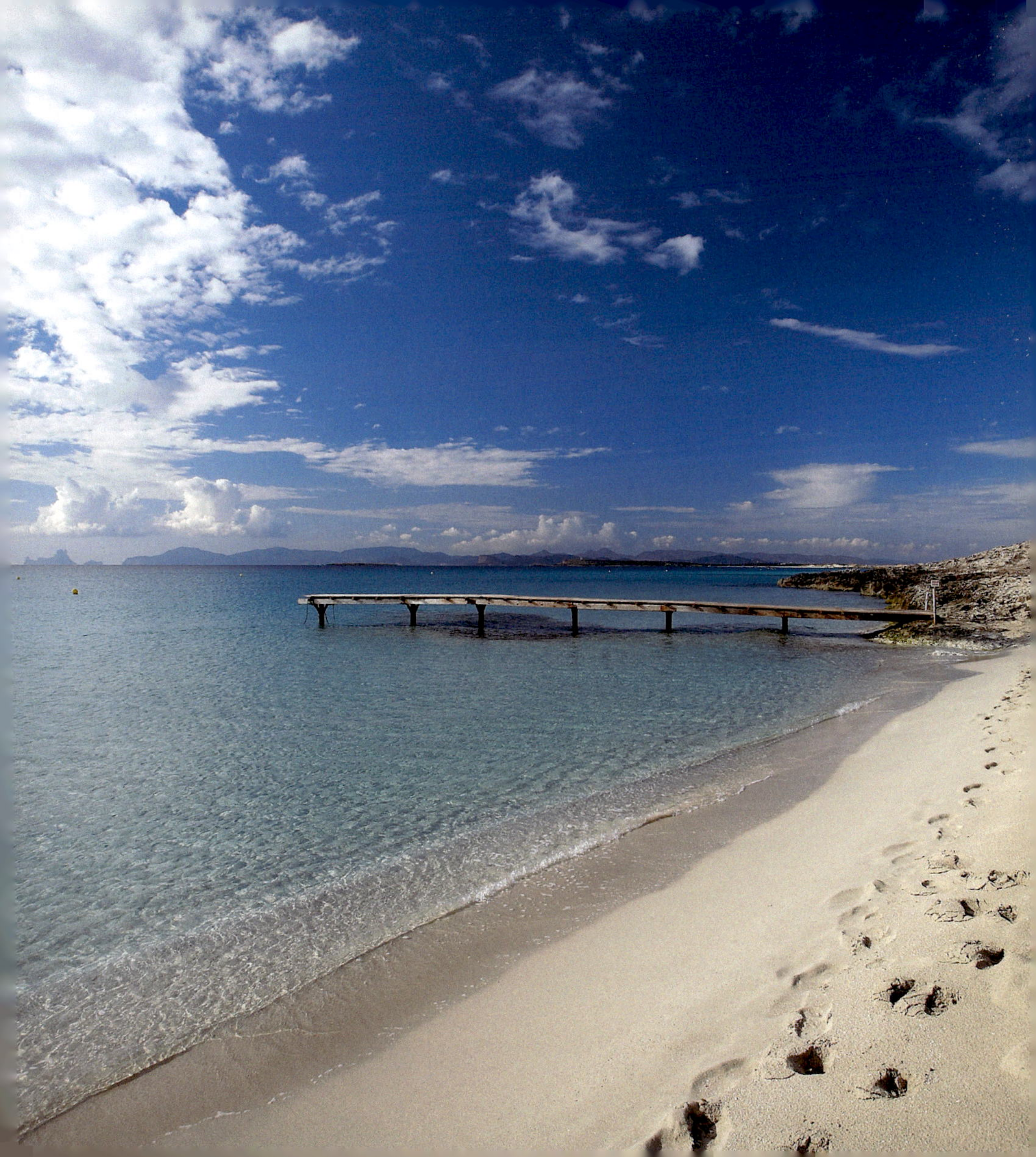

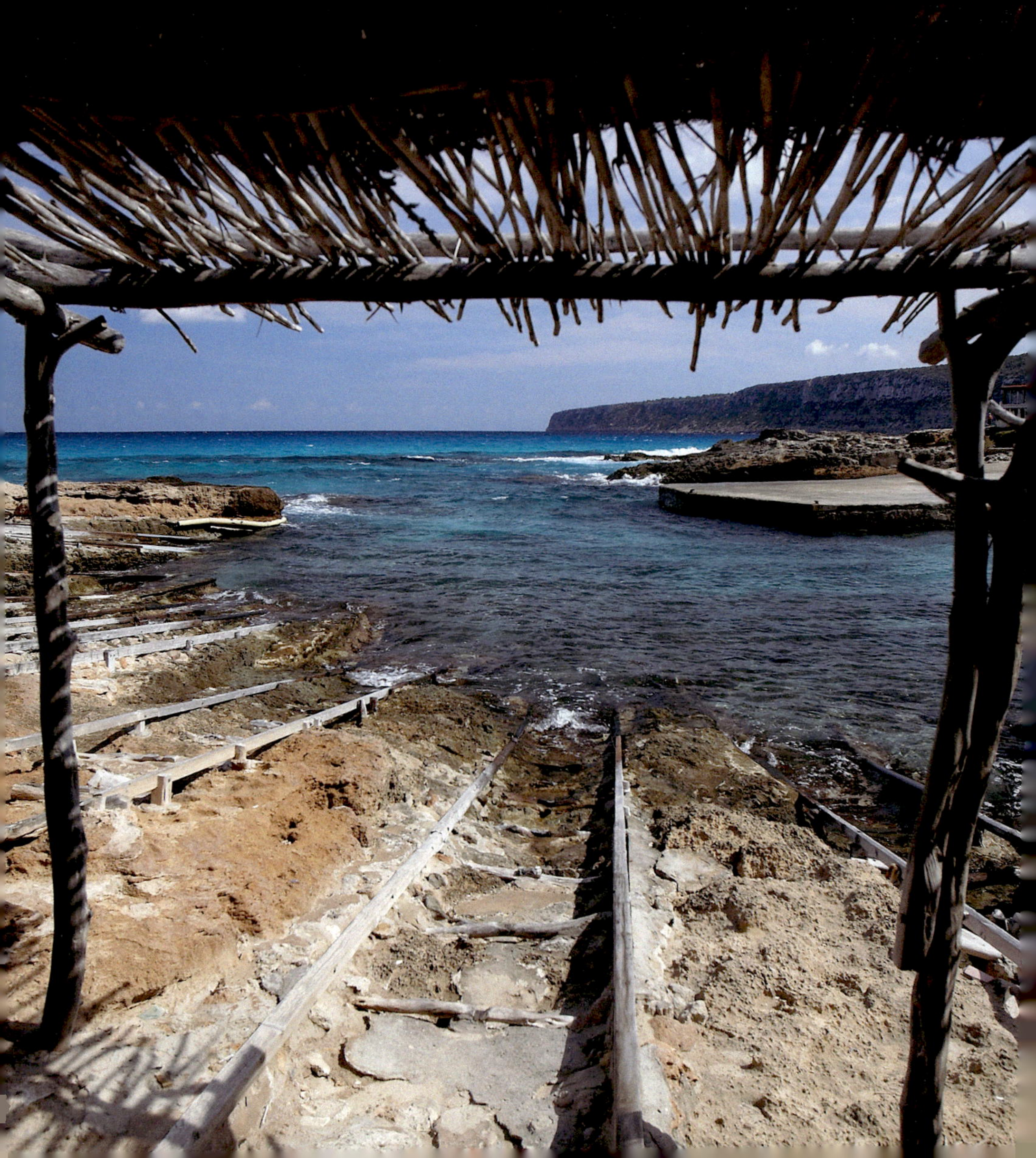

La Savina is the home of the commercial port, from where the ferries depart for the neighbouring Ibiza. In Sant Francesc Xavier is the Town Hall and Consell Insular of the island, as well as the Ethnographic Museum dedicated to the rural and seafaring life. The town church was used as a fortress, and even had its own piece of artillery.

In Sant Ferran de Ses Roques is the now mythical Fonda Pepe, which in the 1960s attracted hippies from all over the world, creating a cosmopolitan atmosphere that can still be felt today and coexists alongside the island's traditions. On the outskirts of El Pilar de la Mola there are small plots planted with vines and a very well conserved mill.

In tourist circles, Formentera is known as "the Caribbean of the Mediterranean", an expression that attempts to synthesise the extreme beauty of its white sandy beaches and crystal-clear waters, such as the beaches of Illetes, Llevant, Migjorn, Cala Saona or S'Espalmador. The heritage of this island is its nature, including the seabed, which forms underwater scenery populated with *Posidonia oceanica*, oxygenated and full of life.

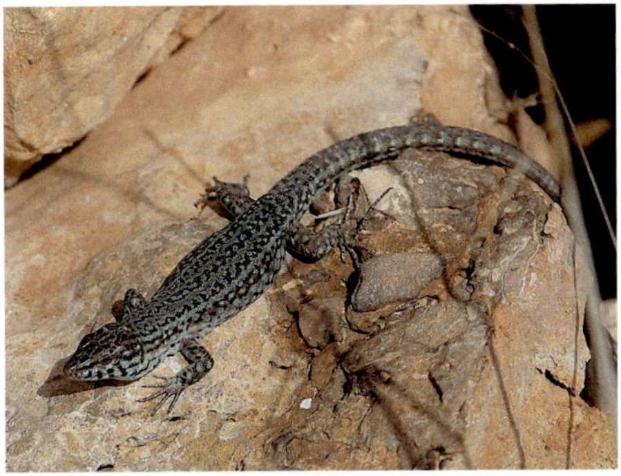

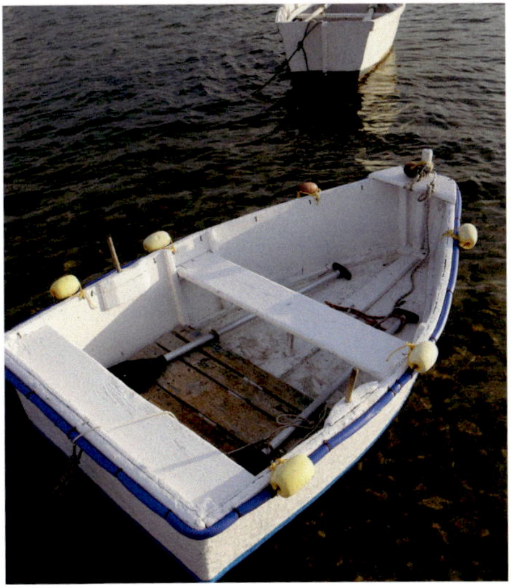

In some coves in Formentera one can still see the old wooden jetties, as in Es Caló de Sant Agustí.

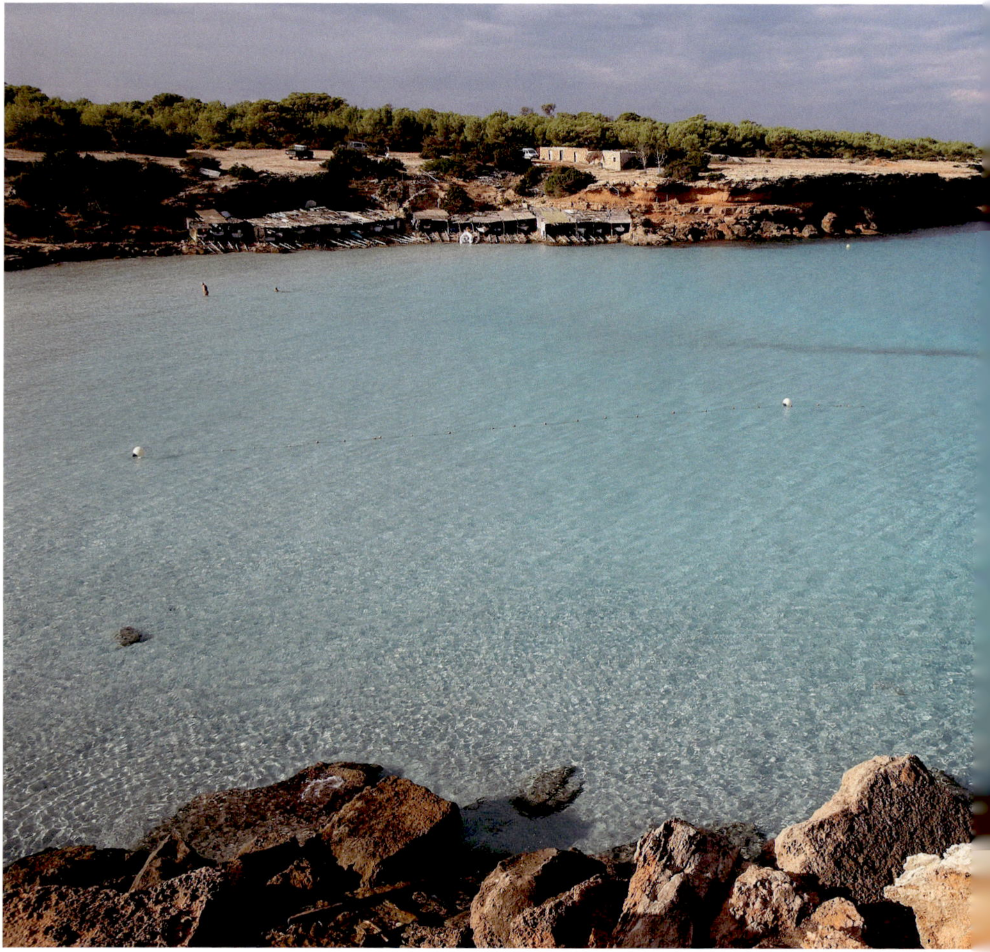

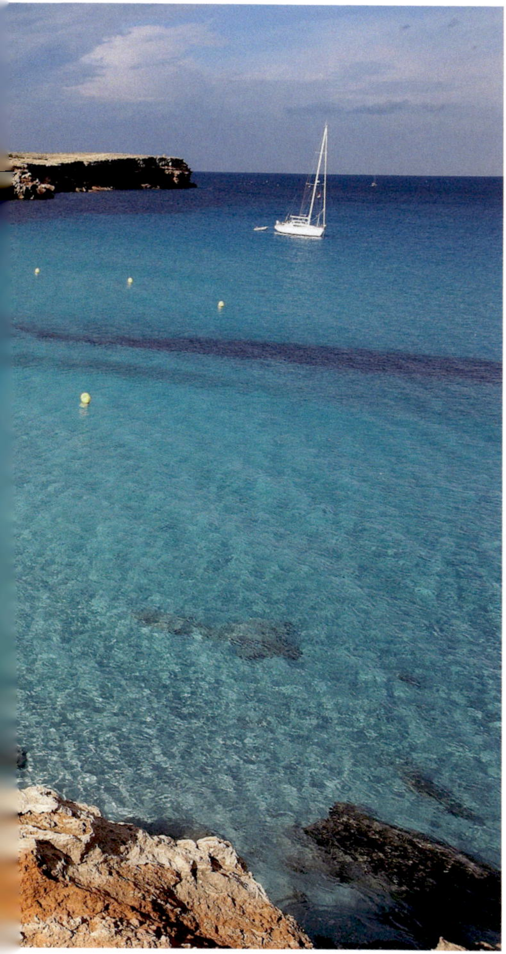

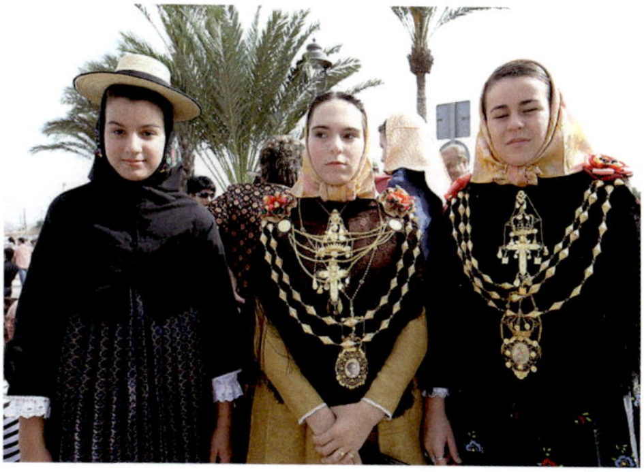

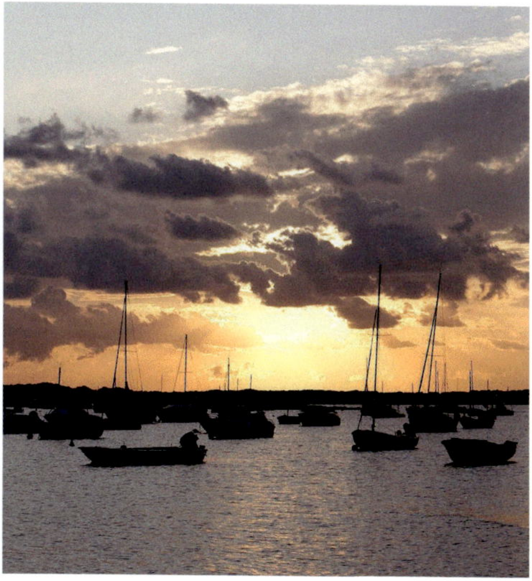

Cala Saona, in the west, in a setting of pine woods and dunes.
Above, women wearing traditional costumes in the festivals of
Pilar de la Mola.

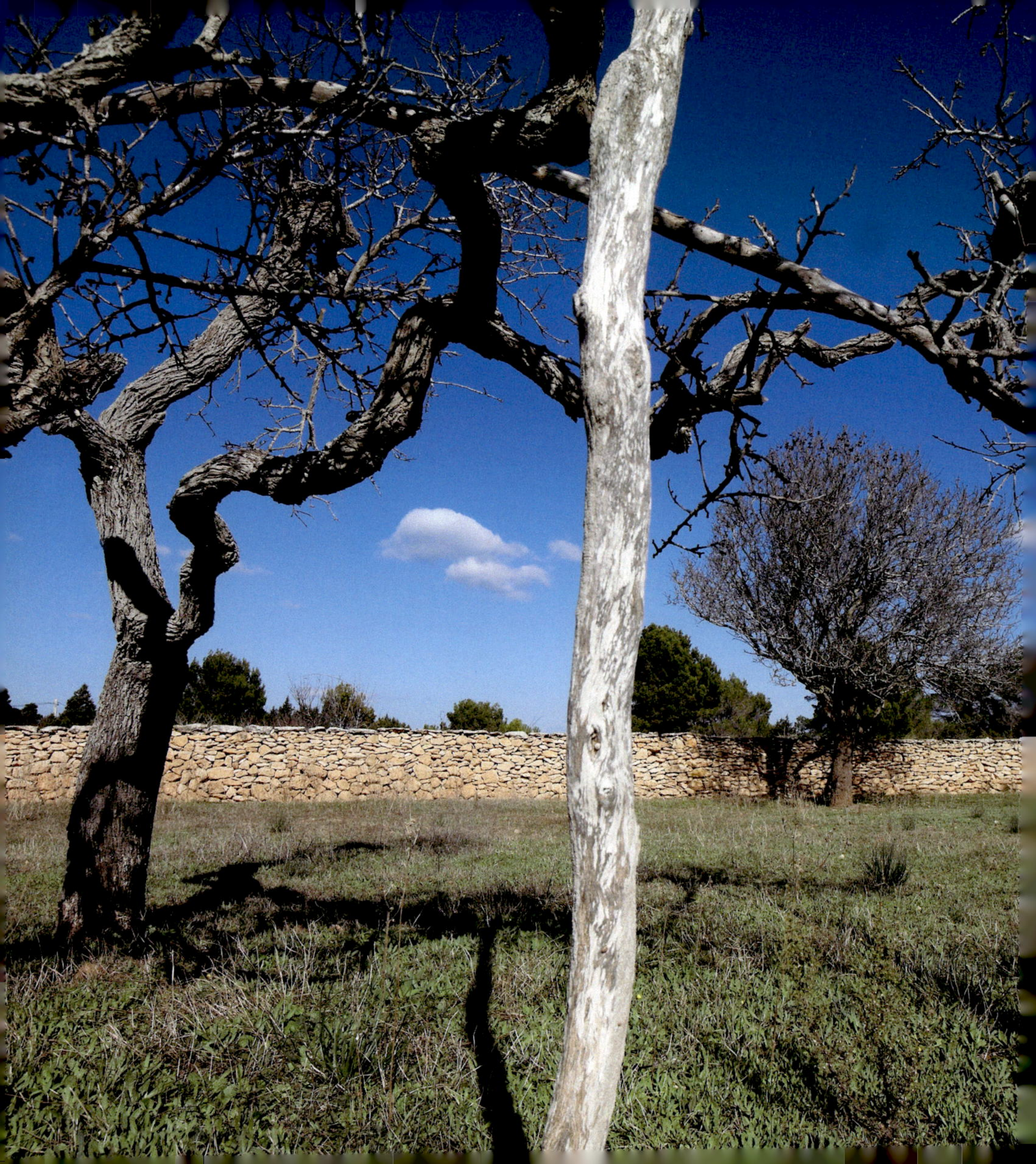

Rural life

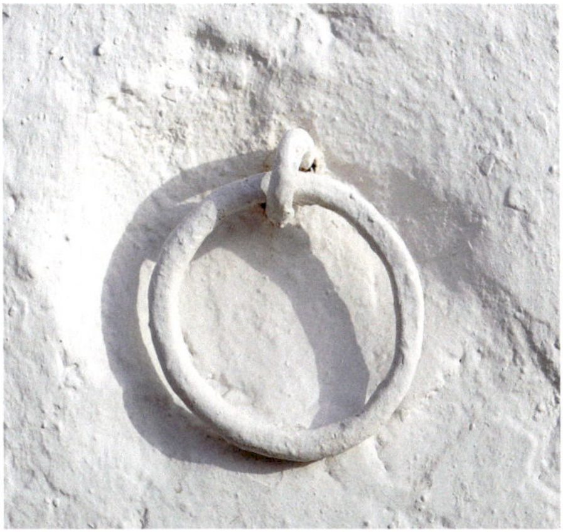

Since Antiquity, the country houses of Ibiza and Formentera have been veritable islands within islands, solitary, spread around the rural geography. All the members of the household, men and women, worked hard to achieve self-sufficiency, and to do that they had to produce a little of everything. This need shapes the landscape and way of life of the Pine Islands.

The main crop was cereals, above all barley and wheat, which in rotational years were replaced by broad beans or peas. Wheat was used to make flour, semolina, noodles, *formigons*, flat breads, bread, biscuits ... Every home had its own wood-fired oven, in which they cooked the bread and flat breads with "something" on top. Wheat, however, was also a currency of exchange, and was used to buy products that were not readily available.

Trees were also a source of food. Carob, almond, fig, olive and apricot trees and some extensions of vines still shape today's rural landscape. Irrigation was important in areas such as the *feixes* of the Pla de Vila and in the orchards of Sant Antoni and Santa Eulària, as well as on the

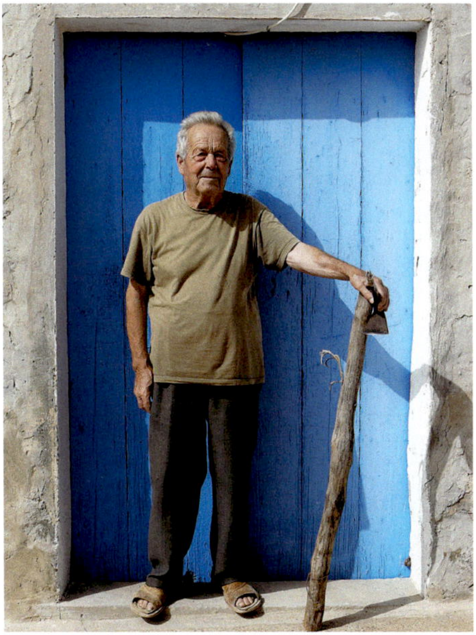

En Joan was the last miller of the flour mill of La Mola, in Formentera. Wheat and flour were subsistence foods.

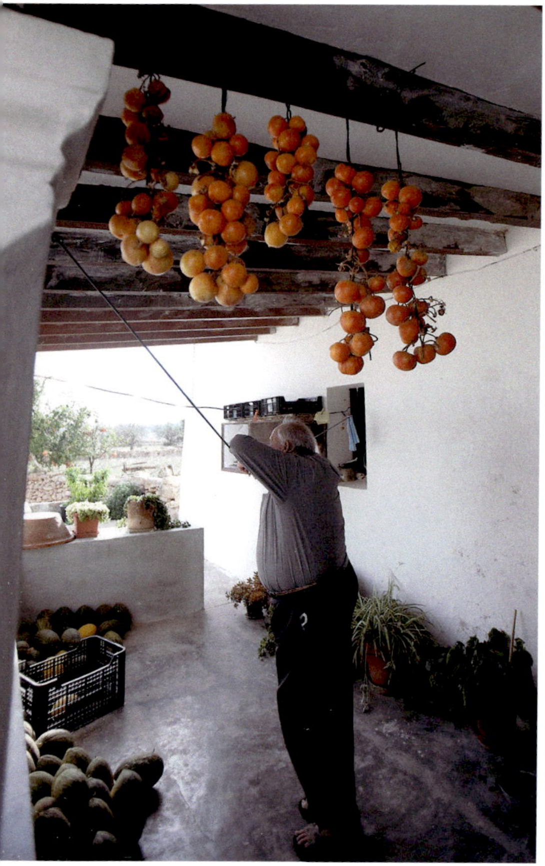

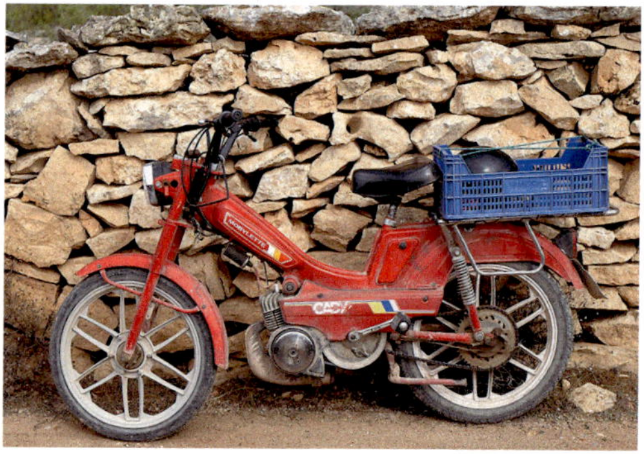

largest pine island. Alongside each house small allotments where organised where they grew fruit and vegetables, the water obtained from the cistern or tank.

The livestock and farmyard animals provided them with meat, eggs, milk and other products, as well as wool, leather and fertiliser. Sheep and goats grazed on the fallow land, and they also bred rabbits and poultry. But the beneficial animal par excellence was the pig, which cost little to raise in money and work, and from which every part use was made of.

Collecting activities complemented the domestic economy: from the forest they obtained wood, firewood, charcoal, tar, candlewood,

Rural life is full of details, such as the *motorino* (above), work and delights such as the tomatoes *de penjar*.

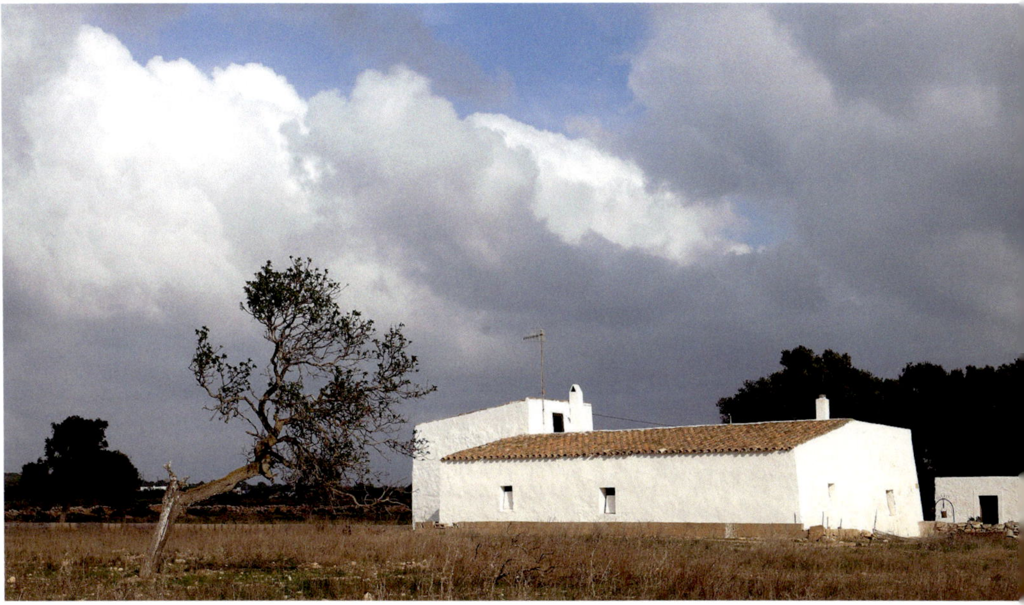

snails, and aromatic and medicinal herbs. The latter were collected above all for Sant Joan, and were fundamental for treating illnesses and making liqueurs, such as the *herbes* and the *frígola*. Hunting, fishing and, in summer, collecting salt from the saltworks were other complementary occupations.

There were festive occasions, often linked to work, such as house-building, the slaughter of the pig or the oil pressing. These activities were undertaken together with neighbours or family members, who were rewarded with a part of the product produced. People also worked together on jobs like whitewashing the church or repairing a path, limekilns or carbon mounds. Despite their toughness, these tasks strengthened relationships and enabled girls and boys to meet each other.

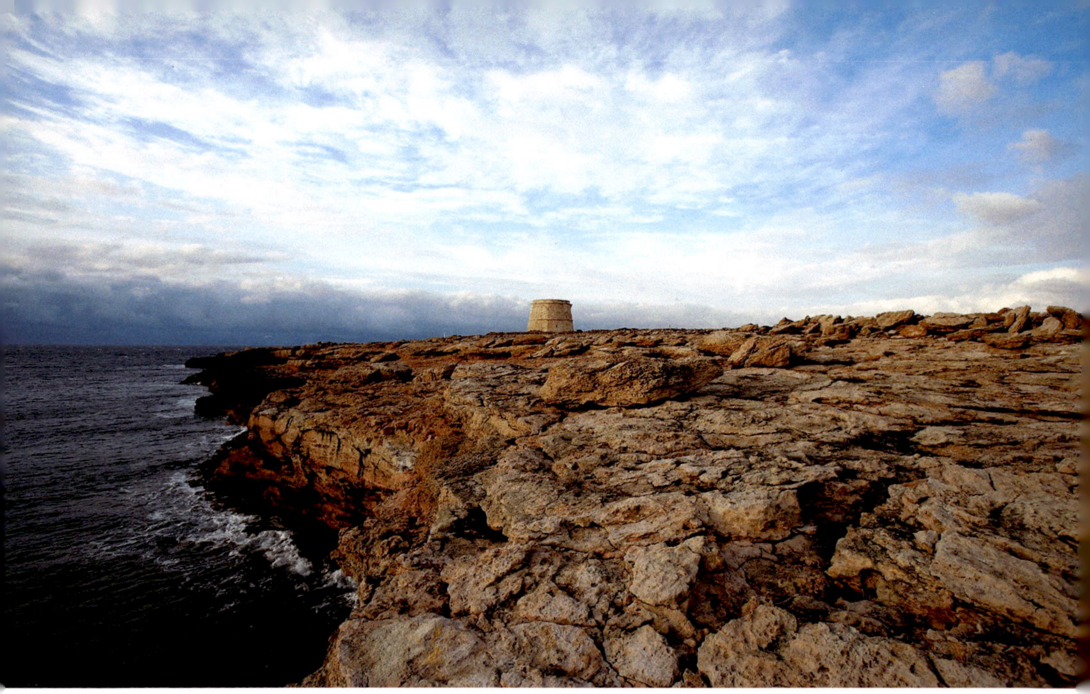

The Pine Islands and the sea

The Mediterranean has conditioned the history, way of life and gastronomy of Ibiza and Formentera, as well as the superstitions: it is said that some sailors who had just had a son sailed around the Es Freus area —which separates the two islands, with shallow waters and dangers— to throw into the water the child's umbilical cord, and thus ensure that their son would never die drowning.

Along the coast one can still see the defence towers, used in former times to warn the population in case of a pirate attack. Many of them housed cannons and keepers who watched out for the arrival of enemies. Their job was to light fires on the roof so that everyone could see the cloud of smoke during the day or the flames at

The coast of Ibiza and Formentera is scattered with defence towers that warned the population in case of pirate attacks.

night. News travelled fast, and people took refuge in the fortified churches, since the Turkish pirates who attacked the Pine Islands razed the crops, killed the peasants or turned them into slaves.

Fishing was a major activity, in the city and the country, but especially for those who lived close to the coast. The small craft, *llaüts* or lateens, and rowing boats, were kept in the dry dock huts that can still be seen in many coves. Many are still used, and are a meeting point for family celebrations, places where one can enjoy good food and a siesta by the sea.

Today commercial fishing is of little importance. In 2007 the fishermen of Vila, Sant Antoni and Formentera caught a total of 515 tons of fish of more than 70 different marine species, above all sardine (*gerret*), little fish (basically used for making stock), octopus and dogfish (*gató*). Just like everywhere else, it is a sector in crisis, which suffers from a lack of generational handover and a drop in catches, due to the over-exploitation of the fishing grounds.

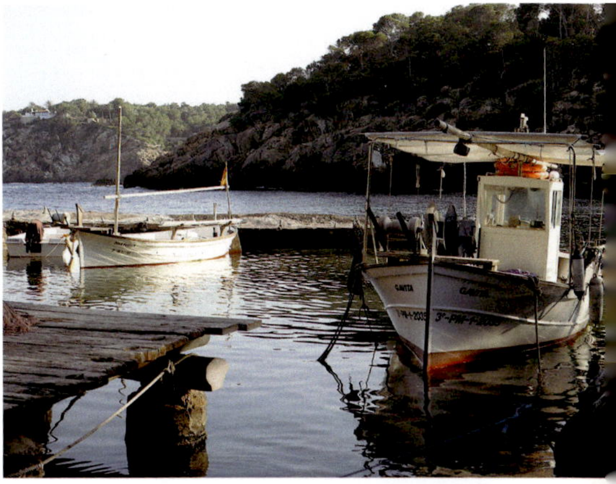

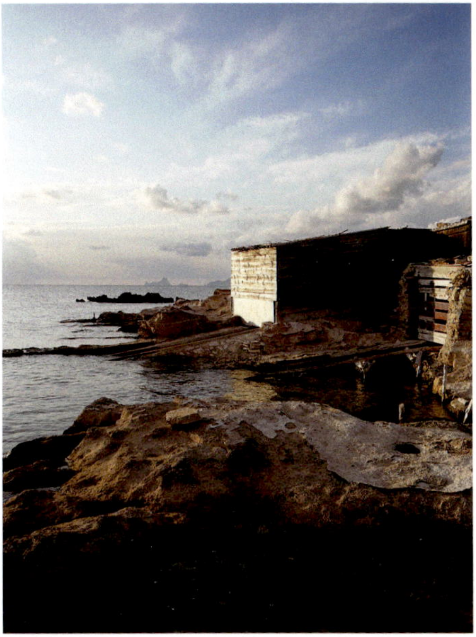

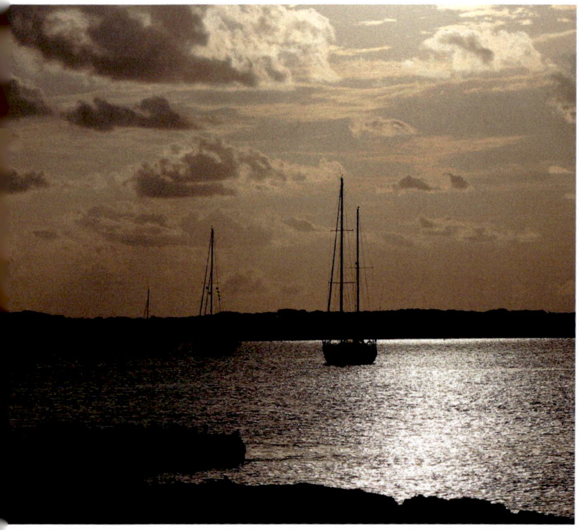

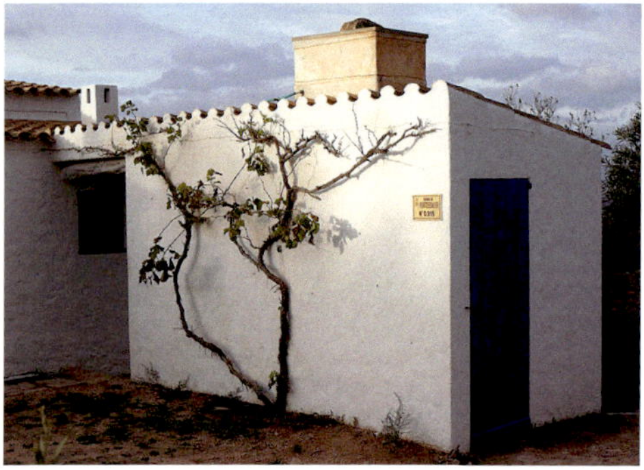

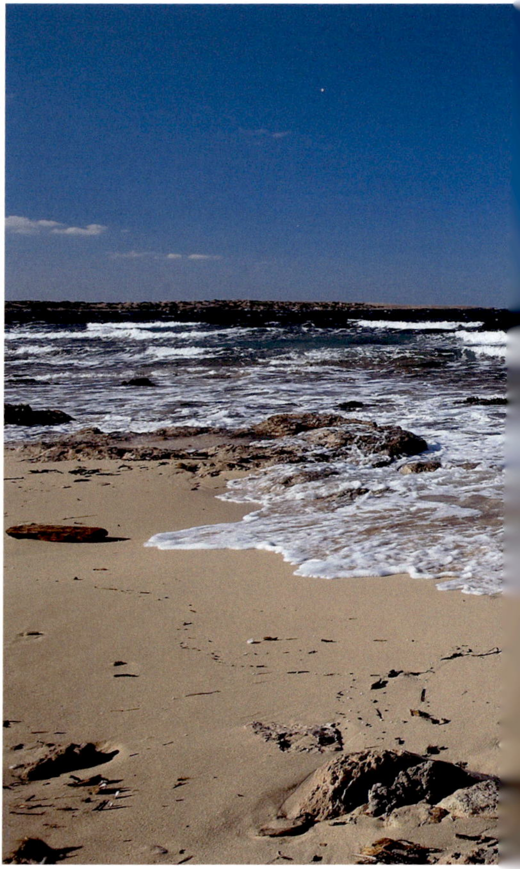

The beauty of the sea, wild and unpredictable, is one of the main tourist attractions of the Pine Islands.

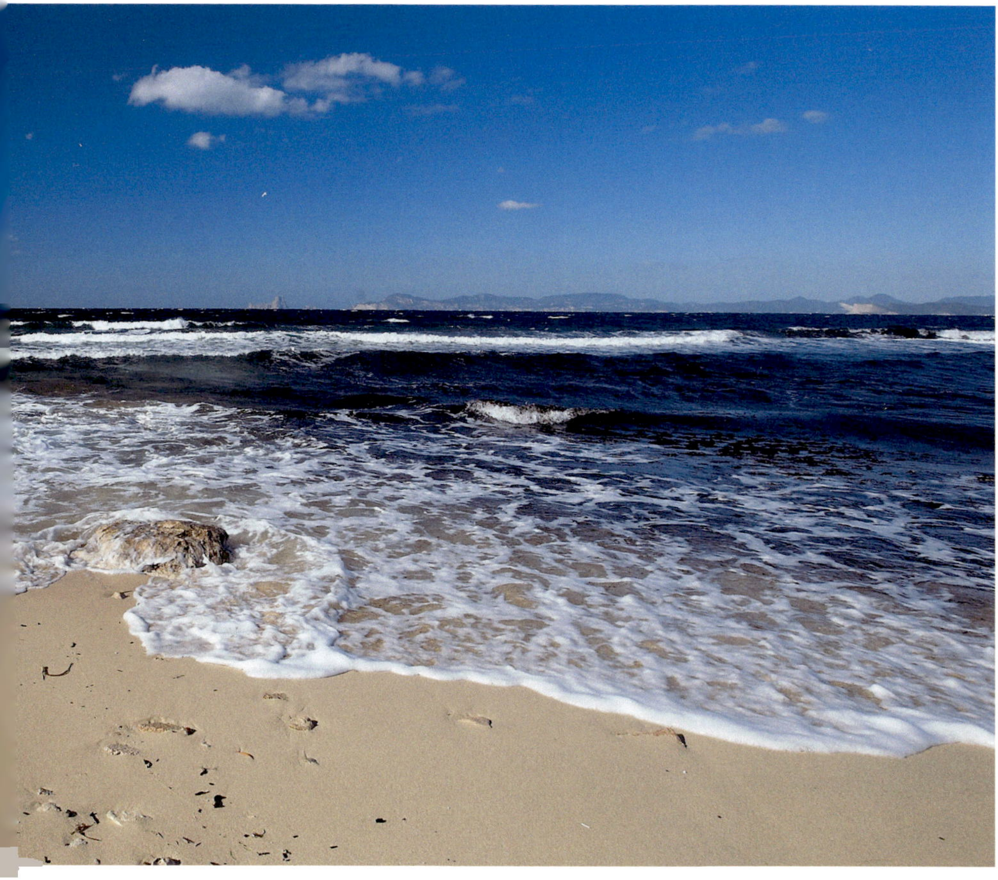

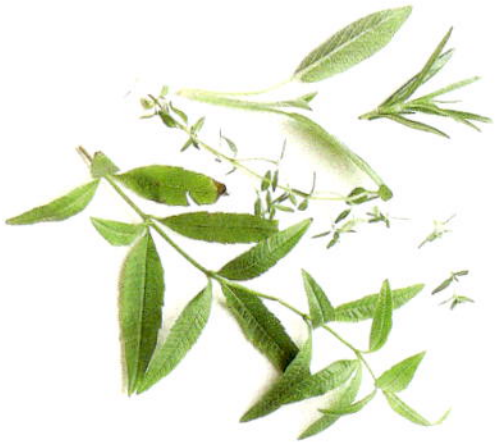

Products of the land and sea, which ingenuity combines with the legacy of the different people who have passed through these islands.
From the land: figs, which are eaten fresh or dried; almonds, which impregnate the Christmas sauce and appear in the spicy sauces that round off stews; grapes, the star of increasingly excellent wines; or wheat, from which are made the delights of the bakery and cake shop, and confectionery oozing with cinnamon and lemon. From the land also comes the animals beneficial to man such as the pig —from which *sobrassada* and other cured meats are obtained—, the sheep and the goat, the milk of which makes aromatic traditionally made cheeses in different stages of maturation.
The sea provides fresh fish and seafood of the like of octopus, ray, parrot fish and sardine, as well as the colourful rock fish and the typical dried fish of Formentera.

Products of the islands

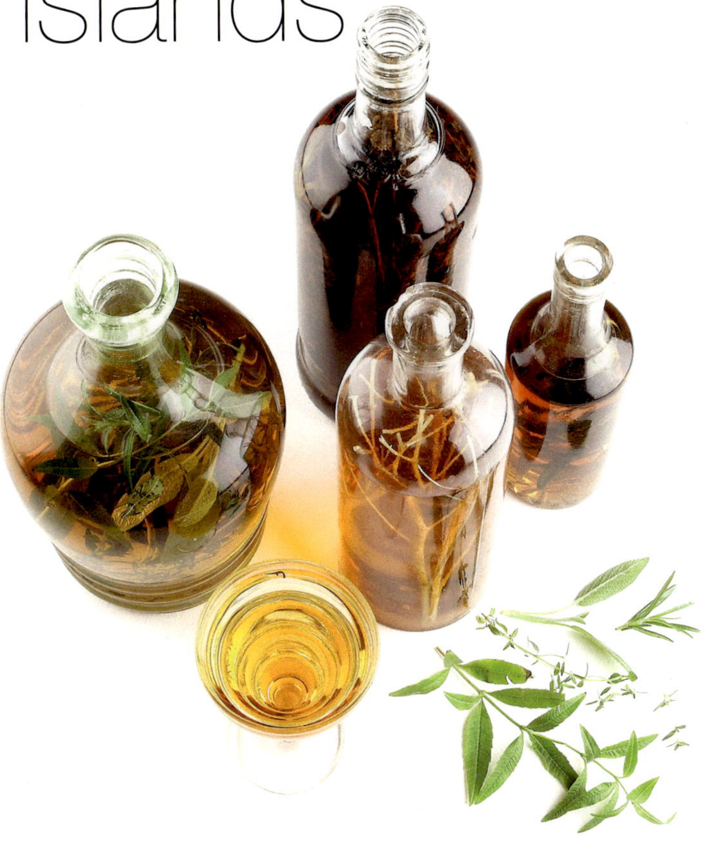

The richness of salt

Salt production in Ibiza is ancestral. Its exploitation began with the arrival of the Phoenicians and Carthaginians, continued with the Romans, and must have been continued with the Vandals and the Byzantines. In the 10th century the Arabs arrived, from whom came the first records that refer to salt-making exploitation during their time on the island. Moreover, documents predating the Catalan conquest bear witness that some Italian city-states already traded with the salt of Ibiza.

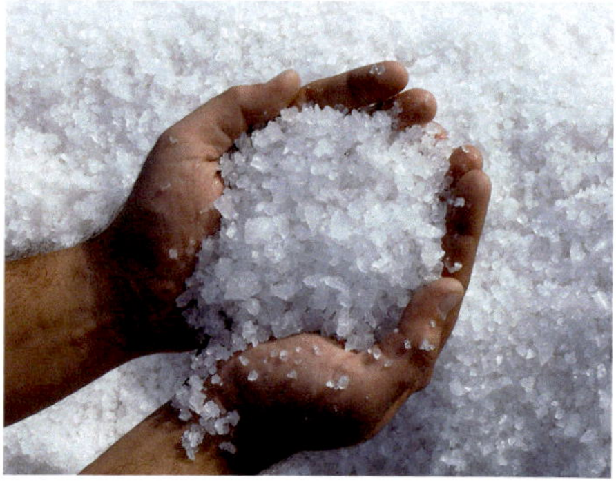

The extraction of salt is the oldest industry in Ibiza, a very tough job that has brought wealth to the island.

With the Catalan conquest in 1235, the feudal lords obtained their share of the benefits arising from the saltworks and the sale of salt. A few years later, however, it was established that the product should also benefit the community of Ibiza and its inhabitants, who were allowed to extract salt freely in exchange for paying a tax. Salt meant wealth for the island, and was the main source of income for its local government body, the Universitat.

In 1709, the saltworks were rented out to the Genoese trader Joan Baptista Visconti, who exploited them until, at the end of the War of Succession, Felipe V appropriated them "by right of conquest". In 1871 they were sold to a private concern, and are currently exploited by the Salinera Española SA company.

Salt extraction and the maintenance of the saltings are very tough jobs, which in the 17th century was done in part by slaves and by prisoners in the 18th century. The magnitude of the human effort involved in extracting salt, even in the 1950s, is immortalised in black and white by the photographer Francesc Català Roca (in the book *Ibiza, 1950*).

The saltworks form one of the most important ecosystems of the Balearics, in which many spe-

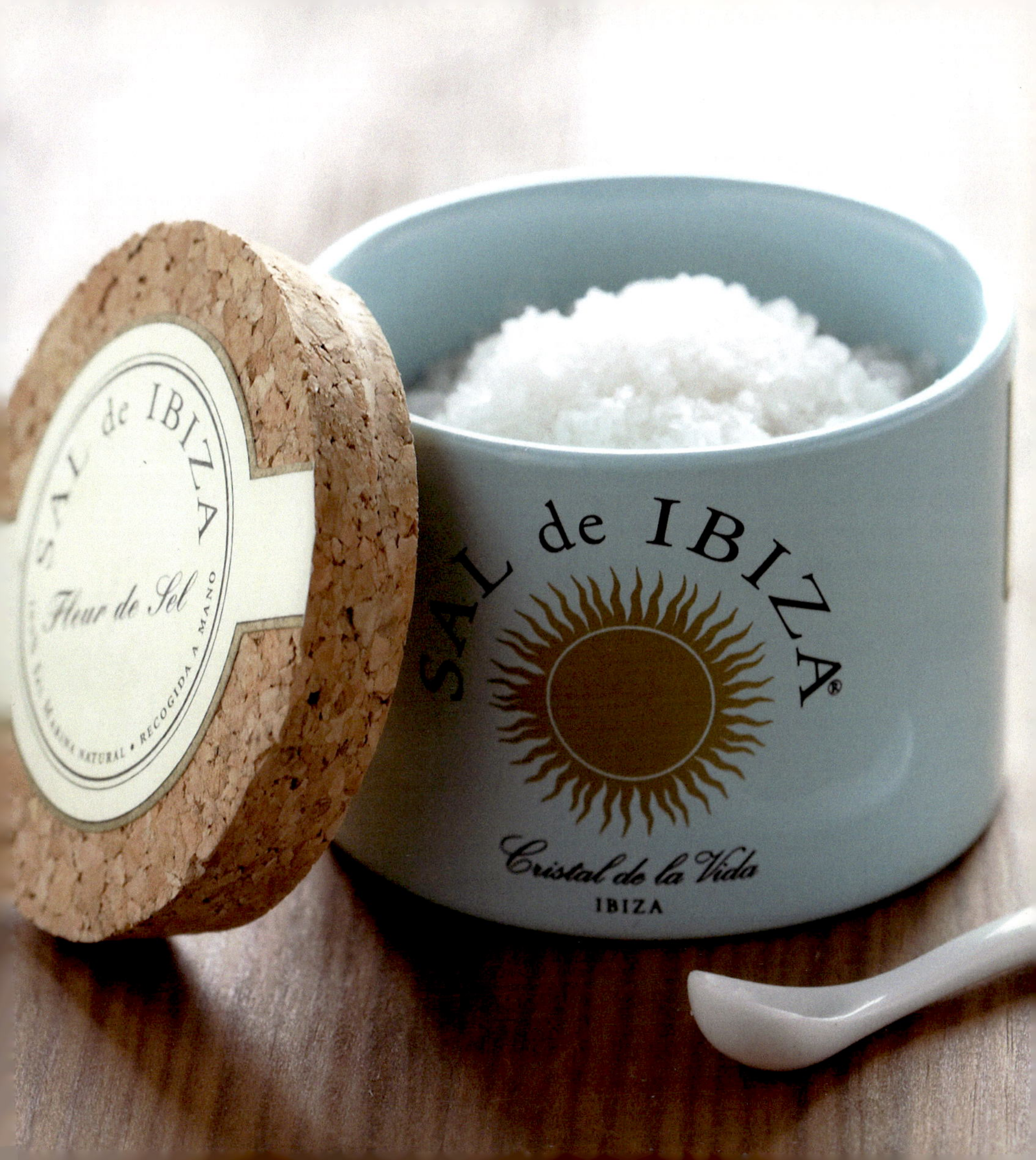
SAL de IBIZA
Fleur de Sel
RECOGIDA A MANO
SAL de IBIZA®
Cristal de la Vida
IBIZA

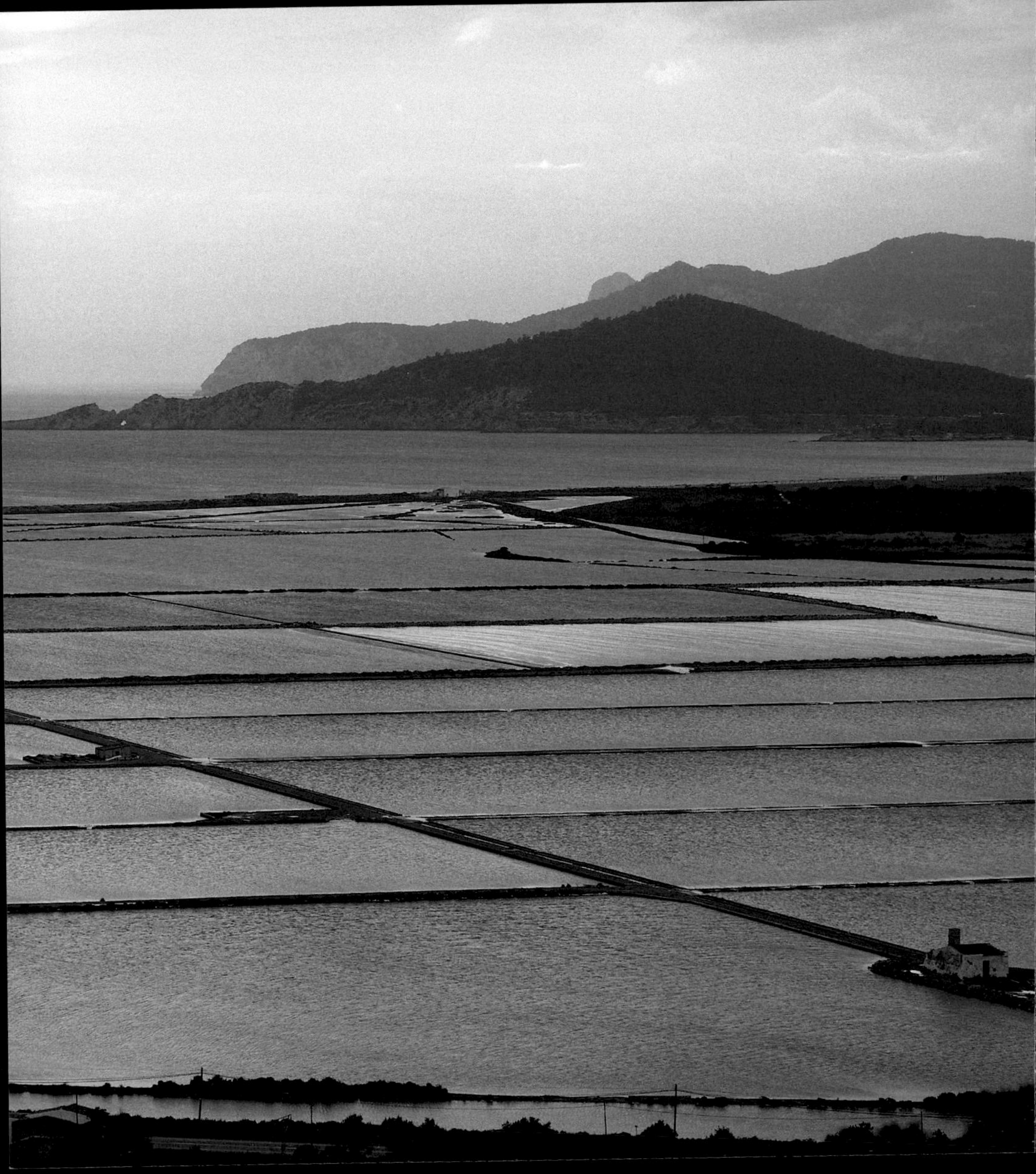

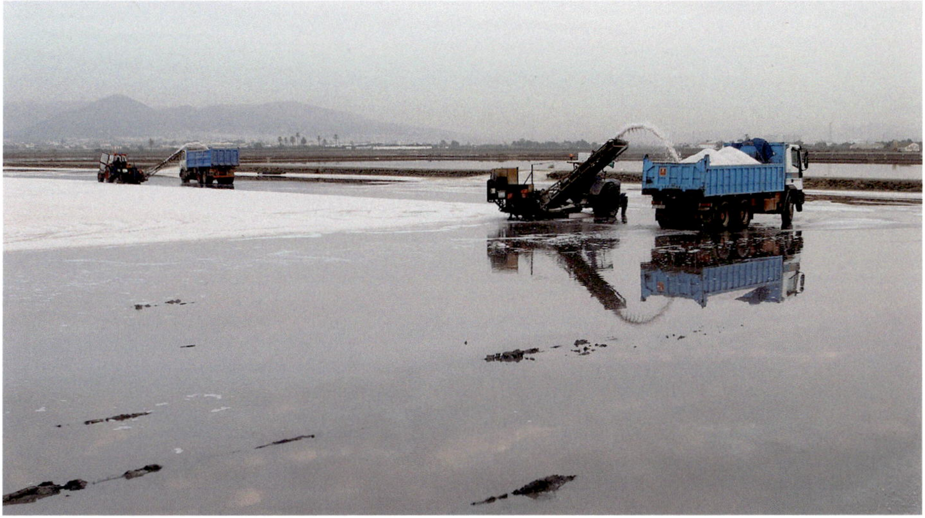

cies of birds stock up and nest. In 1977 the first movement in defence of this space arose, which after a long and popular ecological campaigning struggle was declared a Natural Park on the 19 December 2001.

The saltworks of Formentera. They are located in the north of the island, where a coastal platform is formed with two salt lakes, the Peix and the Pudent. Close to the latter is the important Megalithic sepulchre of Ca na Costa, and it is possible that in prehistoric times this area was already used as a saltworks. The Punic remains also found in S'Espalmador indicate the establishment of a small naval base, perhaps related to the collection of salt.

During the Roman period there was a stable settlement close to the Peix lake. Also, the remains of the Roman *castellum* of Can Blai show the importance of the control of Formentera. By the 13th century, when the Catalans considered

Today, the operating saltworks form part of the Natural Park of Las Salinas of Ibiza and Formentera, to which many species of birds come.

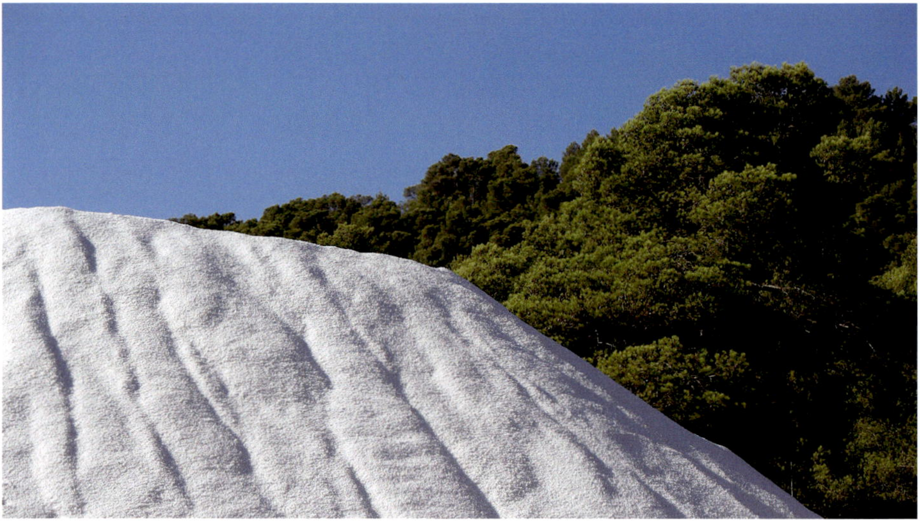

conquering Ibiza, the saltworks of Formentera are referred when speaking of compensation.

In 1715 they passed into the hands of the Spanish Crown, and were sold to private concerns in 1871. In 1983 exploitation stopped, and today they form part of the Natural Park of Ses Salines.

Salt and *flor de sal*. As well as a condiment, salt has also been used for centuries to dry meats, fish and vegetables. Salting food means drying it: the tissues immersed in salt or brine lose water and are protected against bacterial infections. One can do dry salting —as is done with cod, or with fish such as the dogfish, in Formentera—, or in brine, that is salted water —as is done with olives or capers. Adding salt to cured meats or cheeses also prolongs their conservation.

Different types of salt are produced, the most delicate one being fleur de sal, which is still collected in the traditional way.

Today different kinds of salt are commercialised, classified according to their thickness —extra-fine, fine or thick—, damp or dry, and may contain other elements, such as iodine or fluoride.

In Ibiza, a company collects and commercialises the flor de sal that comes from Las Salinas. It is pure sea salt, and contains minerals and trace elements necessary for the organism. It is a product that has become a real delicacy, for its flavour and virtues, and which chefs are increasingly including in their gastronomic creations.

The flor de sal forms on the surface of the water of the saltwork lakes, forming a layer of crystals the colour of which varies from pure white to pale pink. In a good harvest, these crystals represent just 0.2% of the total. They are harvested manually with a type of rake that, with slow and uniform movements, collects them from the surface of the water. They are then left to dry in the sun, and thus preserve the marine properties that give them their value.

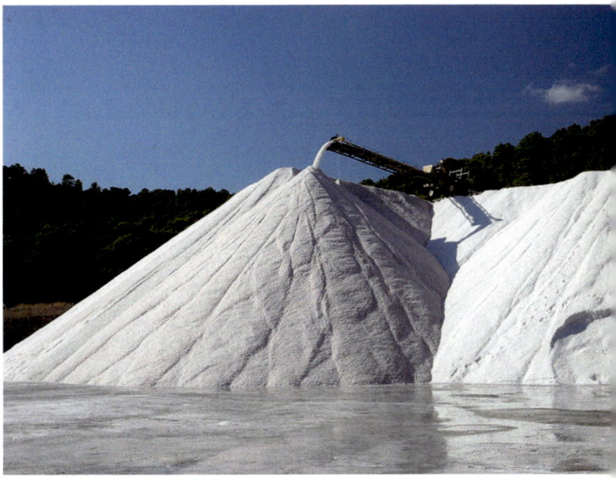

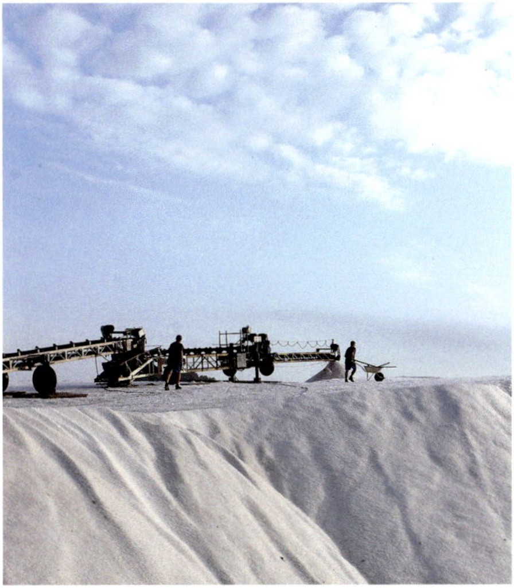

Beneficial fig tree

Along with the almond and carob tree, the fig tree is one of the typical trees of the rural landscape of Ibiza and Formentera. It is usually seen isolated, in the middle of a cultivated field or alongside a path, sheltering beneath its branches a sheep or goat, looping for some shade in the torrid summer afternoons.

The fig tree (*Ficus carica*) has its origins in south-eastern Europe, introduced into western lands in an unknown period. Its cultivation on the Pine Islands without doubt goes back a long way in time, and proof of this is that the Ibiza figs were extolled by the Latin writer Pliny the Elder (1st century AD).

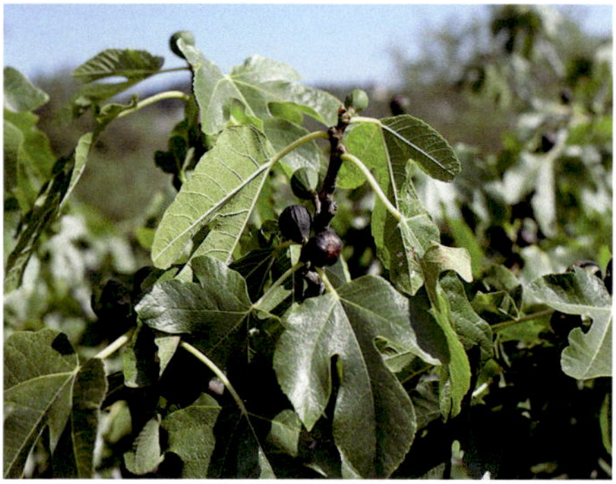

Xereques are the first figs of the season (*figues flors*) separated at the middle, sun-dried and kept in earthenware jars.

This tree can reach 5 metres in height, with a developed and wide crown. In Formentera it is common to remove the main sprout so that the foliage grows below and widely extended. Thus it is easier to pick the figs, the tree is more protected from the North wind and provides shade for the livestock. This practice makes underpinning (*estalonament*) necessary, leading to the startling fig trees of Formentera, which, supported by many sticks, look like mythical trees, designed by Salvador Dalí.

The youngest branches and the leaves have a milky, bitter juice, which is used to curdle milk and get the *recuites*, pieces of cottage cheese with sugar.

It is a tree that is used to the utmost: the production of inflorescences (clusters of flowers) is continuous, which means that on the same shoot there are figs in different stages of growth. When the harvest is picked at the end of the summer, there are still figs that are taking shape, their growth stopping during the winter, and continuing to ripen in spring. These figs, from the year before, are called early figs (*figues flors*).

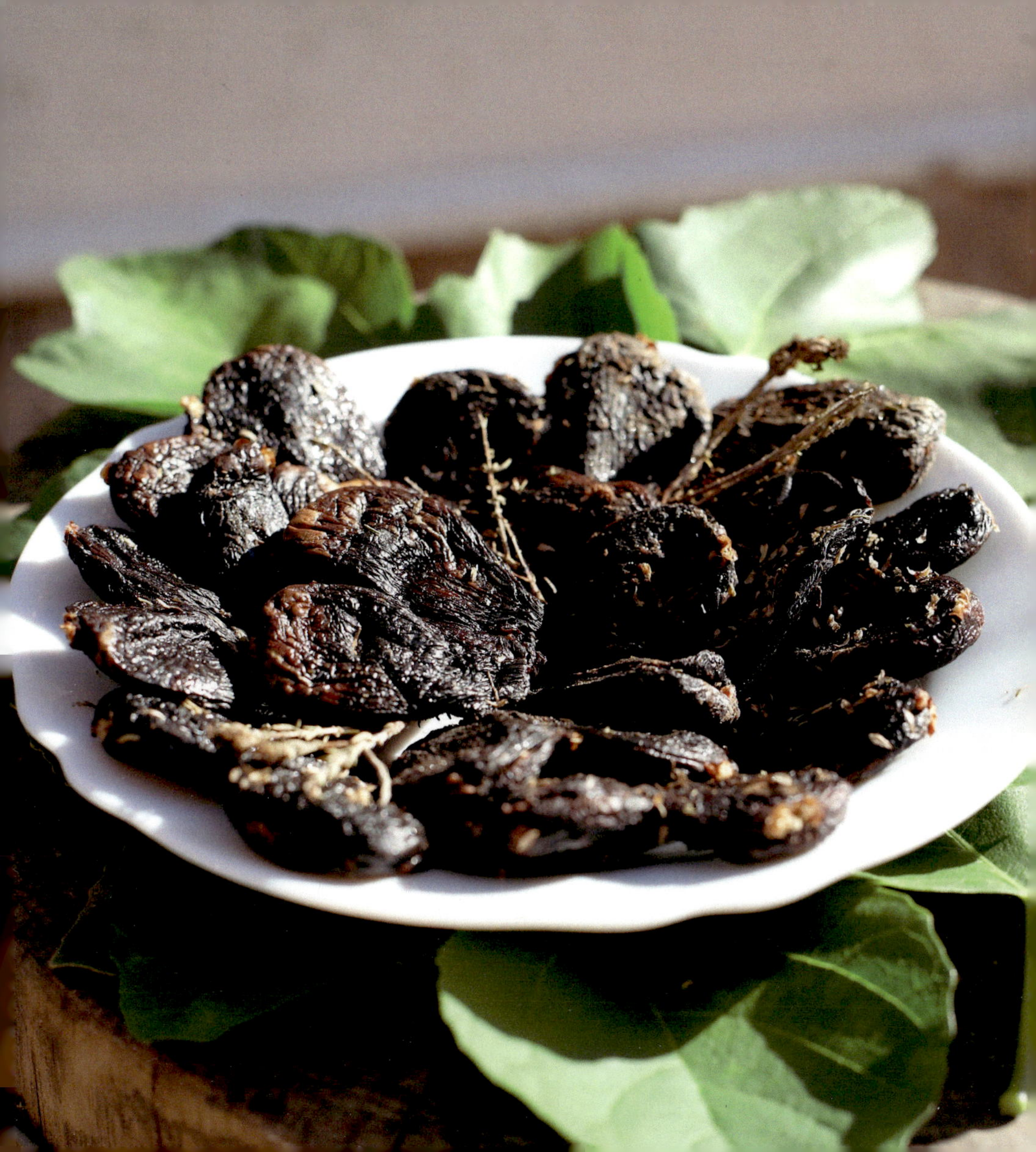

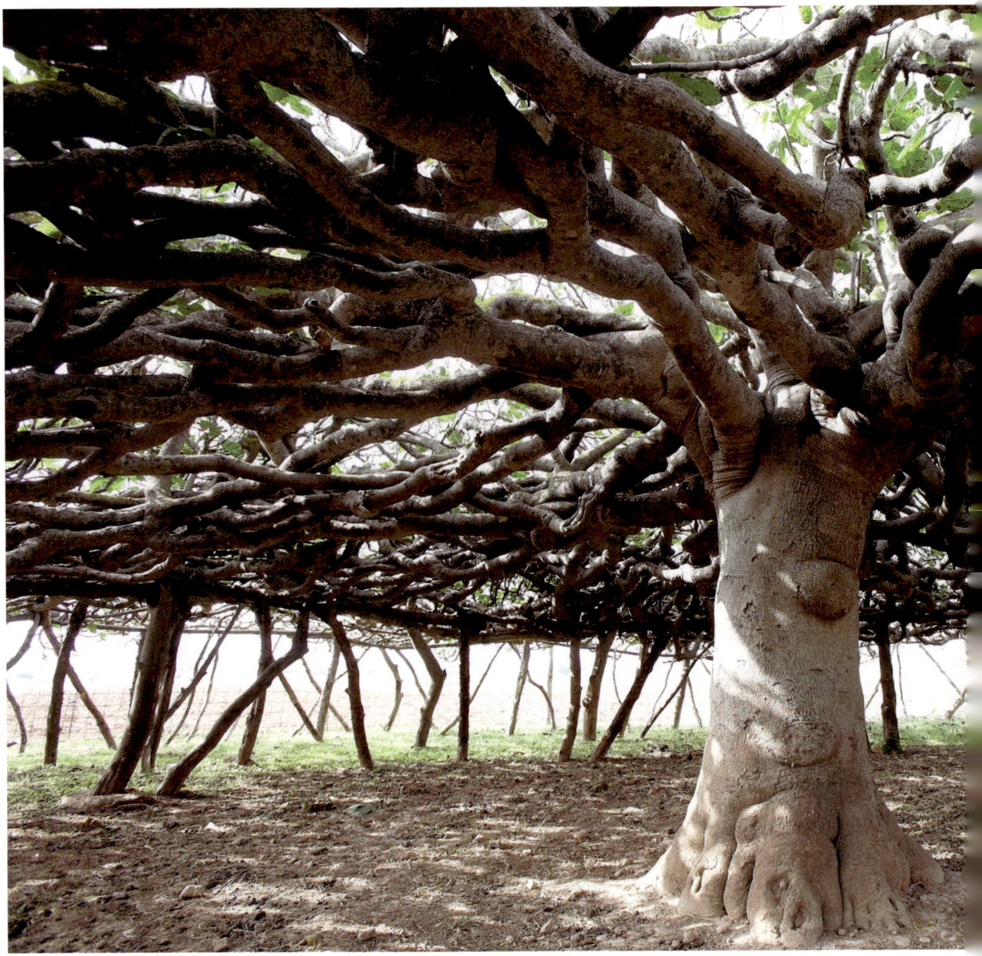

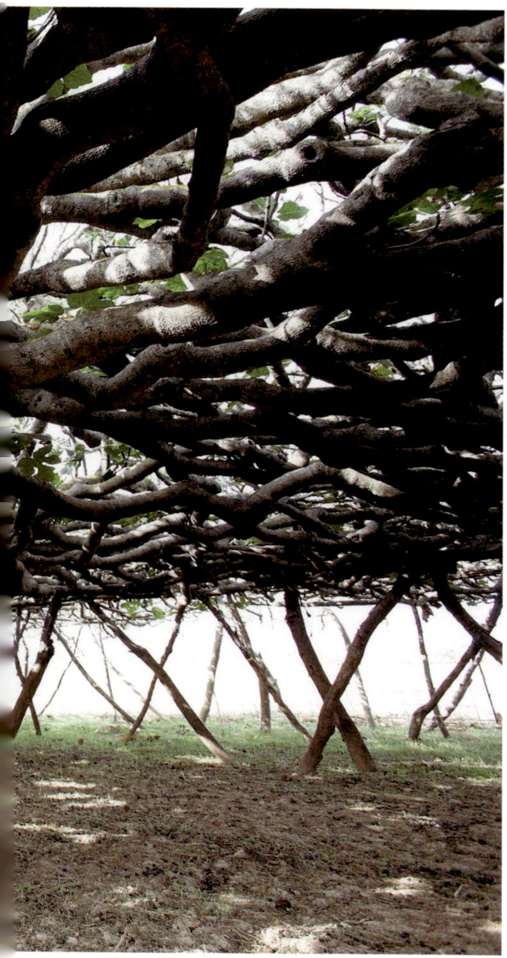

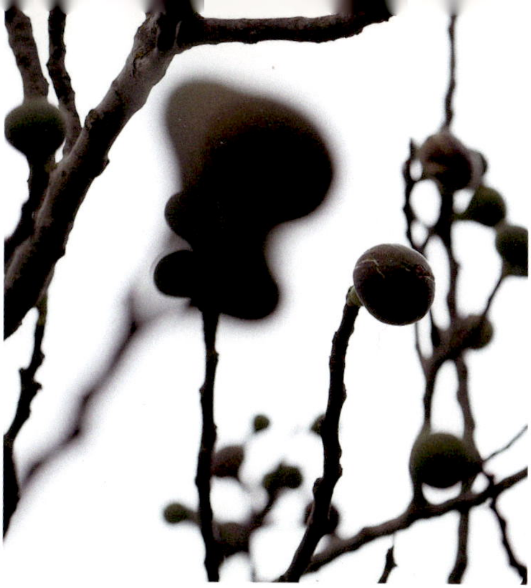

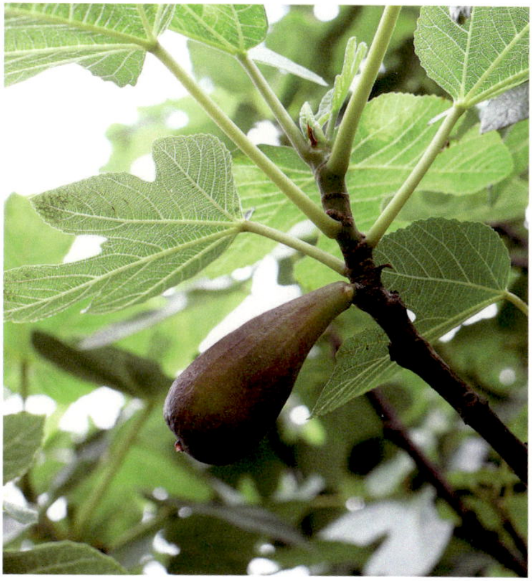

In Formentera the fig trees are underpinned so that the branches do not grow high and can provide shade to the livestock. This is the largest on the island.

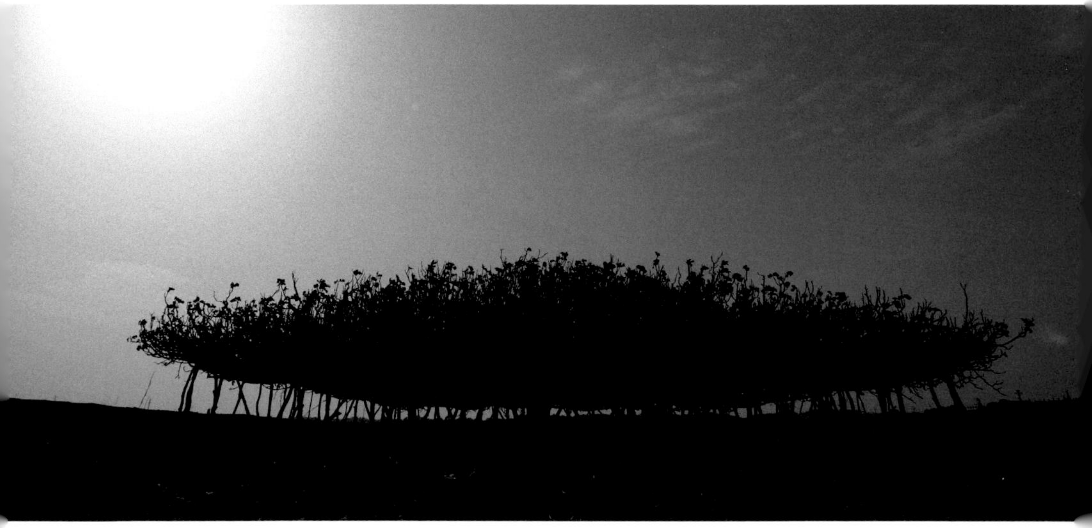

The fig tree was very important in the Balearics at the end of the 19th and early 20th century, and part of the fig production was exported. The enormous variety of names by which they are known here shows the love for this fruit, which has nourished generations: *albocor*, *alcúdia*, *blanca*, *bordissot*, *coll de dama*, *hiversesca*, *lloral*, *martinenca*, *morisca*, *oriola*, *rojal*, *sarrona*... Despite this, its cultivation went into decline due to the lack of manpower and the arrival of tourism—since the figs must be picked in summer.

Today, in the society of abundance, most of the figs are not harvested although they are within arm's reach. Moreover, the ones that reach the market are expensive.

Dry figs and *xereques*. Bread with fresh figs in summer and dry ones the rest of the year was a basic peasant meal. In an agricultural subsistence economy, eating figs represented for many the main energy source in winter. That

The fig, a symbolic tree. Figs are eaten throughout the year, fresh or dry, a basic form of energy.

is why drying figs was a regular activity in all country houses.

The best dry figs were the *xereques*, which today are a very rare typical product. They are made with *figues flors* (the early figs of the season, that ripen for Saint John's Day), opened in half and dried in the sun. Once dry, the pairs are joined, they are lightly baked and, when cooled, placed in layers in a recipient —in the past a large earthenware jar (*alfàbia*)—, alternating with thyme and fennel. The layers are compressed by hand, and when the earthenware jar is full it is closed to avoid contact with the air.

In the past these figs would be opened after Christmas, and it was common to keep the last earthenware jar for the July harvesting. At the time the *xereques* were an energy-filled dessert, accompanied by toasted almonds.

Figs of other varieties were also dried in the sun, but whole, and placed compressed in earthenware jars or boxes, in alternating layers with fennel, thyme and carob leaves. Those that had fallen on the floor were also picked up, dried and kept for pig feed.

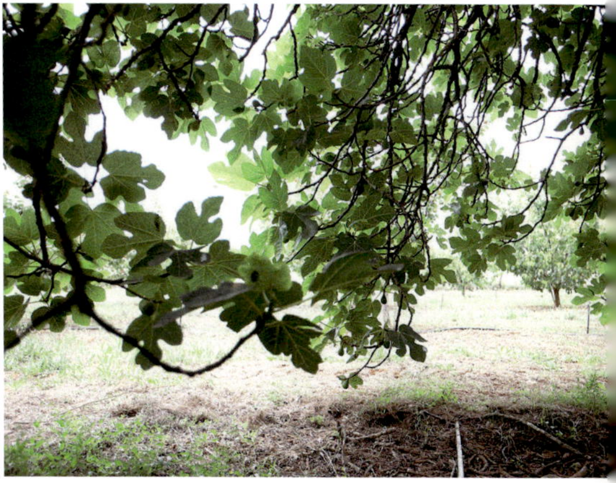

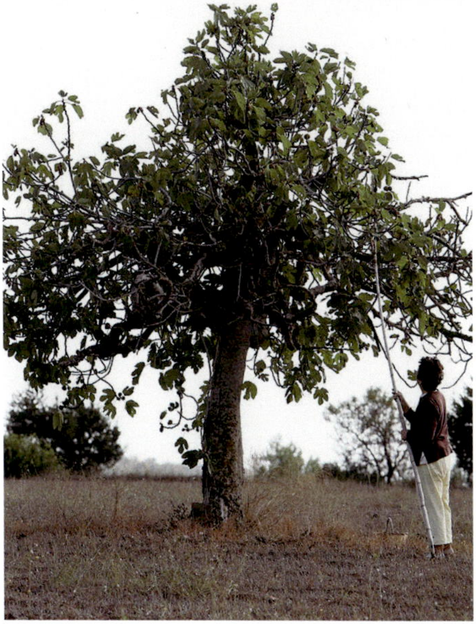

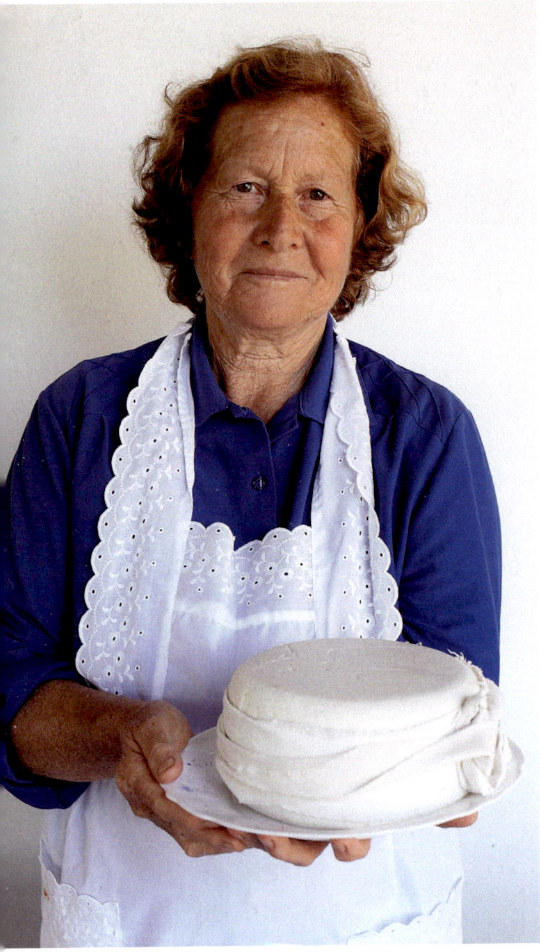

Traditionally made cheese

Turning milk into cheese is one of the oldest food processes known to mankind, arising from the need to prolong the life of foods. Cheese is without doubt the most important dairy product, for both its properties and its excellent flavour.

In Ibiza and Formentera traditionally-made cheeses are produced from goat and sheep's milk, as well as cheeses combining both types of milk. Fresh cheese, with a mild taste, is the one used in traditional confectionery to make products such as flaó, or eaten accompanied by honey as a dessert.

The cheeses can be fresh or mild, medium and mature. The mature cheeses are smeared with paprika, and in the past were kept hanging from the kitchen ceiling, or some pieces were kept in oil to keep them softer.

1 Mature goat's cheese **2** Fresh goat's cheese
3 Medium goat's cheese **4** Mature sheep's cheese

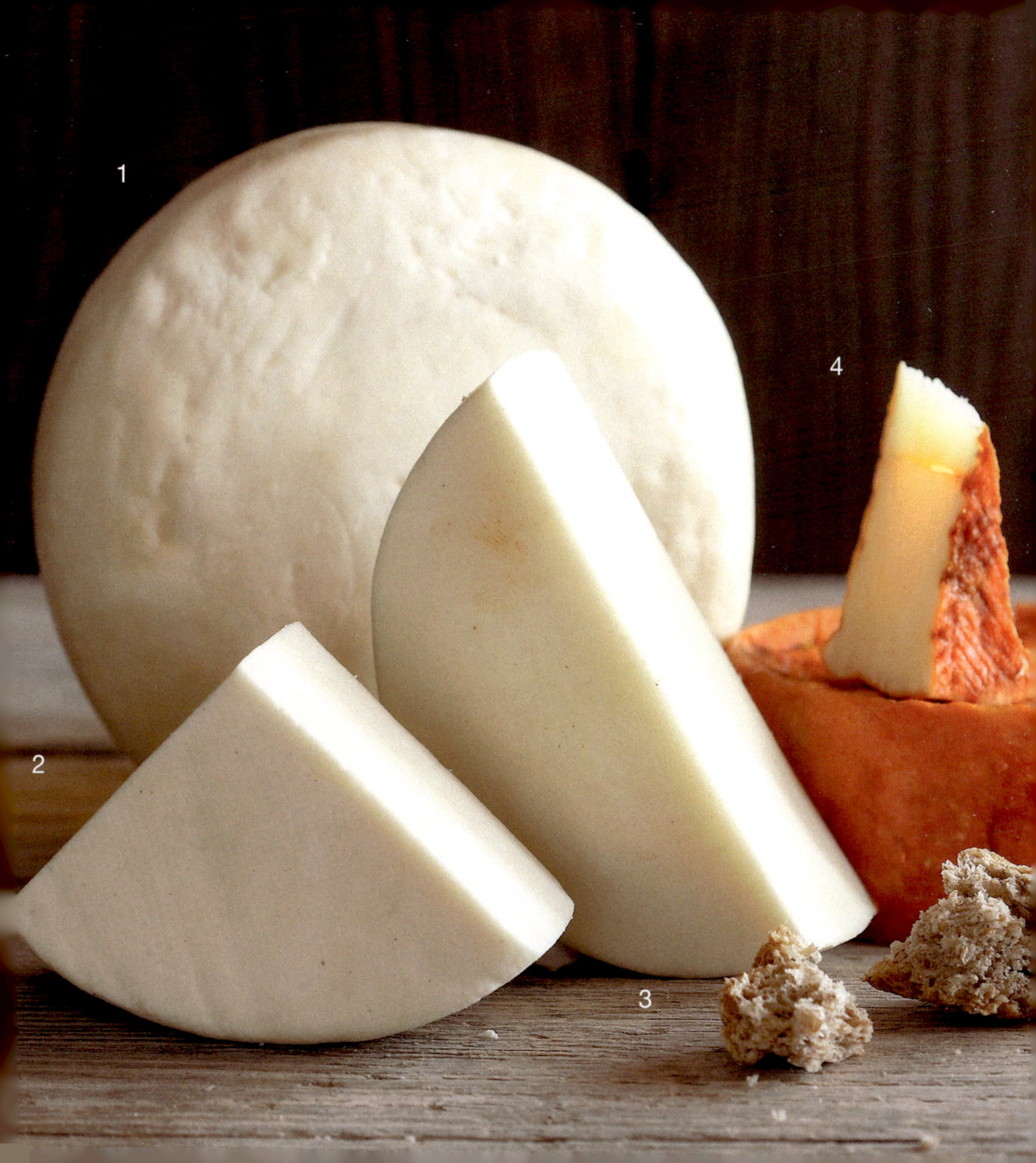
1
4
2
3

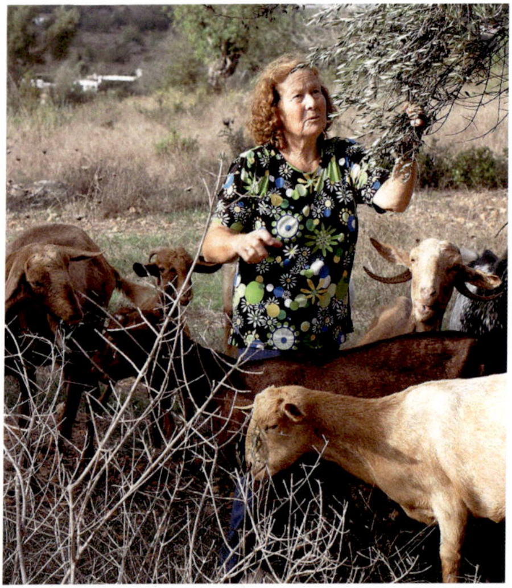

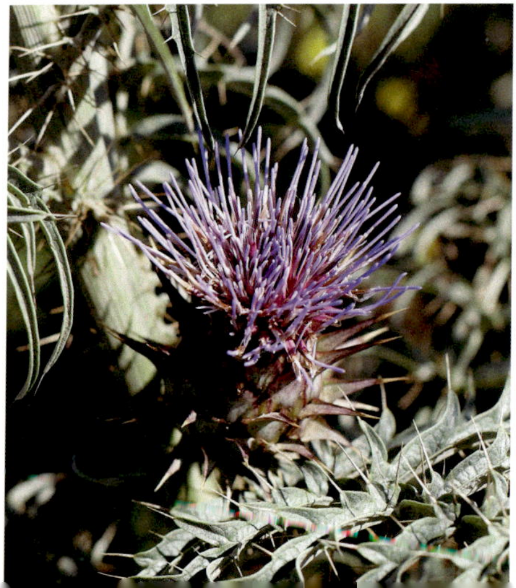

In Ibiza mass-produced cheese is also produced from cow's milk, generally a very compressed mass, creamy, low in salt and with a mild aroma and flavour. It is usually in small pieces, with a soft rind and clear colour. There are also cow's milk cheeses with a reddish rind, due to the addition of paprika, more compact and dryer.

In Formentera traditionally-made cheese is produced from raw goat and sheep's milk, curdled with thistle flower, manually compressed and dry salted. There are two types: fresh —less than 10 days maturing—, and medium, with a maturing period of more than one month. It is a rare product, due to the fact that the livestock exploitations are on a family scale or very small.

L'herba de formatjar. To make cheese on these islands it is essential, as in yesteryear, to use the *herba de formatjar*: the flowers of the inflorescences of the thistle (*Cynara carduncullus*), used to make the milk curdle, both for cheese and cottage cheese. Before, they would pick them on Saint John's Day, dry them and keep them so that they would have enough to last all year. To use the thistle, it is placed in a recipient with water so that it softens during a whole night. Then it is crushed and the juice extracted, which is mixed with the milk.

To make cheese the inflorescences of the thistle are essential, which make the milk curdle.

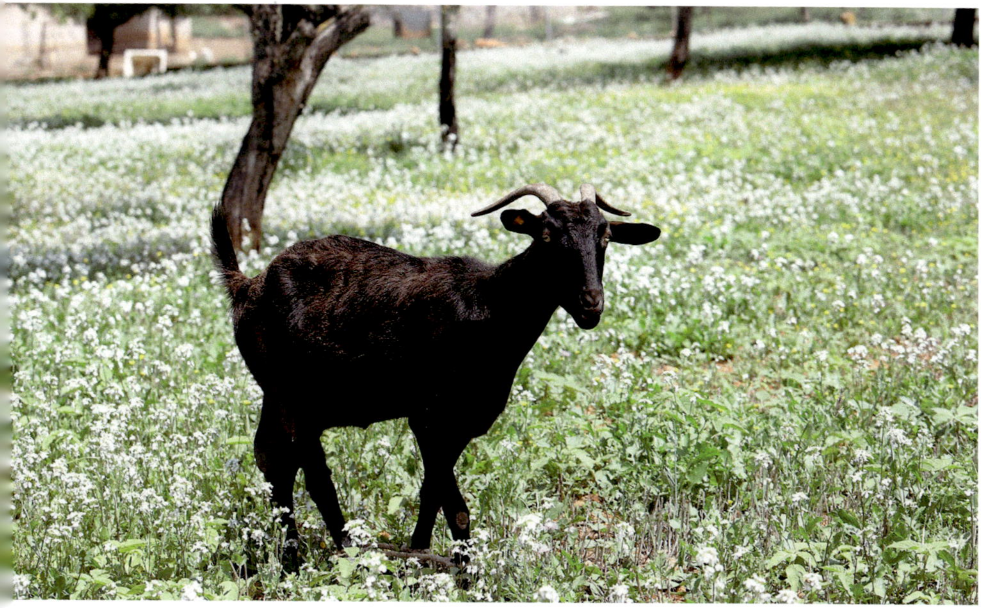

Traditionally it was the women who prepared the cheese. They began making cheese when the lambs and kids had been weaned or sold, and they continued until the females no longer supplied milk. A common custom was to make cheese under the sign of Christmas: if the 25th of December the previous year has been a Monday, they began to make cheese on Monday. The pieces obtained were for home use and were exchanged for other foods or used to pay back favours.

The whey (*xerigot*) that remained as a residue from making the cheese was also used. It was boiled with some mint leaves and, once filtered, the recuita de *xerigot* (the solid part) was obtained, with which *flaoneres*, flat breads, were prepared, or eaten with bread and sugar.

1

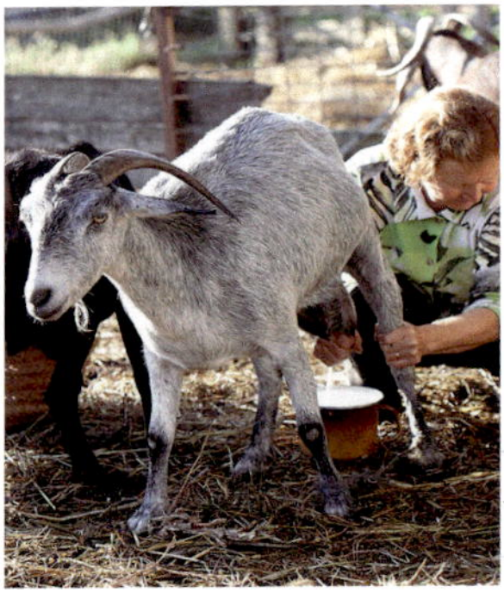

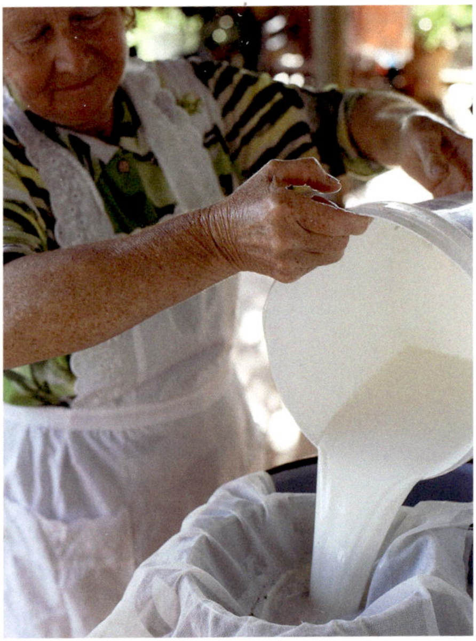

2

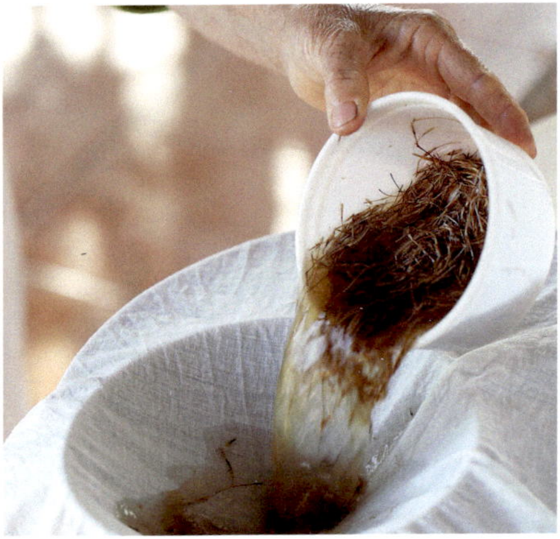

3

¿How to make fresh goat's cheese?

1 Goat's milk. To prepare the cheese, first the milk is obtained, the fresher the better.

2 Filtering. The milk is then filtered in a recipient (*l'olla de formatjar*) to get rid of the hairs and impurities.

3 *Herba de formatjar*. (thistle flower). Then, also filtered, the thistle juice is added wrapped in a tea towel and placed in the pot for a couple of minutes before removing it.

4 Curdling. The cheese-making pot is covered with cloths, so that it preserves the heat (between 15° and 20° C) and the milk will curdle. It is then left to rest covered for between 1 and 2 hours.

5 / 6 Curd and elimination of whey. When the milk has curdled, the curd is broken up by hand, and then removed and compressed again, carefully, so that the whey comes out.

4

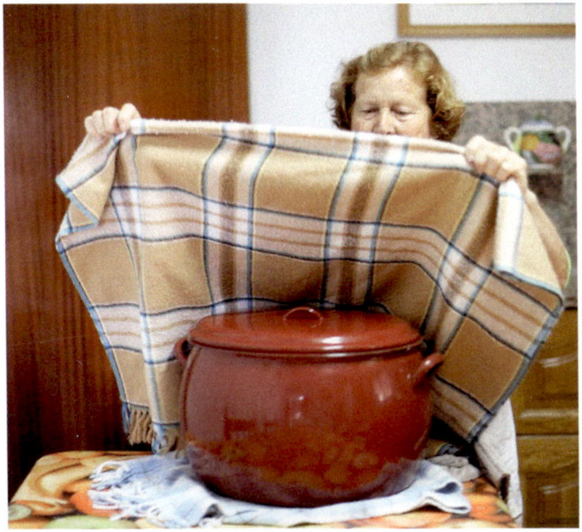

5

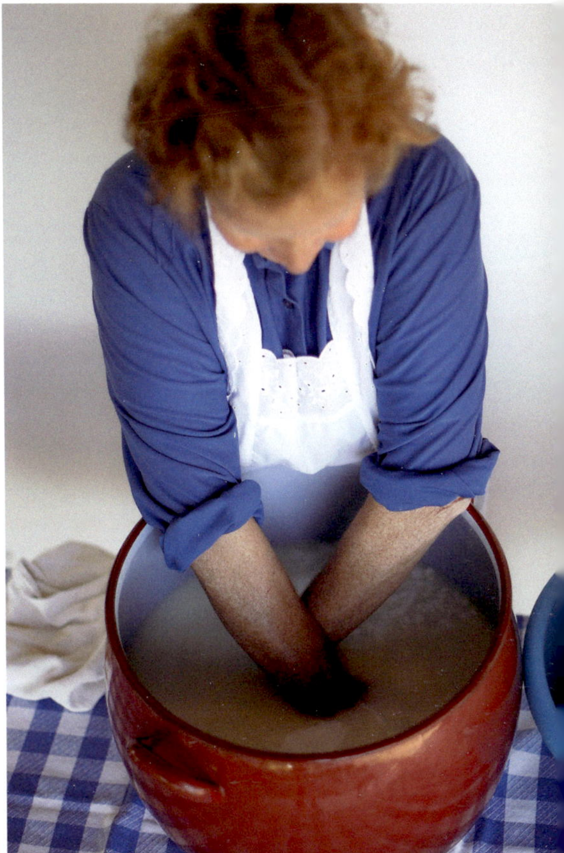

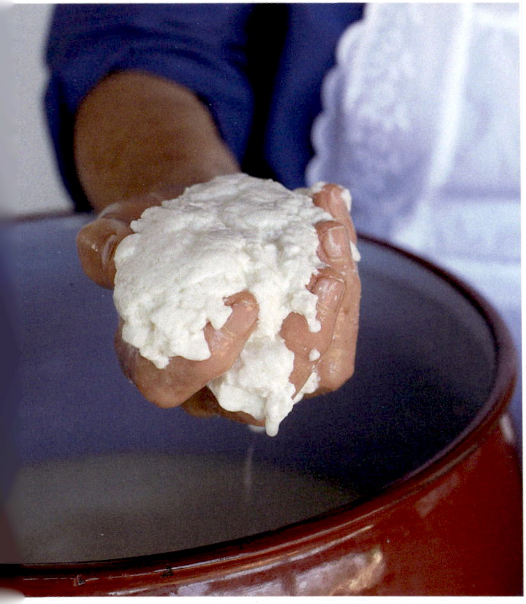

6

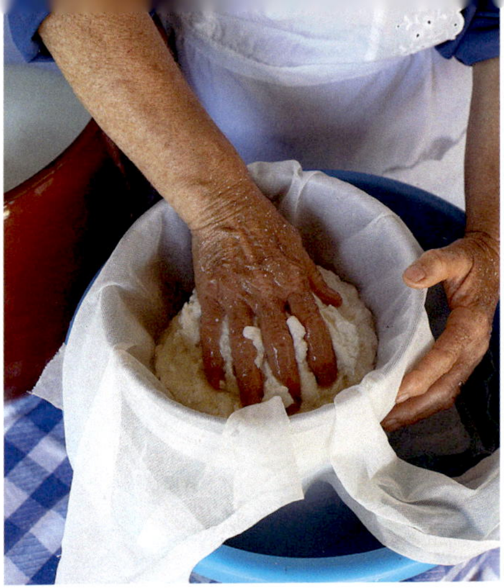

7

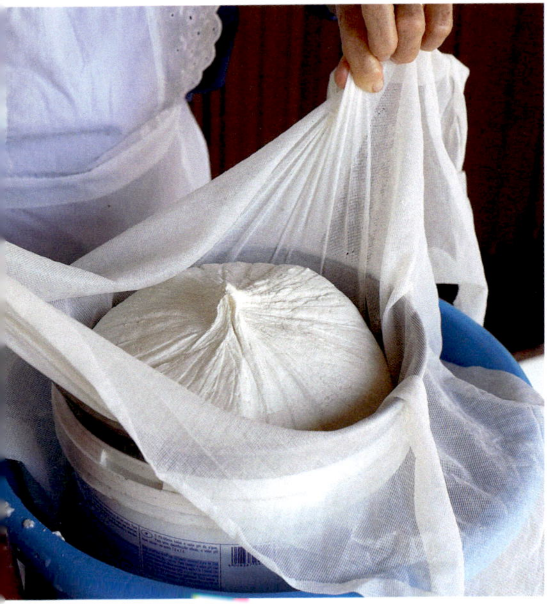

8

7 9 8 10 11

7 Moulding in *escudella*, the bowl. The curd is placed in a colander covered with a tea towel (in the past the *escudella* was used, a semi-spherical ceramic recipient). The mass is compacted by hand.

8 Compacting. Once all the curd is in the colander, it is compacted for the last time in a tea towel, so that all the whey is removed.

9 Salting. The surface of the now shaped curd is coated with fine salt, and it is left to set.

10 Moulding with bandages. The curd is wrapped in a plastic or metallic bandage (in the past they were savin wood), of some 10 cm height and 50 cm long, approximately. It is later covered with a cloth bandage.

11 Maturation. The pieces are left to dry for several days at room temperature. When the cheeses are dry enough, the bandages are removed and they are stored.

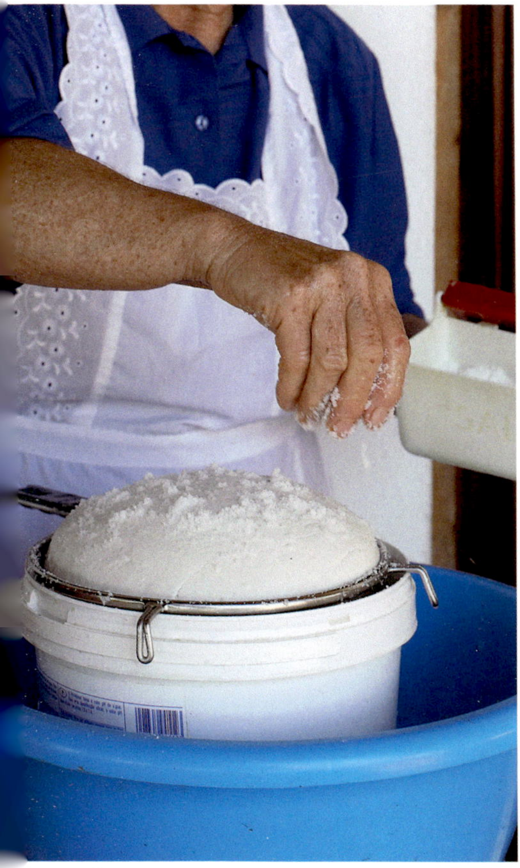

9

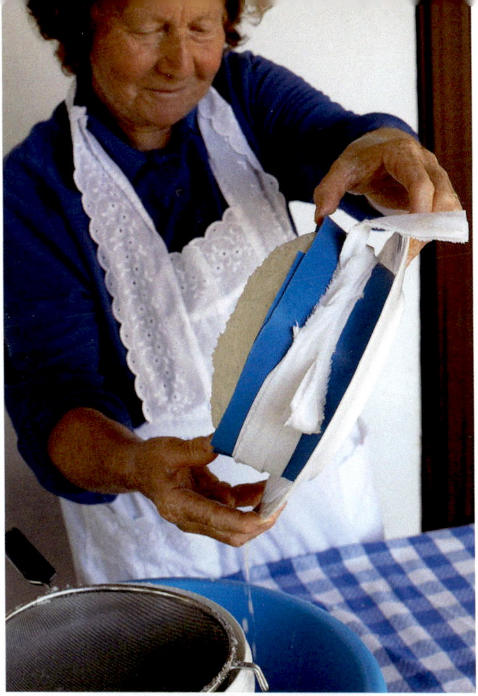

10

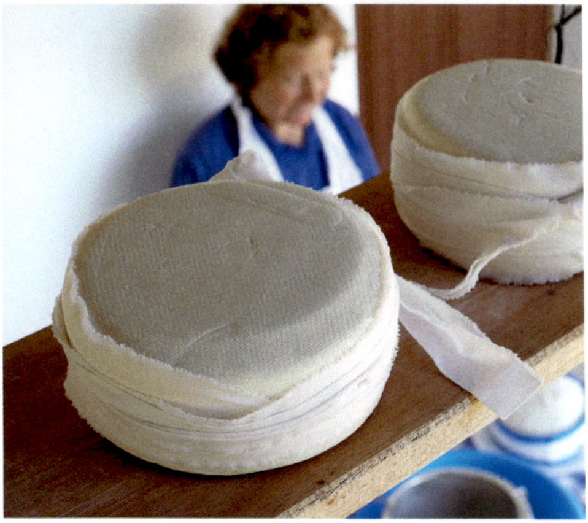

11

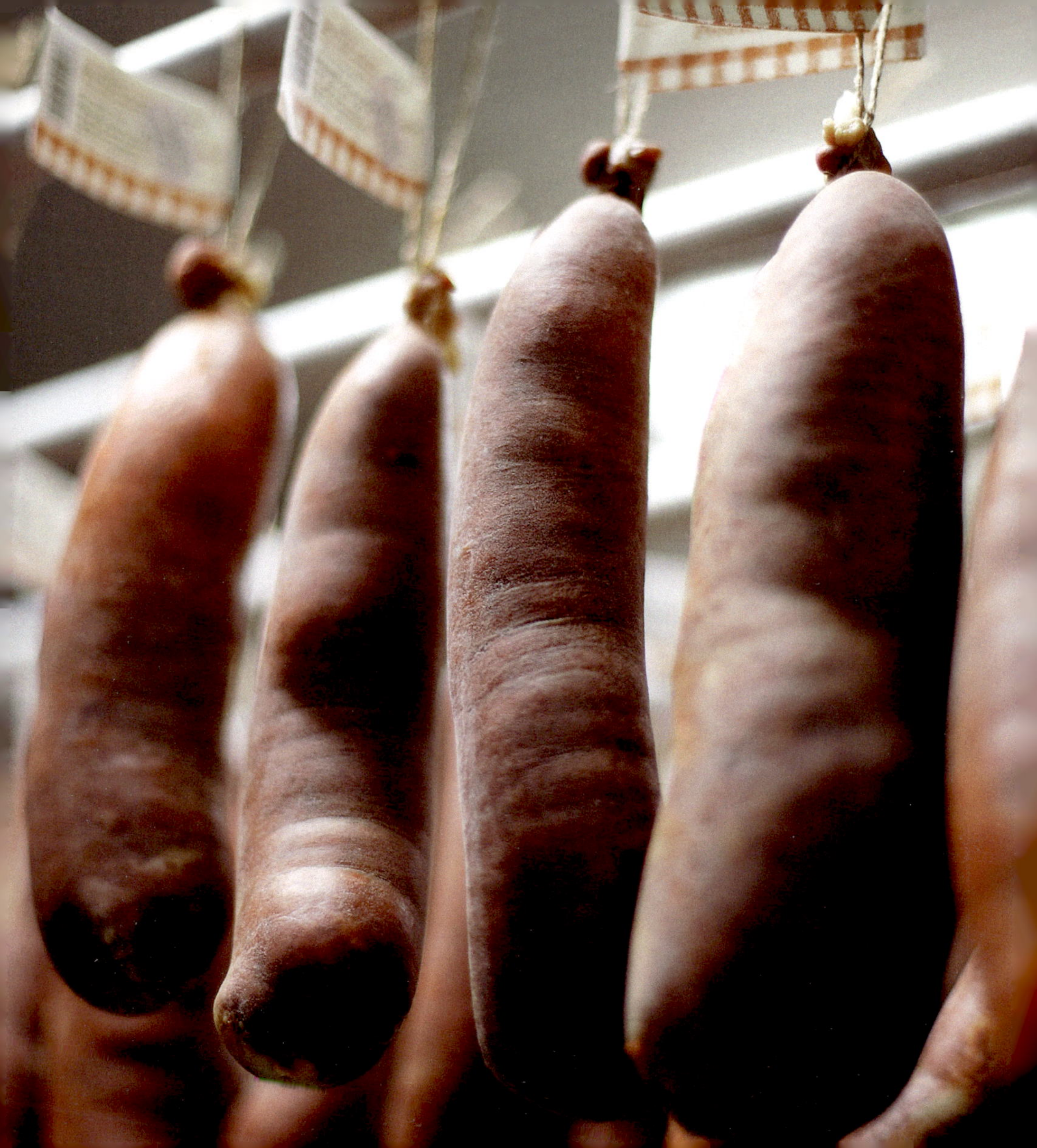

Pork and other meats

In the rural world of Ibiza and Formentera, dry agriculture and orchard farming were combined with raising farmyard animals. The most profitable of all was without doubt the pig: to raise it cost little work or resources. It just had to be kept near the house, fed with leftovers and carob beans, and once sacrificed almost nothing was left to waste. The slaughter, as it still is in the homes where it is carried out, was a festive meeting that was usually held before Christmas.

Meat was obtained from the pig and they made products throughout the year from it. Just like today they made *sobrassada* (cured meat), *botifarra* (sausage), *botifarró* (black pudding) and the sublime *ventre farcit* (stuffed pork belly). The bacon and bones were also salted to conserve them for a long time. The eye teeth were used to smooth down the pita fibre of espadrilles, and even, in the past, were used as buttons on trousers.

When a home wanted to slaughter a pig they invited the family, friends and neighbours. In exchange for their work, the guests were given food: early in the morning they were offered fritters, and there was always bread with *sobrassada* or *botifarró*; when the work was finished and everything tidied up, they ate pork with rice, pork *frita* and the best *sobrassada* from the previous slaughter. Those who had collaborated were given pieces of the cured meats prepared.

The pork meat and products derived from the pig have a fundamental place in the recipe book. Thus, bacon, *sobrassada*, *botifarra* and *botifarró* appear in modest dishes such as *pinya de col ofegada* (sautéed cabbage); *col amb ossos*, where salted pig bones are also added; or the *olla podrida* (hotpot), with potatoes, beans, onion and tomato. They are also used to make broths, such

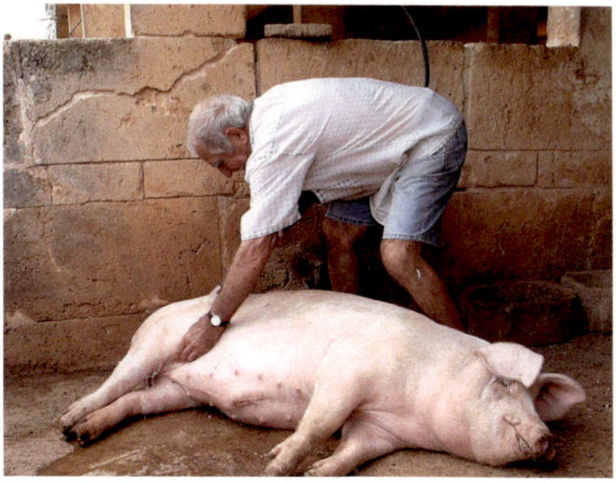

Sobrassada is a cured meat made with the lean pork meat, chopped and highly seasoned. It is then left to dry.

as *sopa i bullit*, with chickpeas, cabbage, celery, onion and tomato —and sometimes salted pig bones—; or rice dishes, such as rice with meat *a la pagesa* (peasant style), where they are combined with lamb and peas. They are, of course, basic ingredients in the renowned *sofrit pagès* (farmer's sauce), combined with other meats, potatoes and spices, or in the *frita pagesa* (farmer's fry), pork accompanied by milk mushrooms and potatoes. Pig's trotters are cooked with an accompaniment of rice with white beans, *sobrassada*, *botifarró* and spices.

Lamb. The sheep is inherent in the landscape of Ibiza and Formentera. As well as meat and milk, it also provided wool. Some documents from the 18th century explain that the women worked on shearing the sheep, spinning and weaving the wool. Then they cooked pomegranate skins, and with this juice dyed the fabric, with which they made clothes for the family.

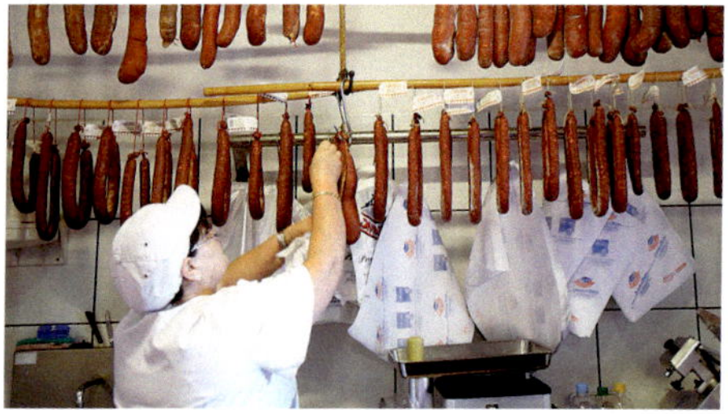

1

1 Sobrassada. It is made with lean pork, chopped and mixed with paprika, pepper and salt. The average curing time depends on the size, between 45 days and 6 months. The *sobrassada* stuffed into the thickest intestine is called *cular*. The new or tender *sobrassada* is preferred for roasting, whole or in slices, and spread over a slice of cottage loaf.

2

2 *Botifarra* and *botifarró*. The *botifarra* is thick intestine stuffed with pork, mainly the meat from the cheek, bacon (*xulla*) and the bloodiest remains, all cut very finely or chopped, mixed with blood, salt and spices (mainly paprika, pepper, nutmeg and fennel) and later cooked. The *botifarró* has the same characteristics, but made with fine intestine. There is black *botifarró* —made with the bloodiest parts of the pig, such as the heart, dewlap and blood, all chopped up and seasoned with spices, stuffed into the intestine and cooked—, and white *botifarró*, with a smooth flavour and with very few spices; to make it lean meat and dewlap are used, all chopped finely and then cooked, stuffed into intestine and cooked.

3

3 *Ventre farcit.* "Stuffed pork belly". It is a highly appreciated sausage, which in the past was kept for a special day. It is very expensive to make: it is the stomach of a pig stuffed with a part of the head of the shoulder chopped, some chopped and some minced, all seasoned with spices, especially black pepper. It is cooked slowly for five or six hours and is meaty and juicy.

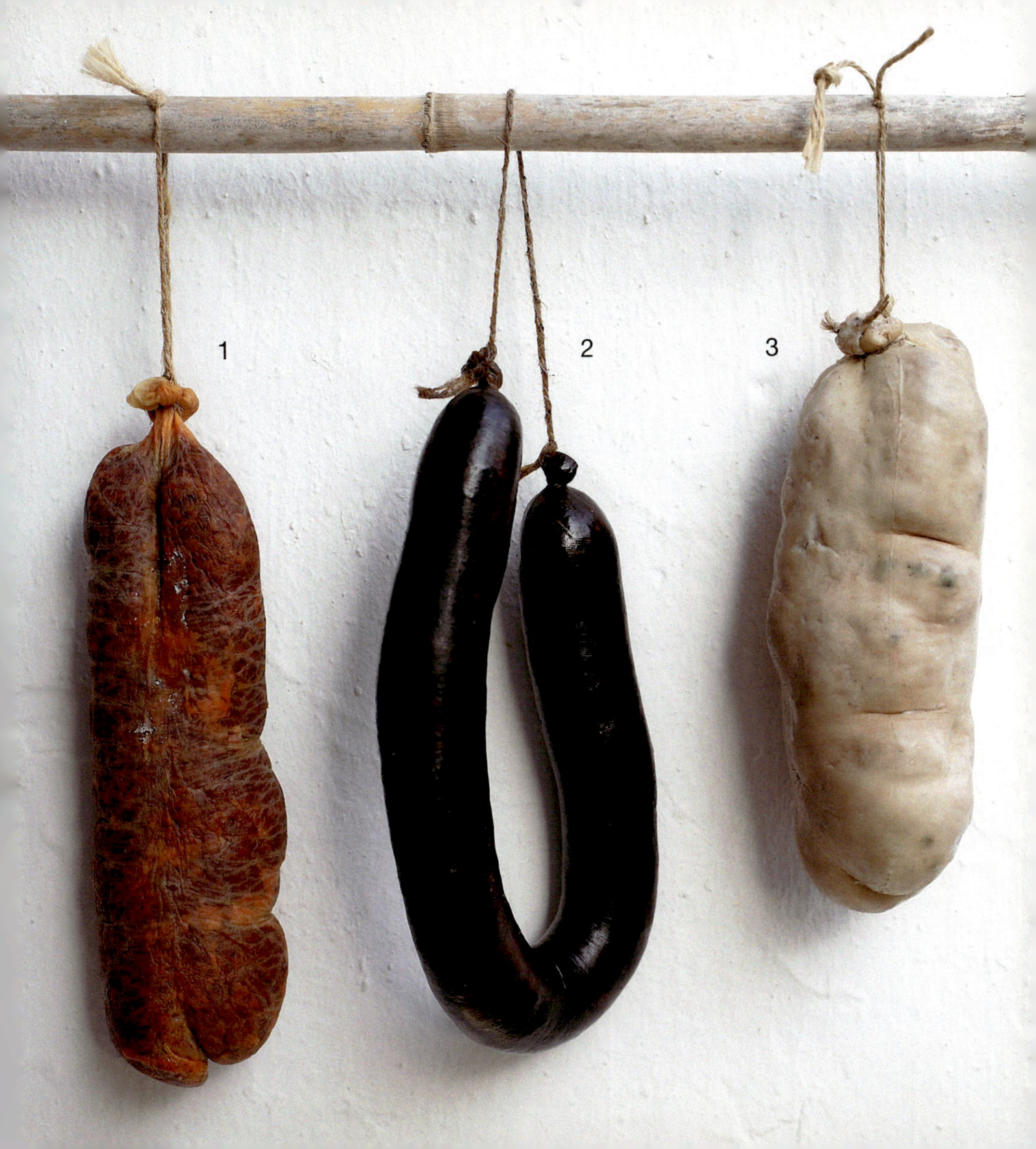
1
2
3

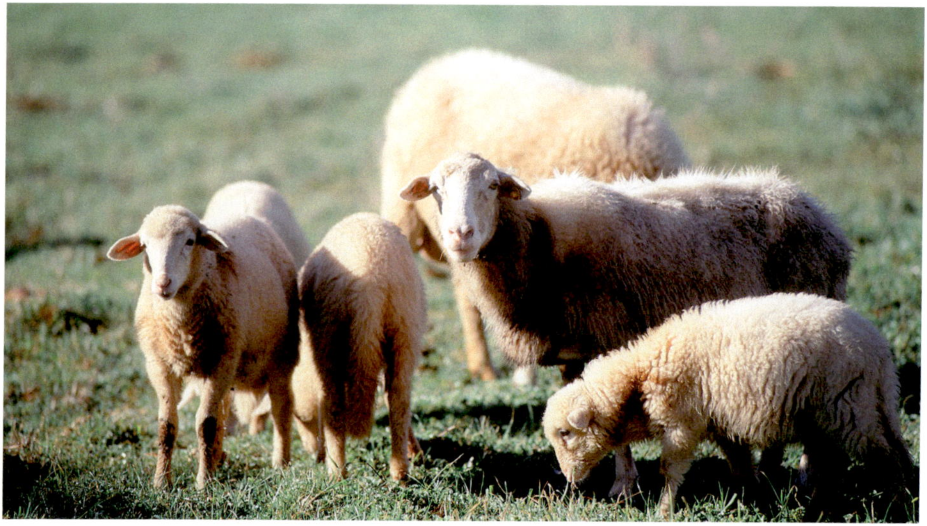

Lamb meat, with a strong taste, appears in many traditional dishes, as does the blood and the tripe. It forms an almost indispensable part of the stocks and broths, such as *sopa i bullit*, or rice dishes such as rice with meat. Minced, it appears in recipes such as stuffed aubergines or, along with other meats, as meatballs. In stews and roasts it is the star ingredient of the sheep's head stew, which is also prepared roast, with potatoes and highly spiced; or the spectacular leg of lamb with peppers, the meat of which is seasoned beforehand. The chops are eaten roast, or with peppers and tomato, or accompanied with vegetables. One of the most elaborate recipes is the leg of lamb stuffed with a mixture of chopped pork, *sobrassada*, pine nuts and garlic.

The lamb's blood, (generally baked beforehand with laurel, salt and pepper) has also been used to prepare dishes such as blood with onion or broad beans. The tripe (liver, lung, heart, etc.)

Lamb, rabbit and chicken are other highly appreciated meats. They are cooked in diverse ways, and appear in stocks or rice dishes.

is the basic ingredient for *frita de freixura*, where they appear finely chopped, fried and combined with potatoes. The kidneys are also prepared in wine or sautéed.

Rabbit and poultry. Rabbit appears in casseroles and stews in which there is a good fried sauce base and final spicy sauce, which include the fried rabbit's liver chopped with a *ñora*, a small spicy red pepper, for example. The meat is often seasoned beforehand, and usually cooked with potatoes, peas, onion or peppers. A delicious rabbit with noodles is also made.

Among the poultry, Chicken features in casseroles and stews, such as chicken with tomato. It can be used to prepare the *frita de carn*. As a sublime dish we should mention the *capó farcit* (stuffed capon), stuffed with a mixture of onion, garlic, pig's ear, shoulder, *sobrassada*, *botifarra*, raisins and pine nuts, green beans and carrots (among other variants).

With the chicken tripe the *frita de menudets* is prepared. Partridge is cooked with cabbage or marinated.

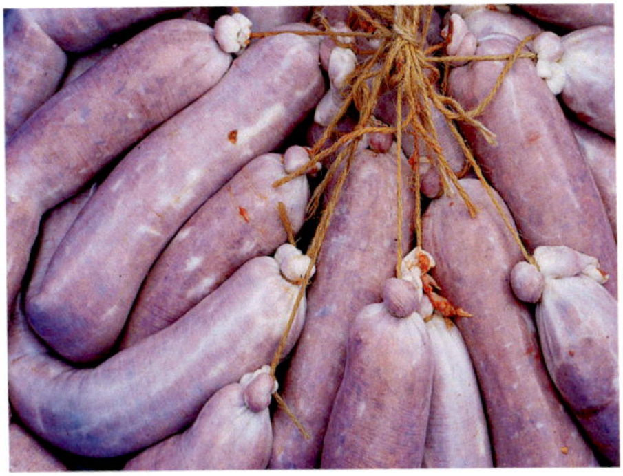

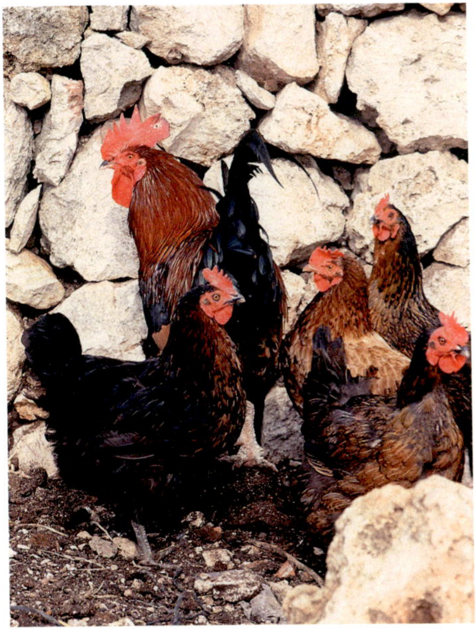

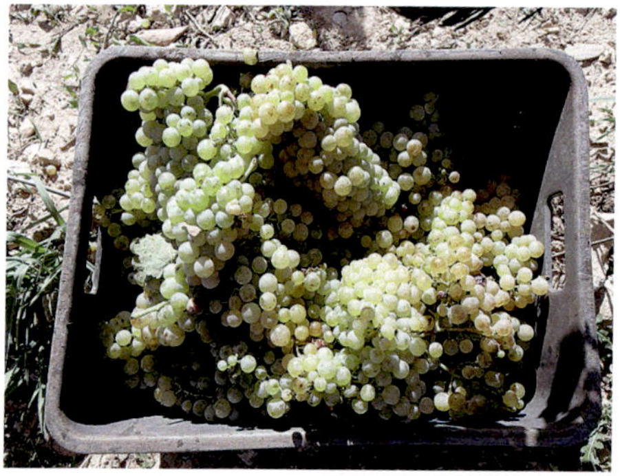

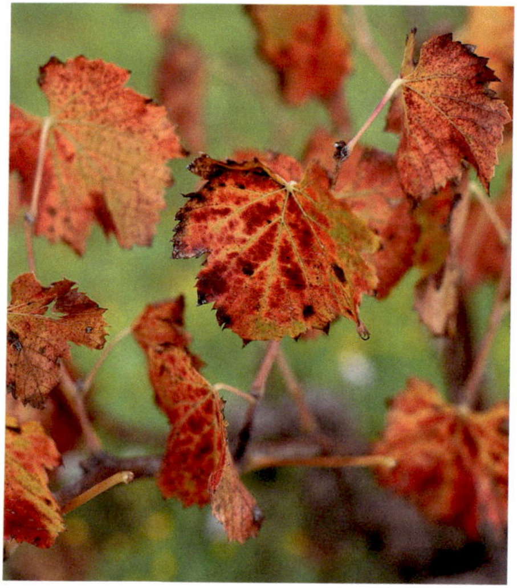

The wine sector is recovering the splendour of bygone times, with a commitment to quality wines.

Local wines

The production of wine is one of the most promising activities of the Pine Islands. This is nothing new, though, since wine production on these islands dates back a long time. In Ibiza it began in the 7th century BC, during the period of the Phoenicians and some historians point out that in this period the majority of the wine drunk on the eastern part of the peninsula came from the island. Later on, the Romans introduced new cultivation techniques and improved the fermentation processes.

The age of splendour, however, was the 19th century: when the phyloxera plague affected the French vineyards, France —large wine consumer and producer—, had to import it from elsewhere, including Ibiza. The island's production was thus reactivated. According to Archduke Louis Salvador, in 1867 the surface area of vineyards was more than 54 hectares, and production some 232 hectolitres of wine. At the end of the 19th century, however, phyloxera also reached Ibiza, something that, added to the community incentives to pull up vines, meant that the sector experienced a crisis. However, the farmers never stopped producing wine for their own consumption.

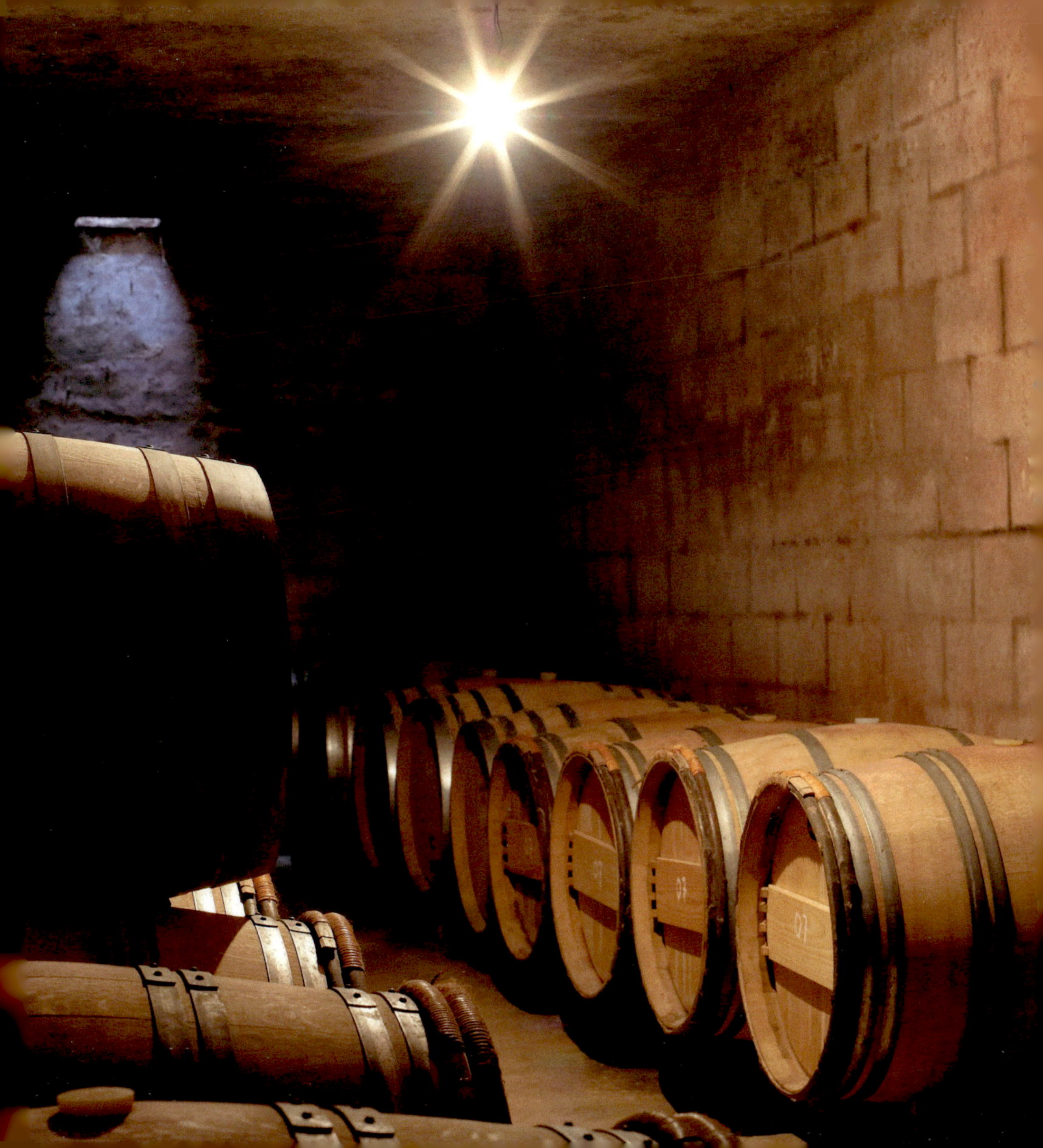

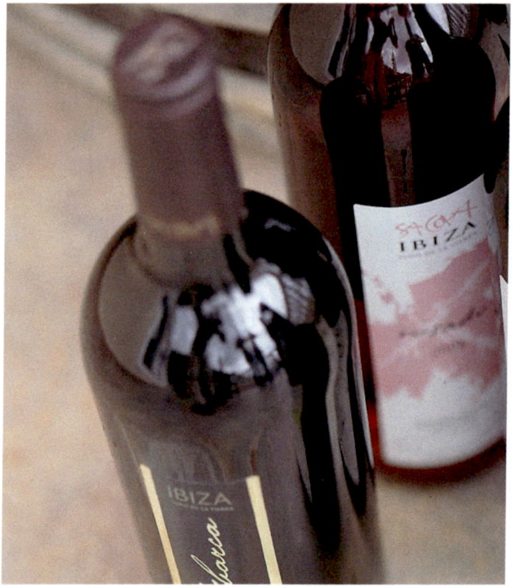

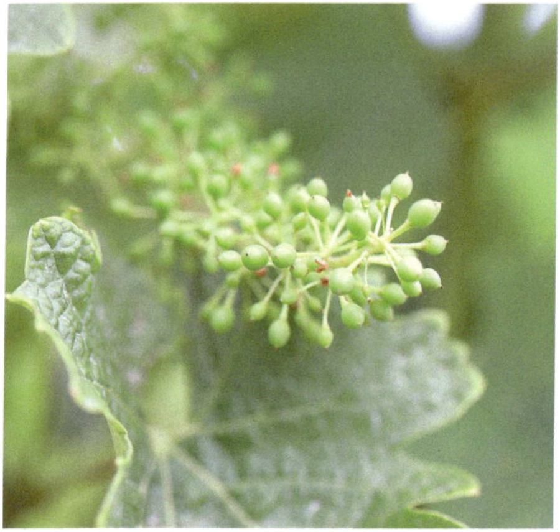

In the 1990s the sector began a recovery process: some wine producers modernised their cellars, and in 1996 the winemaking county of "Ibiza" was created, regulating the mention "Vi de la Terra Eivissa" (wine from Ibiza). Under this geographic sign feature the red wines made from the Monastrell variety, very well adapted to the island. They are cherry or bigarraeu coloured wines, bright and transparent, in which the aromas of mature fruits dominate. In some cases thyme is prominent, traditionally used to avoid the fermentation casks from blocking. Among the white wines feature those made with Macabeo as the main variety, with a solid lemon or straw yellow colour, with aromas of mature fruit and flowers.

In December in Sant Mateu d'Aubarca the popular Festa del Vi (wine festival) is held, where the farmers present the new wine.

The wine of Formentera. Grape growing and winemaking are agricultural activities with a longstanding tradition on the island. It was undertaken in the 13th century, and probably continued until the 15th Century, the century when Formentera became depopulated due to the plague. The island was repopulated four centuries later, and

"Vi de la Terra Eivissa" and "Vi de la Terra de Formentera" are geographic identifiers for some island wines.

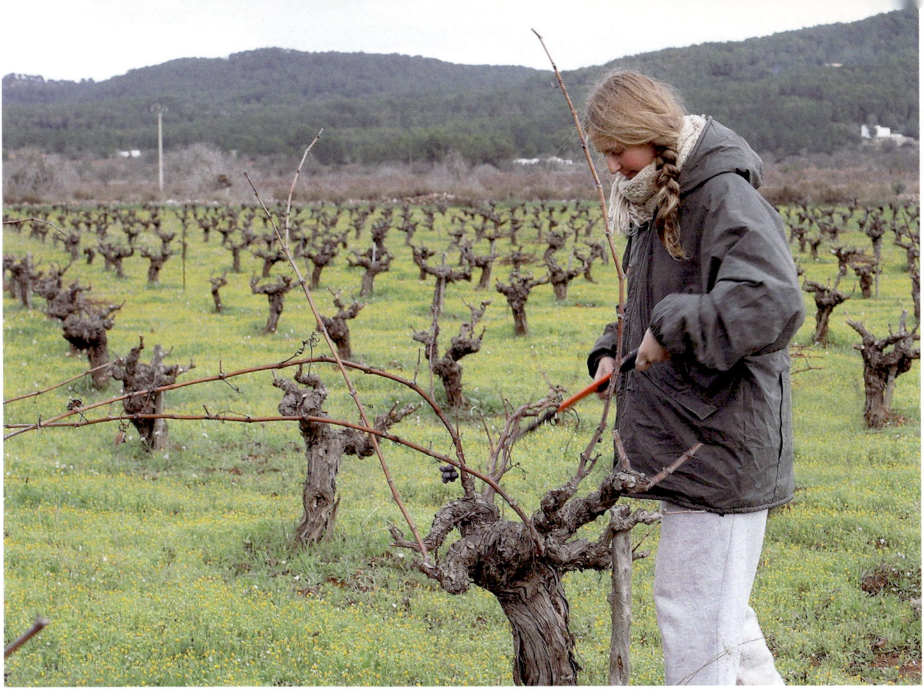

the winemaking activity gradually increased. According to Archduke Louis Salvador, in the 18th century there had been 79,000 stocks sewn, and the production was 11,400 litres of wine. With the construction, at the end of the 19th century, of the Ca'n Marroig cellar, production increased. Today there are two cellars on the island, situated in La Mola and Cap de Barbaria.

"Vi de la Terra de Formentera" (wine from Formentera) is the geographic sign that designates the traditional wines made from the Monastrell, Fogoneu, Tempranillo, Cabernet Sauvignon and Merlot varieties, and with the whites, Malvasía, Prensal Blanco, Chardonnay and Viognier. The reds are characterised by their redcurrant colour and violet tones, they are bright and clean, and the aromas of mature fruit predominate.

Every year a competition is held of the wines made by the farmers, the central event of the festivals of Sant Francesc and Sant Ferran.

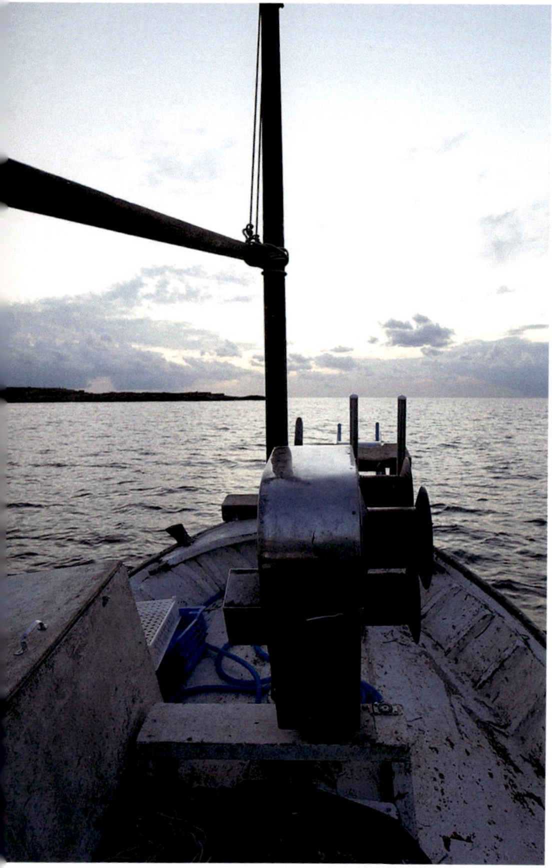

The universe of fish

Ibiza and Formentera have traditionally lived facing the sea, making full use of all its food resources. This is reflected in the veritable gastronomic universe that makes up the dishes in which, as the main ingredient or otherwise, fish and seafood appear. Some fish, like cod conserved in salt, are no longer subject to mass consumption since the appearance of the fridge. Other species, such as the smooth-hound shark or sea urchin, have suffered the consequences of overfishing and are today protected.

Nevertheless, in private homes and restaurants —both along the coast and inland— one can still enjoy exquisite fish and seafood dishes. Moreover, in Formentera fish salted and sun-dried is prepared as it was centuries ago. Let's look at some of the more representative fish of this cuisine.

Fishing in Ibiza and Formentera is mainly carried out by fishermen with small craftsman-built boats.

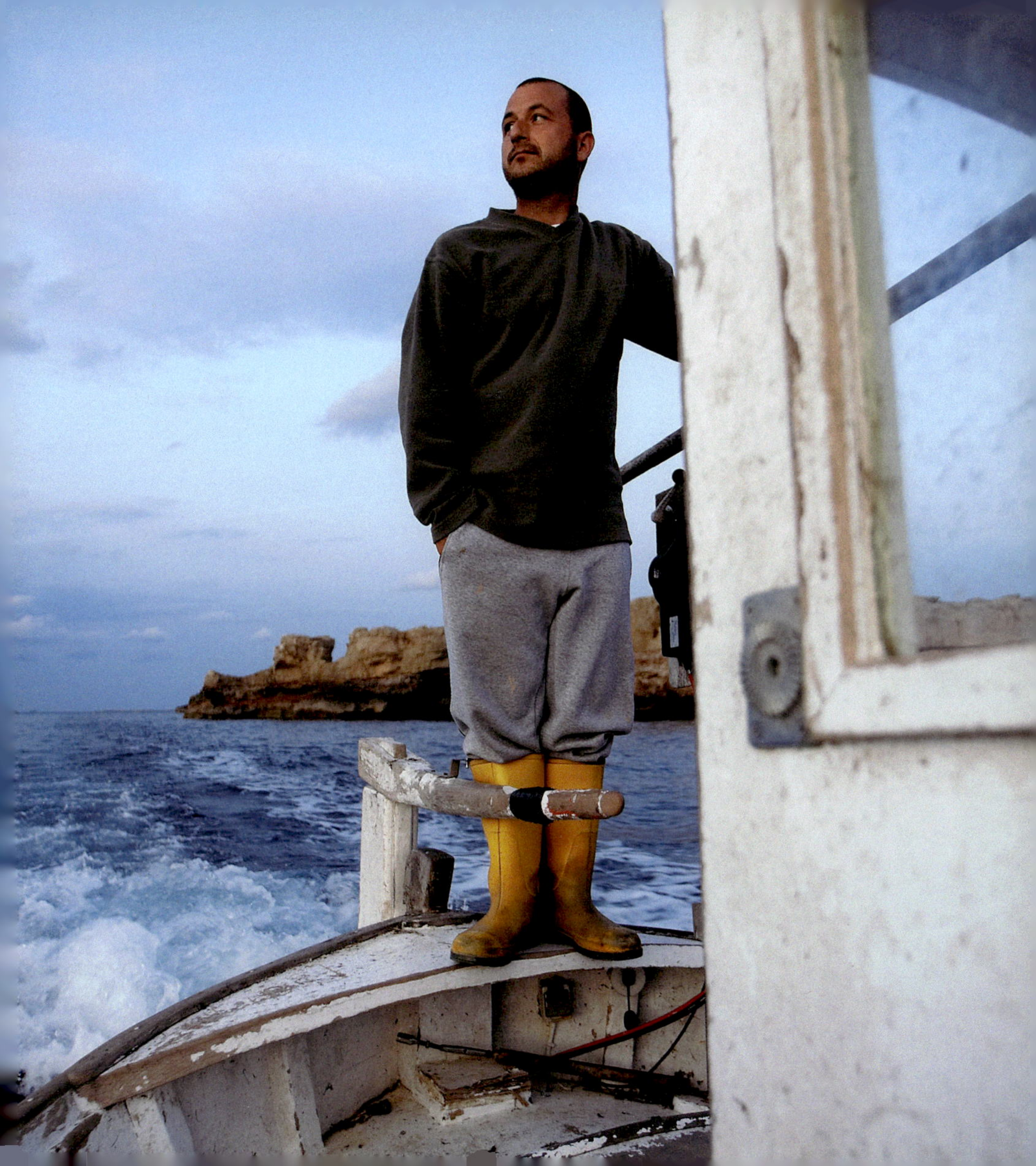

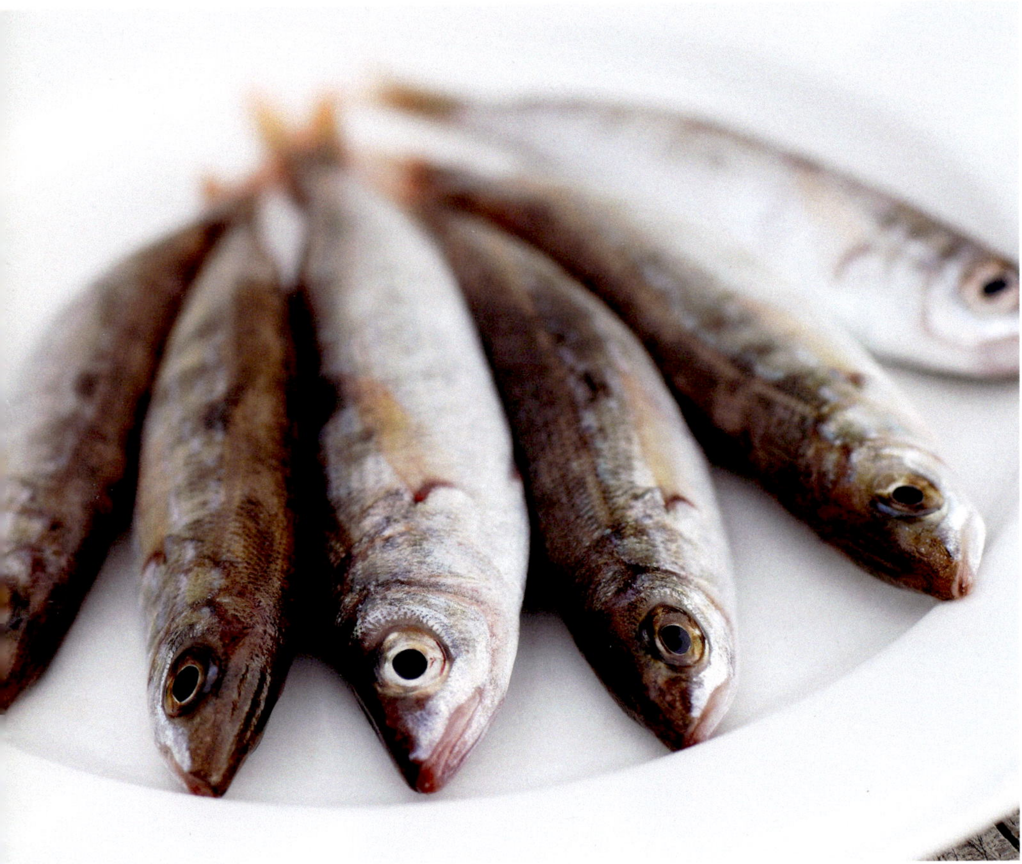

Sardine or *gerret*. On the right, a recently caught skate, with its characteristic marks on the back.

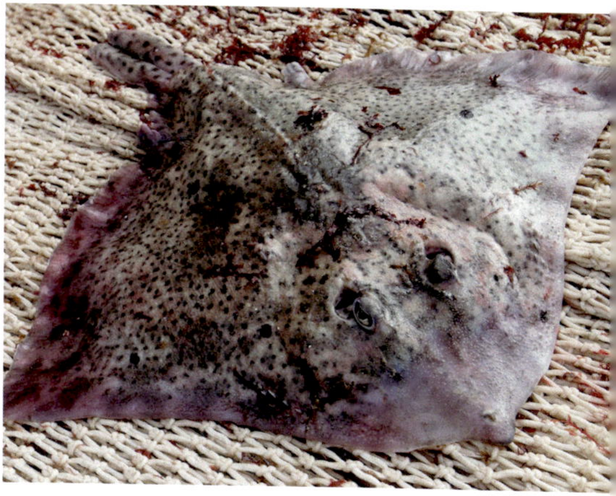

Thornback skate *(Raja clavata)*. It belongs to the scaleless group of fish. In ancient Greece, skates were not highly thought of: it was said that the sting of some of them was fatal, and they were taken live from the sea and the barb stuck into a tree and it withered. At that time, different species were mixed together under the name of skate which today are distinguished. In fact, skates do not have a barb, but other similar species do.

From the skate we eat the fins, a mild-flavoured meat, easy to separate from the cartilage and excellent when fresh. In the markets you can find more than a dozen species, but the thornback skate is the most valued in the kitchen. It has a rhomboid shape, thin tail and many and varied spots on the back. The skin is tough, difficult to remove, but in the market it is already skinned and cut. In Ibiza and Formentera it is prepared fried —usually previously seasoned in lemon, vinegar and salt—, or the excellent *borrida de rajada* is prepared.

Another much-used scaleless fish is the **dogfish** (*Scyliorhinus canicula*). When returning to port, the sailors spent the time skinning these small sharks that they later sold on land, and they kept the takings, without giving a part to the shipowner. Sometimes the price of this fish was so low that it was better just to throw it overboard. In the Pine Islands the dogfish is used to make meatballs (*pilotes de gató*), savoury fat breads and rice dishes.

Sardine *(Spicara smaris).* They say that the best sardines are those caught during the winter, close to the coast, with traditional fishing boats. These delicious examples are females about to reproduce.

It appears to have been the fish, among others, that the Romans used to make the main sauce of Roman cuisine, the *garum*, which accompanied nearly all the dishes and was made with marinated fish, sun-fermented and seasoned with spices.

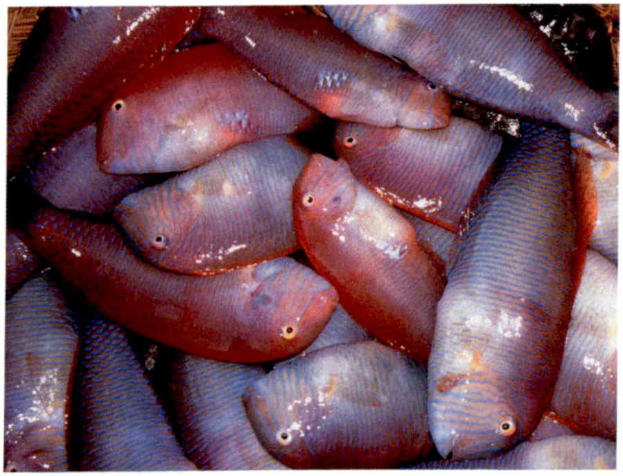

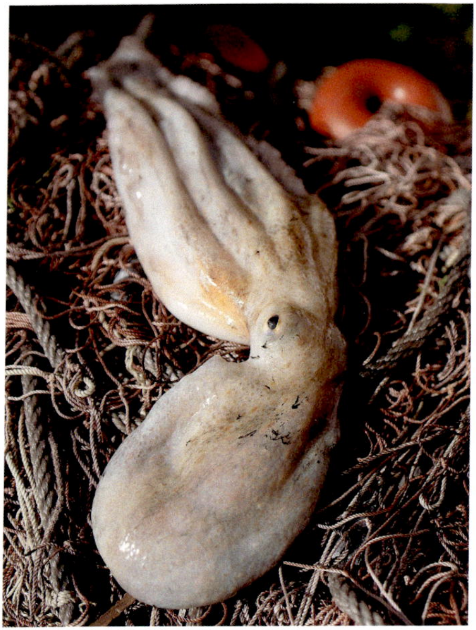

Barbecued to the heat of the coals with salt and lemon, the gerret is excellent, splendid pickled, and fried with garlic, superb. In Ibiza and Formentera the typical dish is *gerret de matança* — the dish served on the day the pig is slaughtered, prepared the night before—, which is made with this fish fried, placed in layers and alternating with a generous fry mix of parsley, garlic and lemon juice. It is also eaten pickled or barbecued, and meatballs are made with it (*pilotes de gerret*), as well as with rice.

Cleaver wrasse (*Xirichthys novacula*). It lives on sandy seabeds of between 2 and 50 metres depth and has the special ability of being able to bury itself when sensing danger. Its mouth is armed with strong teeth, the two front ones being very well developed and they project outwards. It is a fish with white, delicate, exquisite and mild meat.

It is caught seasonally, above all with baited fishing line and small lead weights. The traditional fishermen also catch it with small multiple hook fishing lines. It is one of the most appreciated species for sports fishing.

It is much sought-after in the market, which has led to the illegal fishing of the species with dragnets on the sandy areas. Today a close sea-

Raors or cleaver wrasse (above) and octopus. On the right, coloured and varied rock fish.

son has been declared with a limitation of catch. The star recipe for this fish (*raor*) is the simplest: coated in flour and fried.

Octopus. Octopuses, sepias and squids are soft-bodied animals, close relatives of the land snail. As they possess feet in the head they are called 'cephalopods'. In cooking they require a low flame and careful treatment. They never disappoint if sautéed combined with the extensive list of fry-sauces. From one day to the next the stews can become tastier and more tender, a sublime characteristic of the food that requires being left to stand.

In the Mediterranean different types of octopuses are commercialised, but the most valued is the common octopus (*Octopus vulgaris*), which lives along the coast.

The Greeks liked octopus, and the Hellenic formulas for cooking it with red wine have not changed much since Antiquity. Once boiled, it is sautéed in a sauce made of onion and tomato to which is added wine, vinegar, rosemary, laurel, black pepper, nutmeg, cinnamon and cloves. In the Pine Islands it is also eaten as a stew with onion, peppers or sauce, among other variants.

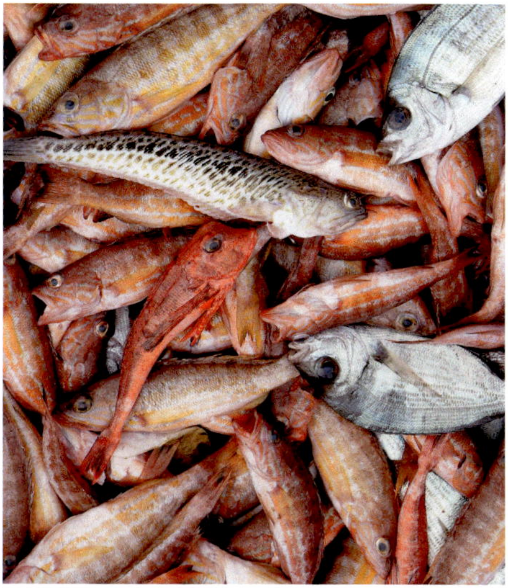

Rock fish. Sheltered on the seabed around the rocks are a cluster of species of a very different appearance and magnificent flavour. These fish have the honour of being the main ingredients of dishes such as the famous fish stews of Ibiza and Formentera. They are fishes such as the large-scaled scorpion fish, horned boxfish, tub gurnard, or Atlantic stargazer, to name just a few, large enough to eat grilled or stewed. You can save the heads to make stock, and thus make use of almost all the animal. Eating fresh fish is a luxury, and you would be well advised to steer clear of those who only use it, crushing it, to make stock.

Dried fish. Since Antiquity, most of the population of Formentera, as well as working the land, devoted their time to fishing, when there was an abundance, examples of scaleless fish were salted and sun-dried. Today dried fish is still prepared and commercialised, but now a gastronomic speciality of the island.

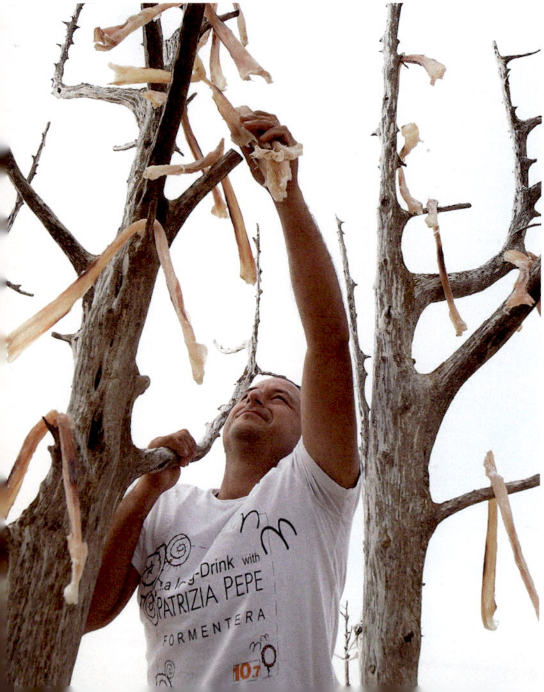

The fish used are the cartilaginous species, with a tough skin and scaleless, such as the skate and the dogfish. The process is carried out with the skin on the fish. First the innards are removed and the piece cleaned well with seawater; It is then cut into fillets, which are covered with thick salt, for 2 to 7 hours according to the size of the fish; the salt is then removed, cleaning the pieces with seawater; and then the fillets are hung on the ends of dry savin branches, called *parreres* —from where the dried fish gets its name on the island, *peix de parreres*. The drying time varies between 1 and 4 days, according to the size. At night they are usually placed indoors to avoid the humidity.

Dried fish remains conserved for months. It has a hard texture, a strong smell of the sea and a salty taste. The most typical way of eating it is in a peasant salad: mixed with roast aubergines and red peppers and boiled potatoes, all lubricated with a fine olive oil.

In Formentera, the fillets of small fish are left to dry hanging from the branches of a dry savin trees.

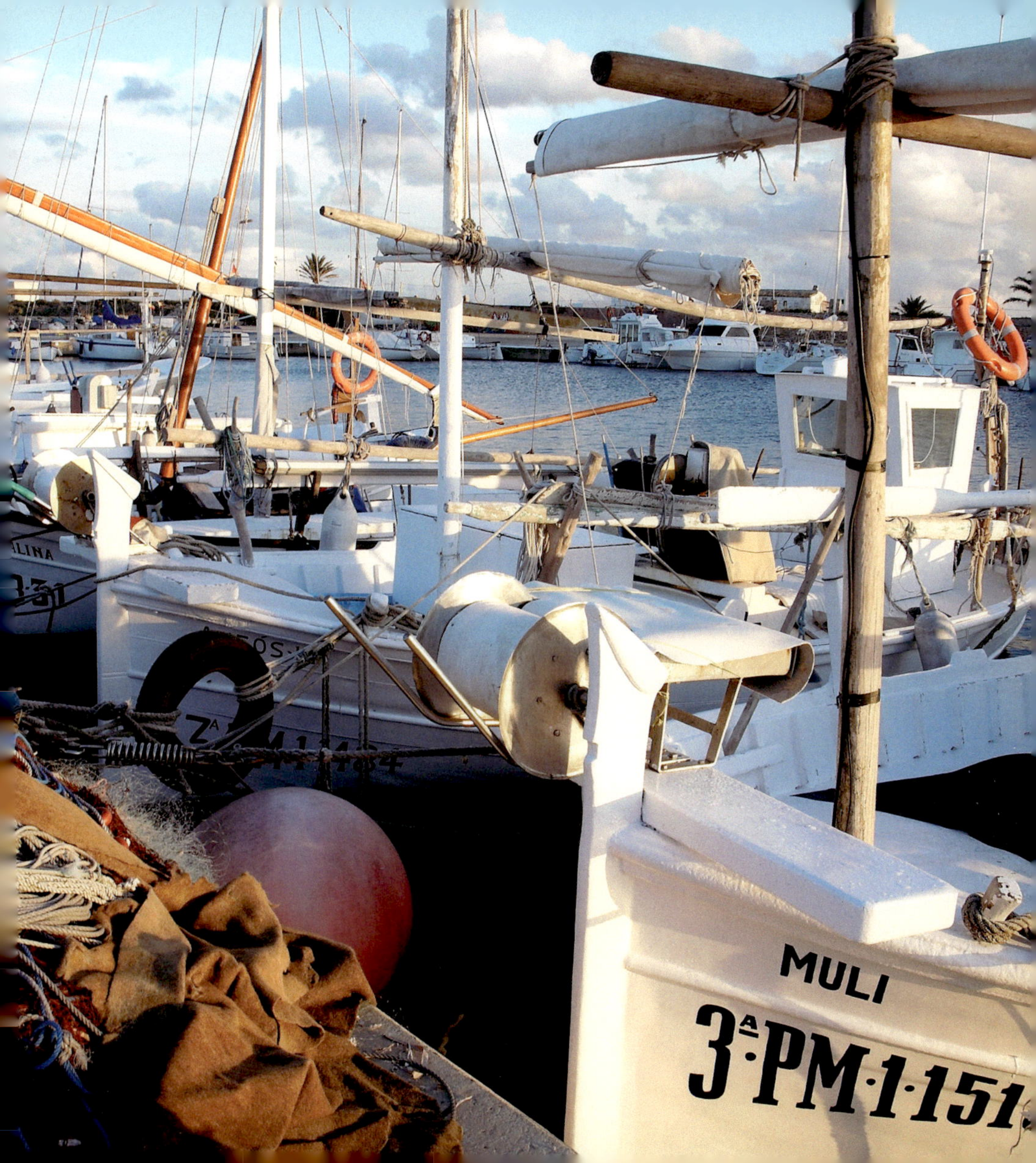
MULI
3ª·PM·1·151

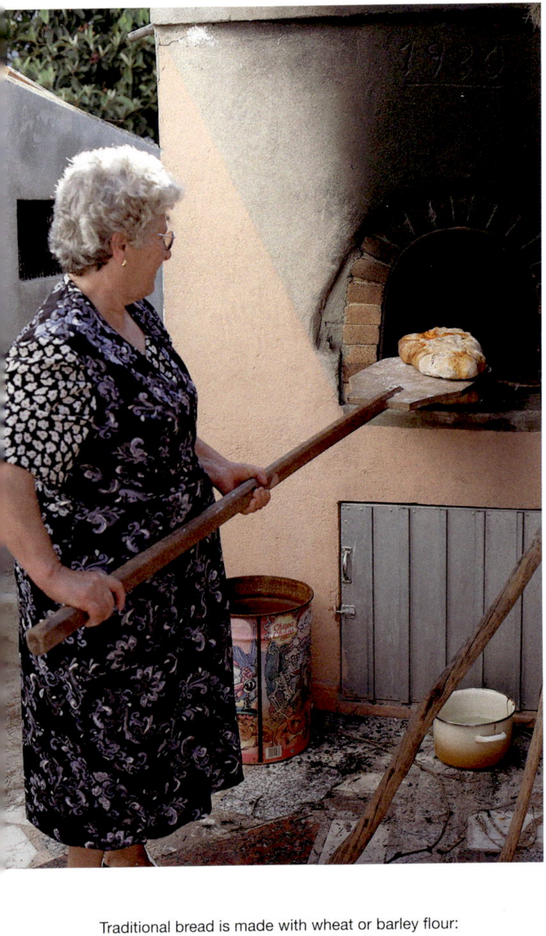

Traditional bread is made with wheat or barley flour: Some bakers add aniseed to the dough.

The art of baking and cake making

Strolling around the countryside of Ibiza and Formentera you can still see in some houses the wood-fired oven as an indispensable element of traditional architecture. In the past, bread and other dough-made delights, both sweet and savoury, were made at home. Today, the bakeries and cake shops of these islands preserve all their flavour and variety.

Bread was a basic source of food on the Pine Islands until relatively recently, as the flour mills that are still conserved bear witness. Bread was made at home once a week, and sometimes it was spiced up with a little aniseed, as they still do in some bakeries. From traditional bread making, with wheat or barley flour, came other products such as *bescuit*, bread baked twice so that it was dry and lasted a long time. The flat breads were baked on the same day as the bread was made, and were covered with the ingredients available at that moment. Sometimes other savoury delicacies were baked, such as *cocarrois* and *panades*.

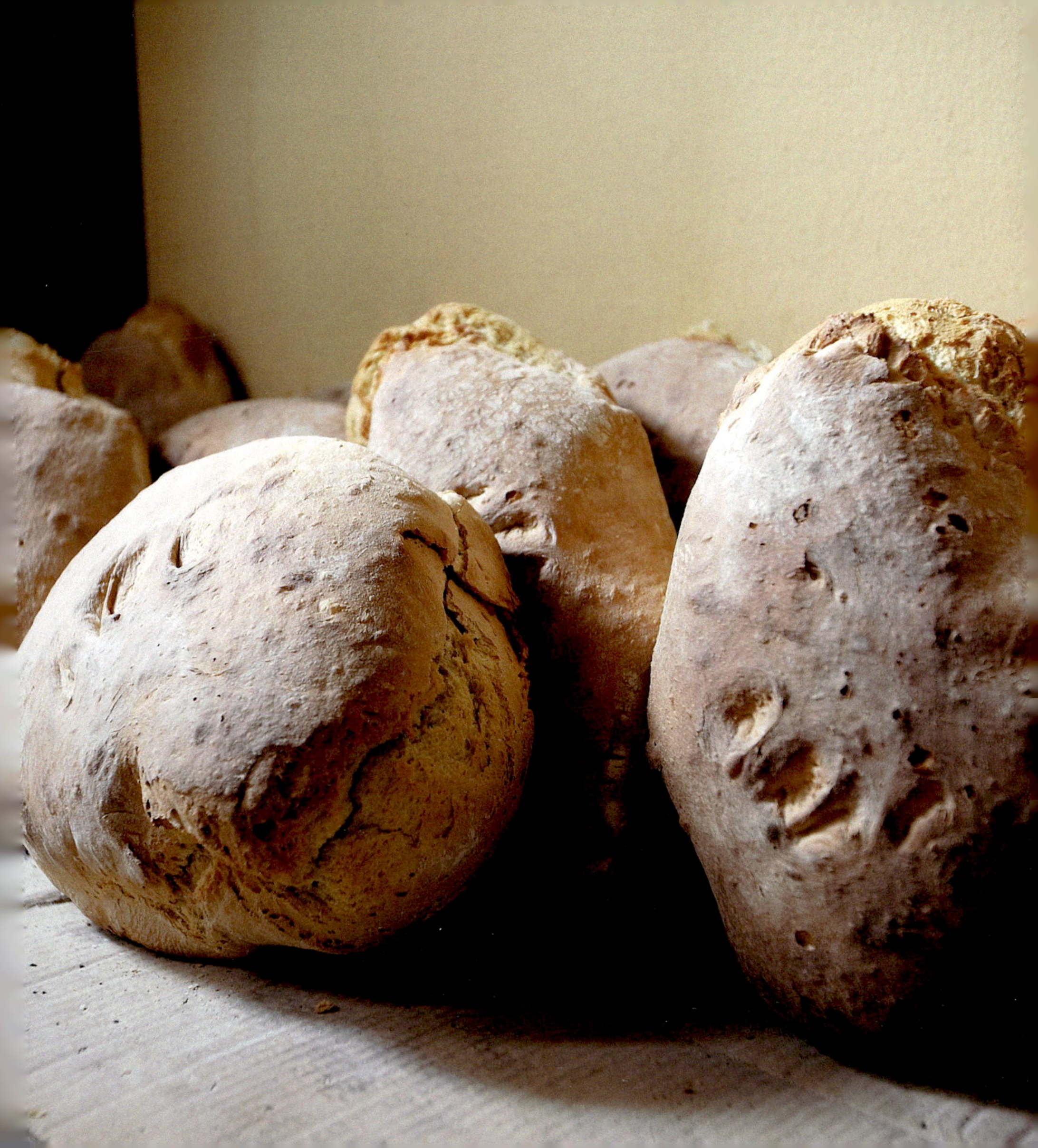

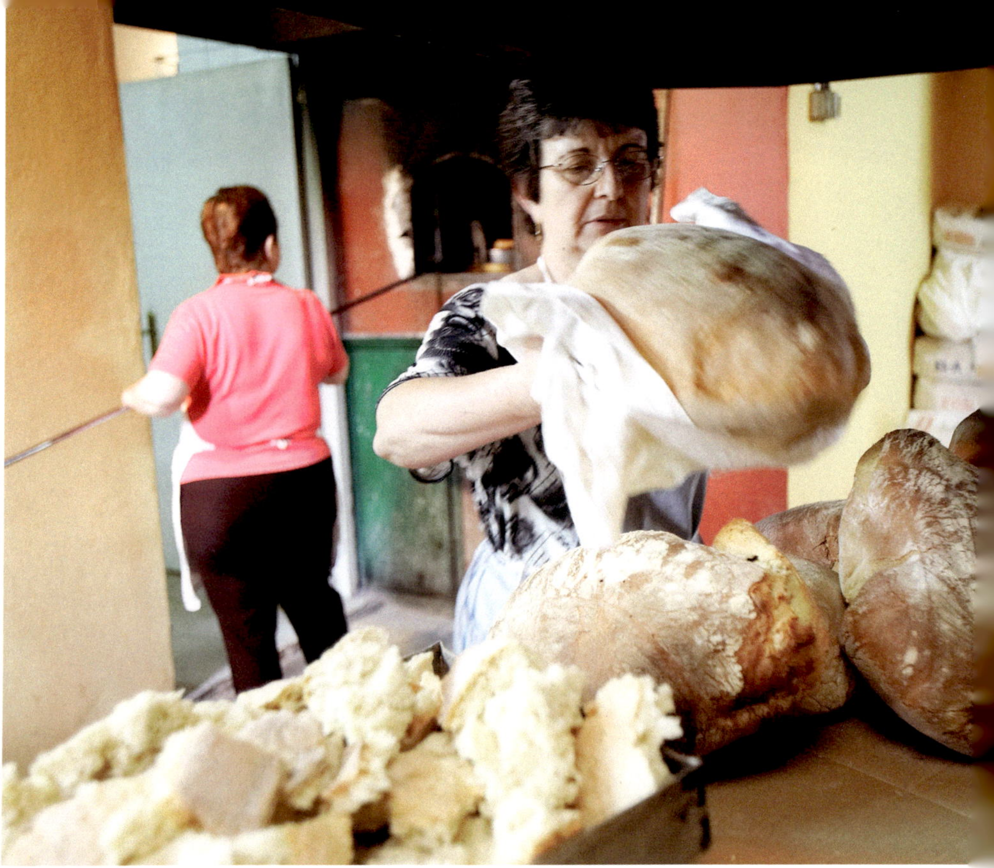

The star of cake making is the *flaó*, having become a symbol for these islands. Its peculiarity lies in the combination of ingredients, which include fresh cheese and mint. In the past it was a typical Easter cake, which was when the best cheeses were produced, but today it is eaten all year round.

In the area of sweets we should also mention the *bescuit de Nadal* or *coc*, the sweet flat bread prepared above all at Christmas time, to dip into

Bread is as essential in salads as are pepper, tomato and onion, or that of dried fish in Formentera.

the *salsa de Nadal*, the Christmas sauce. With the *bescuits* or dried *ensaïmada* pastries —broken up in milk and mixed with sugar, eggs, cinnamon and grated lemon— a cake is prepared with a similar taste to that of the local variant of bread pudding, called *greixonera*.

They also make fritters (*bunyols*), *orelletes* —pastries in the form of a large ear—, *robiols*, almond fairy cakes and, in Formentera, the *pensats i fets*, sweet fried dough sprinkled with sugar and cinnamon.

The sweet flat breads are open to an infinite number of variations, and are often perfumed with aniseed, cinnamon and grated lemon. They may be baked in the oven and coated with sugar, or fresh fruits and jams added. They are round or rectangular, and their variety reflects the local gastronomic imagination: flat bread, *coc*, pork scratchings, cheese, fresh apricots, cherries or the peculiar potato *cóc* —with a dough made of cooked potato, yolks and whites of eggs beaten separately, yeast and sugar.

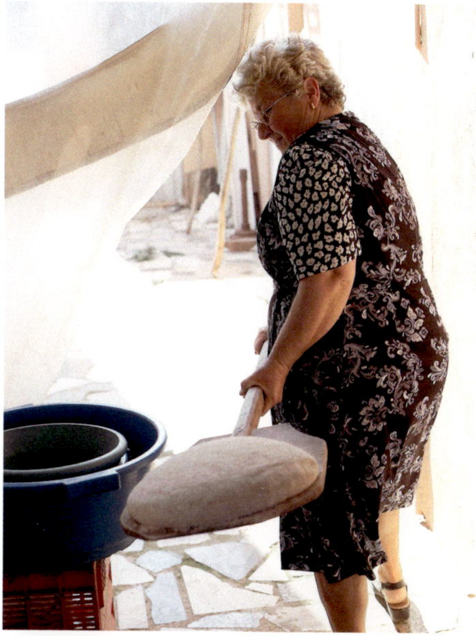

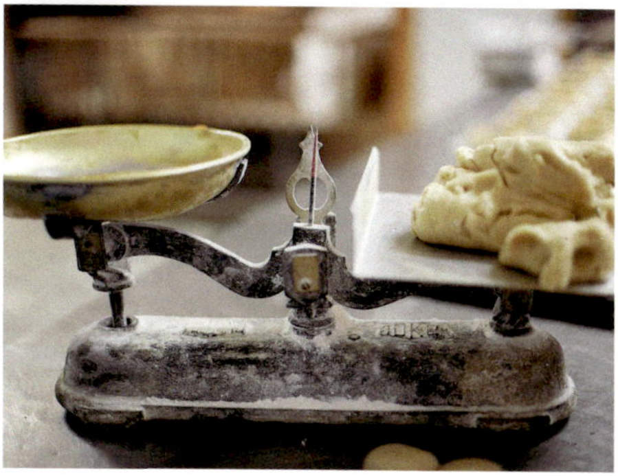

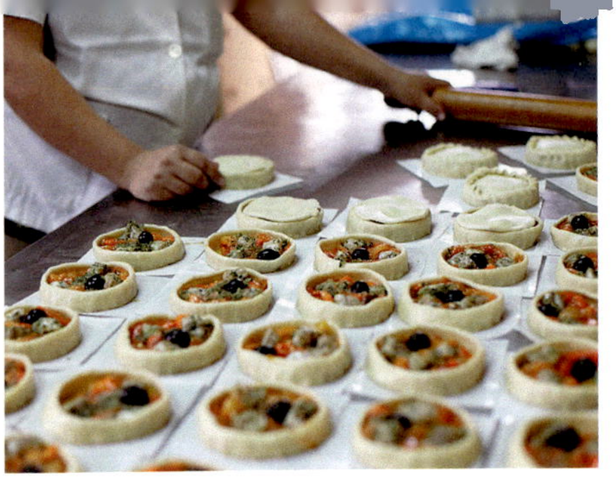

Savoury delights

1 ***Crostes.*** *Crostes* or *crostes de bescuit* are pieces of bread cooked twice, so that they are dry and can be conserved for a long time. In the past, this type of bread was used to feed the crews of the boats during crossings. Today they form part of some salads with tomato, onion, peppers and other ingredients, and in Formentera they are the essential ingredient of the dried fish salad.

2 **Filled bread roll.** A delicious snack, the bread roll filled with *sobrassada* and baked. It is often heated slightly before eating, which enhances the flavour of the *sobrassada*.

3 ***Panada.*** Unleavened bread in the form of a cylindrical box, which can be filled with meat —generally lamb—, or fish, sometimes accompanied by peas.

4 **Flat bread with peppers and dogfish.** The *coca* is a dough made of flour, water, oil and a little yeast, baked with different ingredients on top, which give it its name. The one in the photo is covered with roast red peppers and pieces of dogfish. However, there are countless possibilities: with tomato and onion, Swiss chard, pork scratchings or bacon and *sobrassada*, etc.

5 ***Cocarroi.*** Small flat bread folded over itself, forming a semi-circle. It is made with a dough of flour, water and lard and filled with spinach or Swiss chard with pine nuts, raisins, spring onion and chopped garlic. There is also fish *cocarrois*, replacing the vegetable with fish with few bones, such as hake or grouper, baked and seasoned.

6 **Flat bread with peppers and black olives.** Another variant of the savoury flat bread, in this case with baked red peppers, black olives and a mixture of garlic and parsley. Sometimes a little fried fish is also added.

7 **Bread.** The farmer's loaf is large and round. When it is lengthened it is called *coc*. Same bakeries add aniseed to the dough, and others barley flour. You should try the farmer's bread with tomato in the bars of the villages, accompanied, for example, by a cured meat from the island.

8 / 9 ***Galetes fortes.*** Large savoury biscuits, round in shape, made of hard, crumbly dough. They can be made with refined or wholemeal flour, and are unleavened. They are added to salads and spicy sauces. In the past they were for the boat crews, since they lasted a long time.

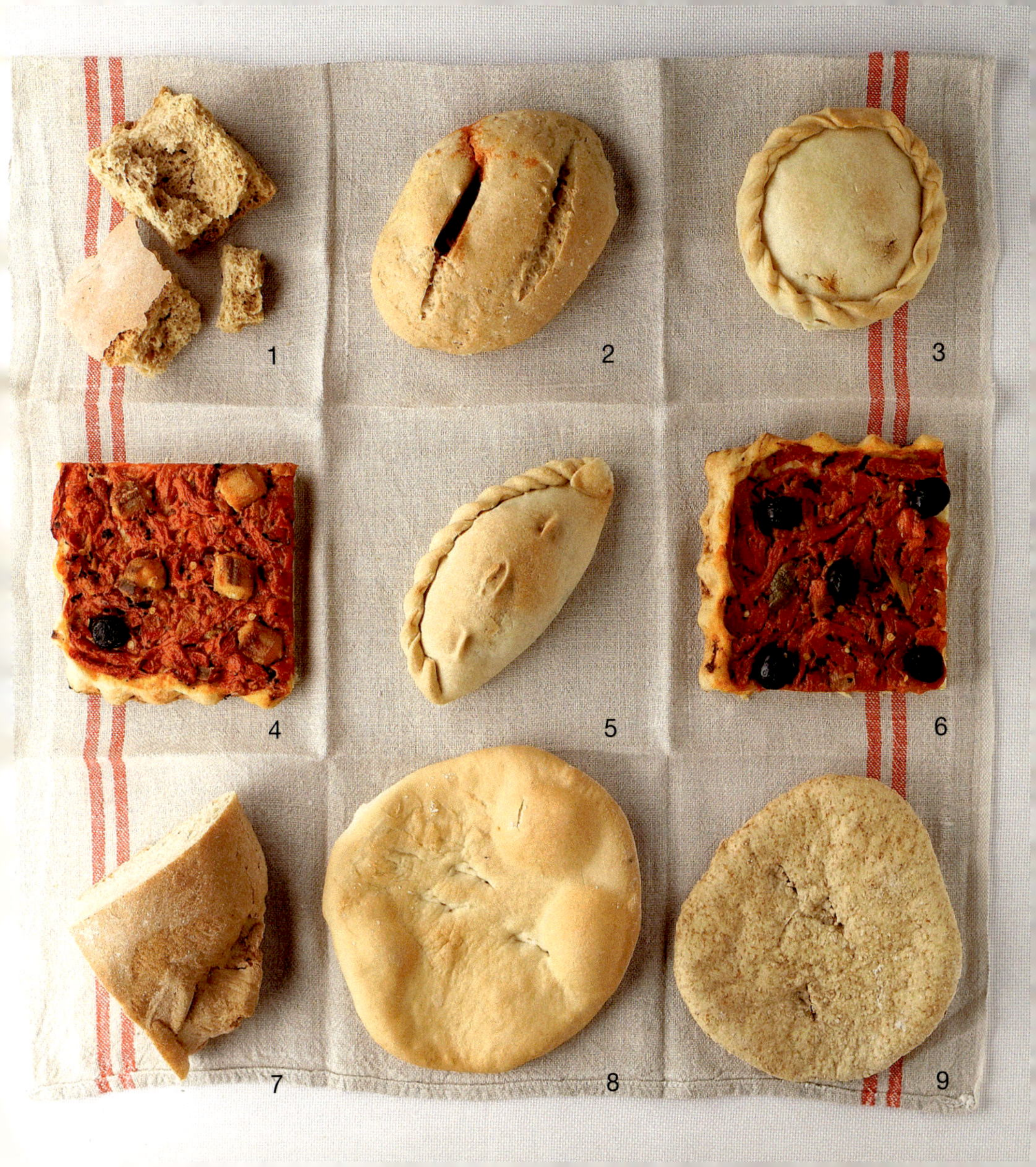
1
2
3
4
5
6
7
8
9

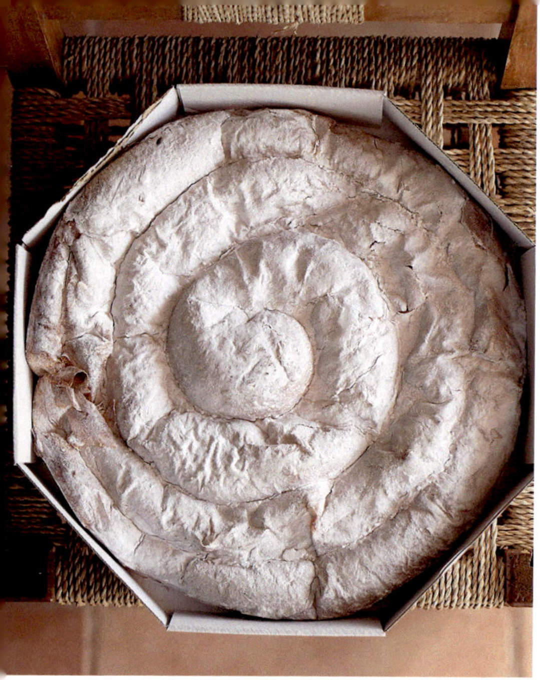

1

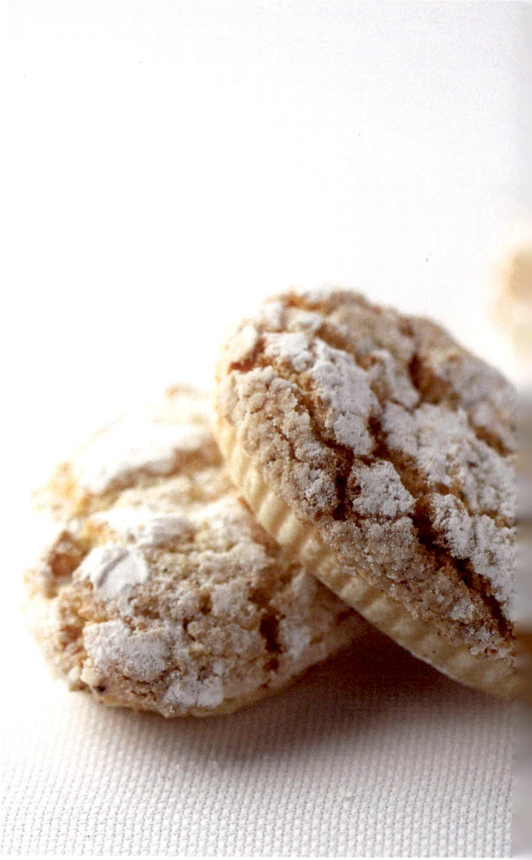

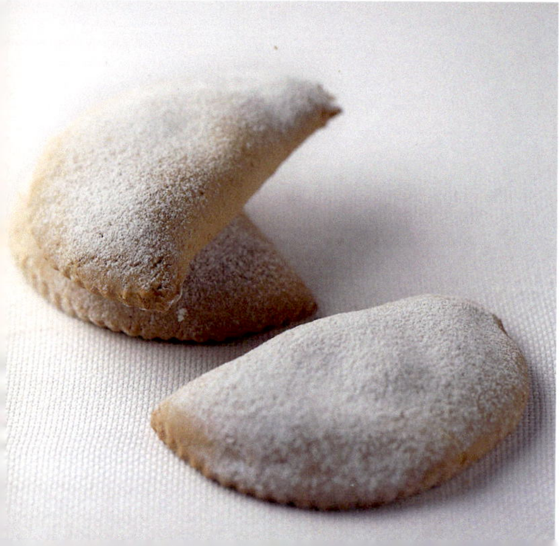

3

2

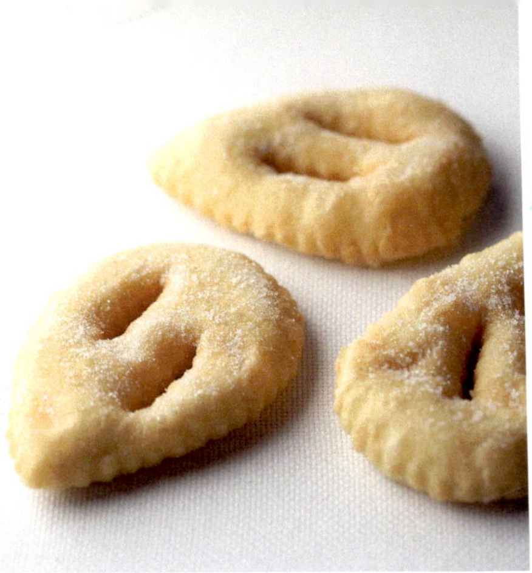

4

Sweet delights

1

1 ***Ensaïmada.*** Sweet pastry with a characteristic spiral form and covered with icing sugar. It is made in different sizes from a dough of flour, sugar, yeast, eggs and lard (*saïm*). Traditional *ensaïmades* did not have a filling, but today they are filled with cream, nougat, pumpkin and syrup, and other sweet fillings.

2

2 Almond fairy cakes. These oval-shaped cakes are made with a lot of chopped almonds. They are very sweet, and the taste of the almond is very prominent. They are crispy on top and sprinkled with sugar.

3

3 ***Robiols.*** Pieces of dough made from fine flour mixed with oil, pork lard and egg, and perfumed with grated lemon peel, aniseed and cinnamon. They are semicircular in shape, and have different fillings: pumpkin and syrup, cottage cheese or jam.

4

4 ***Orelletes.*** Sweet fried dough and moulded in the shape of a human ear, which is where it gets its name from. It is a pastry common at parties and celebrations. It is made with flour, eggs, sugar, pork lard or oil, sweet aniseed, yeast and grated lemon peel. They are shaped and fried in a deep pan with a lot of oil on a low flame. They are later sprinkled with sugar.

5

5 Fritters. *Bunyols* are very popular at festivals and family celebratuons. They are prepared with dough made from water, flour, milk, eggs and cinnamon, which is then fried. They are in the form of ring-shaped doughnut, and when cooked are covered with sugar. In Formentera some fritters are made that are called *pensats i fets*, which can be made even tastier with potato and orange juice.

5

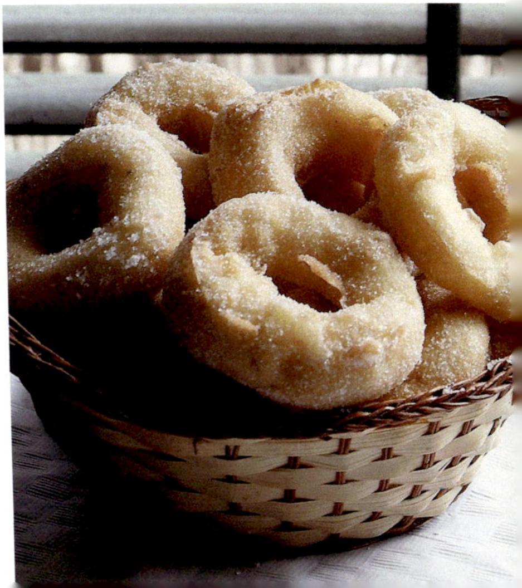

1

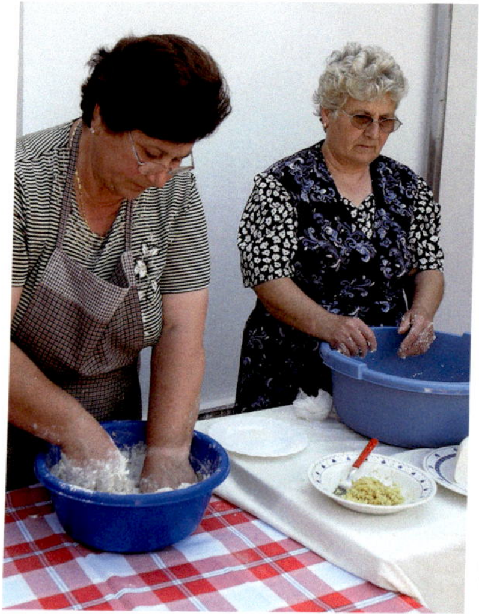

2

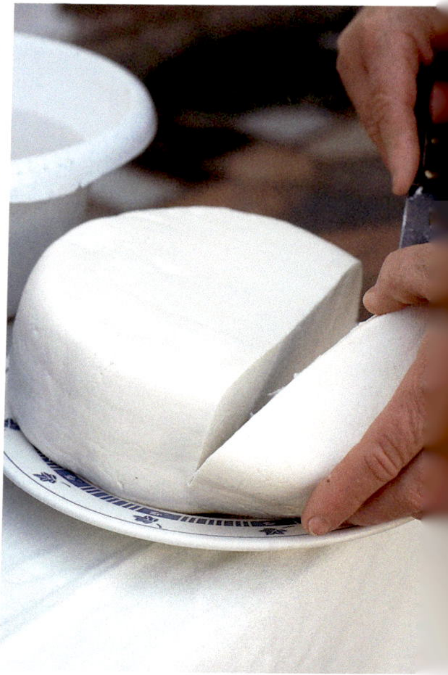

*F*laó, step by step

1 Preparation of the base. The base for *flaó* is a dough made with flour, sugar, eggs, yeast, grated lemon peel and aniseed.

2 Fresh cheese. The filling for the cake is what gives it its peculiar taste and texture, and has a basic ingredient fresh cheese, of goat, sheep or cow.

3 Crumble the cheese. The first step for the filling is to crumble a large portion of the fresh cheese in a recipient.

4 The filling. Then the rest of the ingredients are added: oil, sugar, eggs, grated lemon peel, a splash of sweet aniseed and, above all, some mint leaves (*herba-sana*). The dough must be well kneaded so that all the ingredients are well mixed together, until obtaining a smooth texture.

5 Mint. The mint is essential, and is used for the filling and the final decoration of the *flaó*. It must be fresh, recently picked, and only the leaves of the plant are used.

3

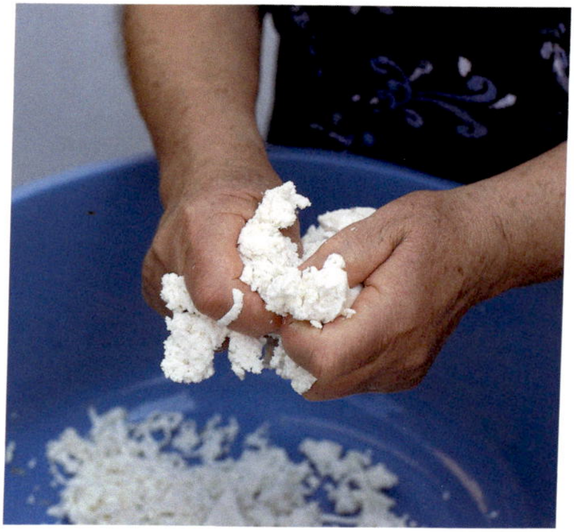

4

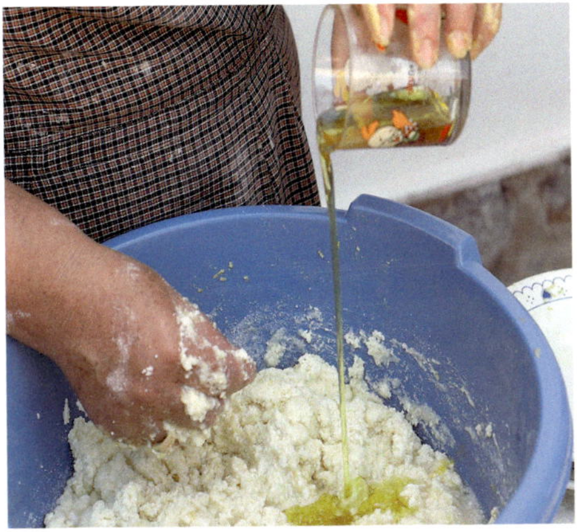

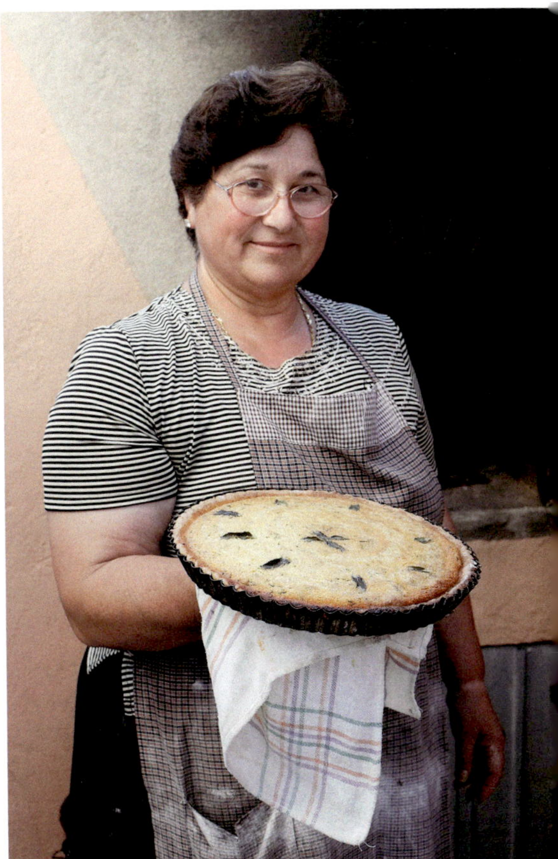

5

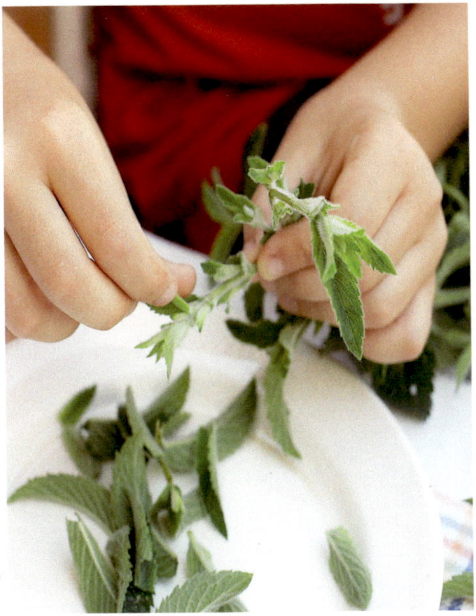

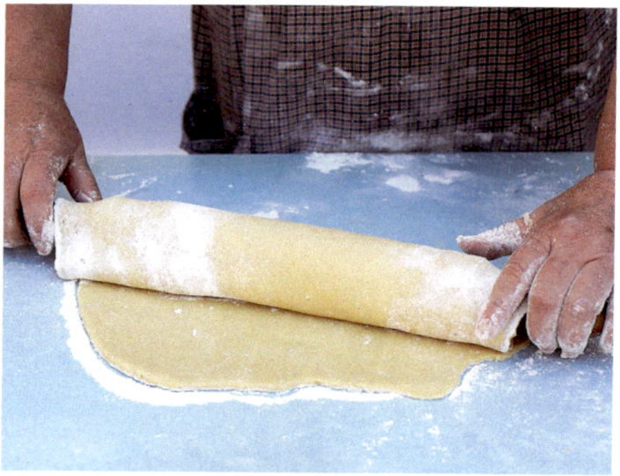

6

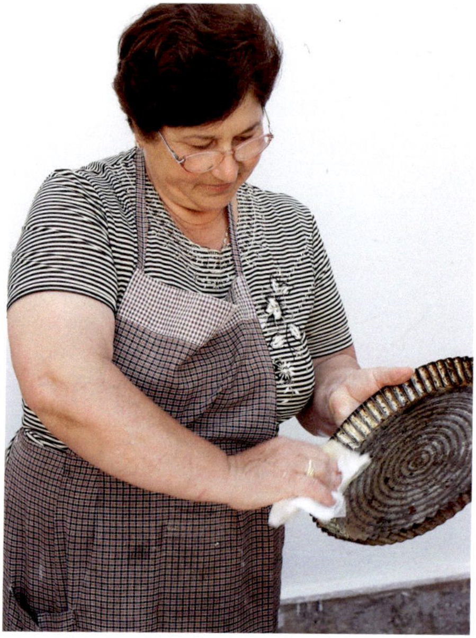

7

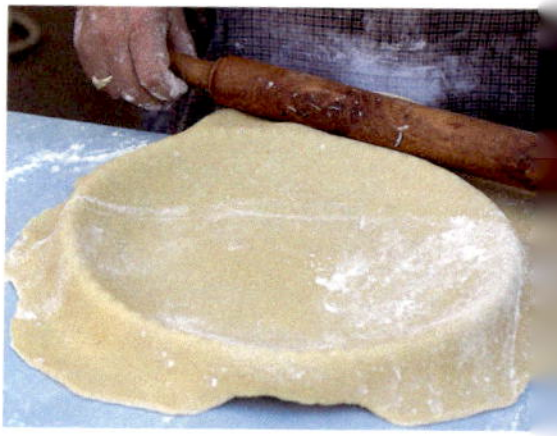

8

6 Kneading. Once the base is kneaded, it is spread very thin using a rolling pin.

7 Greasing the mould. The mould for the *flaó* is then greased, the typical mould being round, not very high and the contour undulating.

8 Spreading the base. The dough is spread over the mould and cut at the edges. The dough left over is often used later to make *orelletes*.

9 Adding the filling. Place the filling for the *flaó* with a ladle, spreading it uniformly.

10 Final touch. The presentation of the cake is important. A mixture of well-beaten egg yolk with oil and sweet aniseed is spread over the top. Finally, the mint leaves are placed decoratively over the cake.

11 Cooking. It is finally placed in the wood-burning oven. To cook in a gas or electric oven it must be done in a bain-marie.

12 Sugar. When the cake is done and has cooled, a little sugar is sprinkled on top.

9

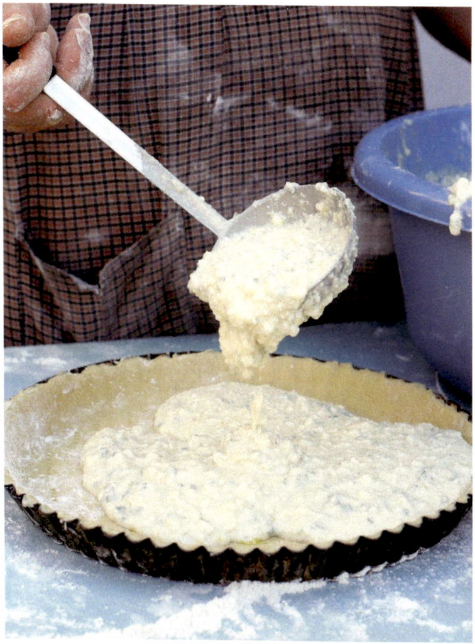

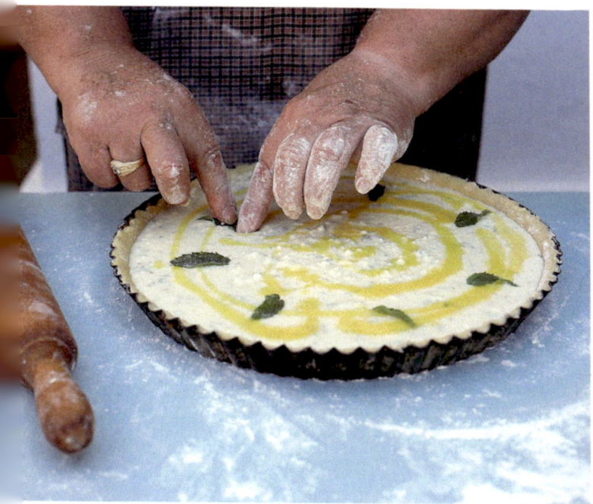

10

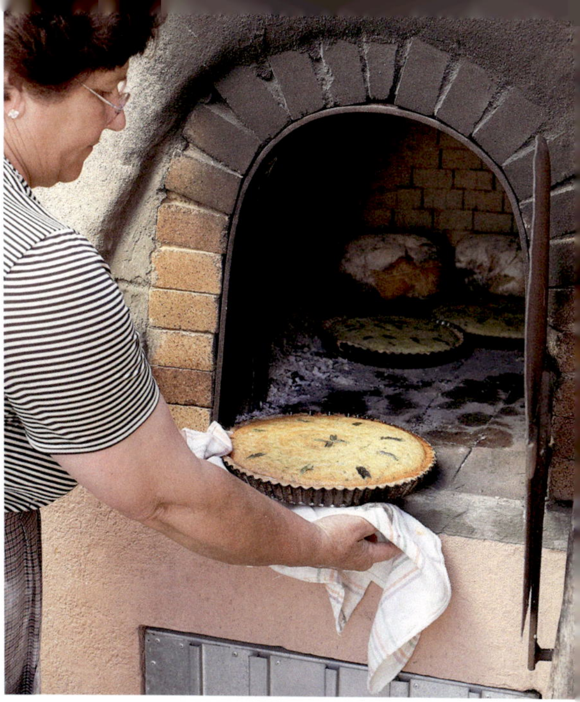

11

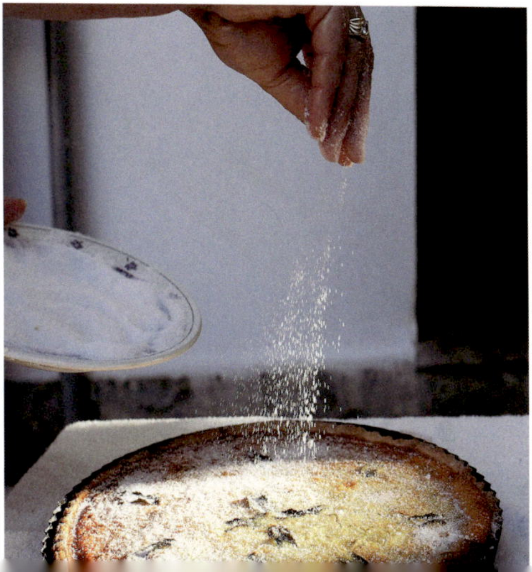

12

Herbs and liqueurs

Since Antiquity the islanders have been well aware of the medicinal properties of many wild plants —such as fennel, mint, rosemary or camomile—, for centuries used in the form of herbal tea to fight some illnesses. Given the bitter taste of some of these plants, they began to add sugar to the teas. This custom was maintained by preparing an excellent local medicinal liqueur: the sweet herbs.

The herb liqueur began to be produced in a homemade form about two hundred years ago, when wine production increased and the copper stills were at hand to prepare distillations. Today many families maintain the custom of preparing their own herb drinks: there is nothing simpler than placing a small bunch of aromatic herbs in a bottle and leaving it to macerate with aniseed, preferably sweet, with a little dry too. It is made in May and June, when the plants that form part of the preparation are in flower.

The amount and composition of the herbs vary according to the recipe of each home. When ready, the bottles should be kept in a cool and dry spot for at least three months. Once empty, they can be filled with aniseed again, since the herbs still conserve many of their properties.

Today in Ibiza there are three companies that make Hierbas Ibicencas with a geographical identification: the Marí Mayans distillery —the oldest, which was founded at the end of the 19th century in Formentera, moving years later to Ibiza—, Can Rich of Buscastell and the Aniseta liquor factory.

The control regulations of geographic identification define the herbs as an aniseed flavoured alcoholic drink obtained basically from the extraction of aromas from diverse plants from the area

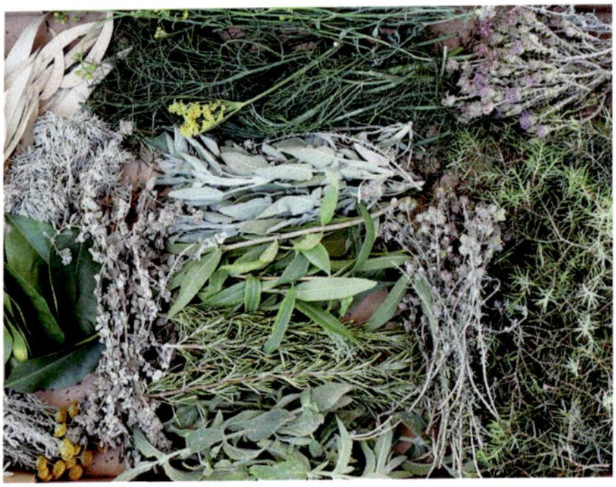

The exact composition of the herbs is a family secret that is passed on from generation to generation.

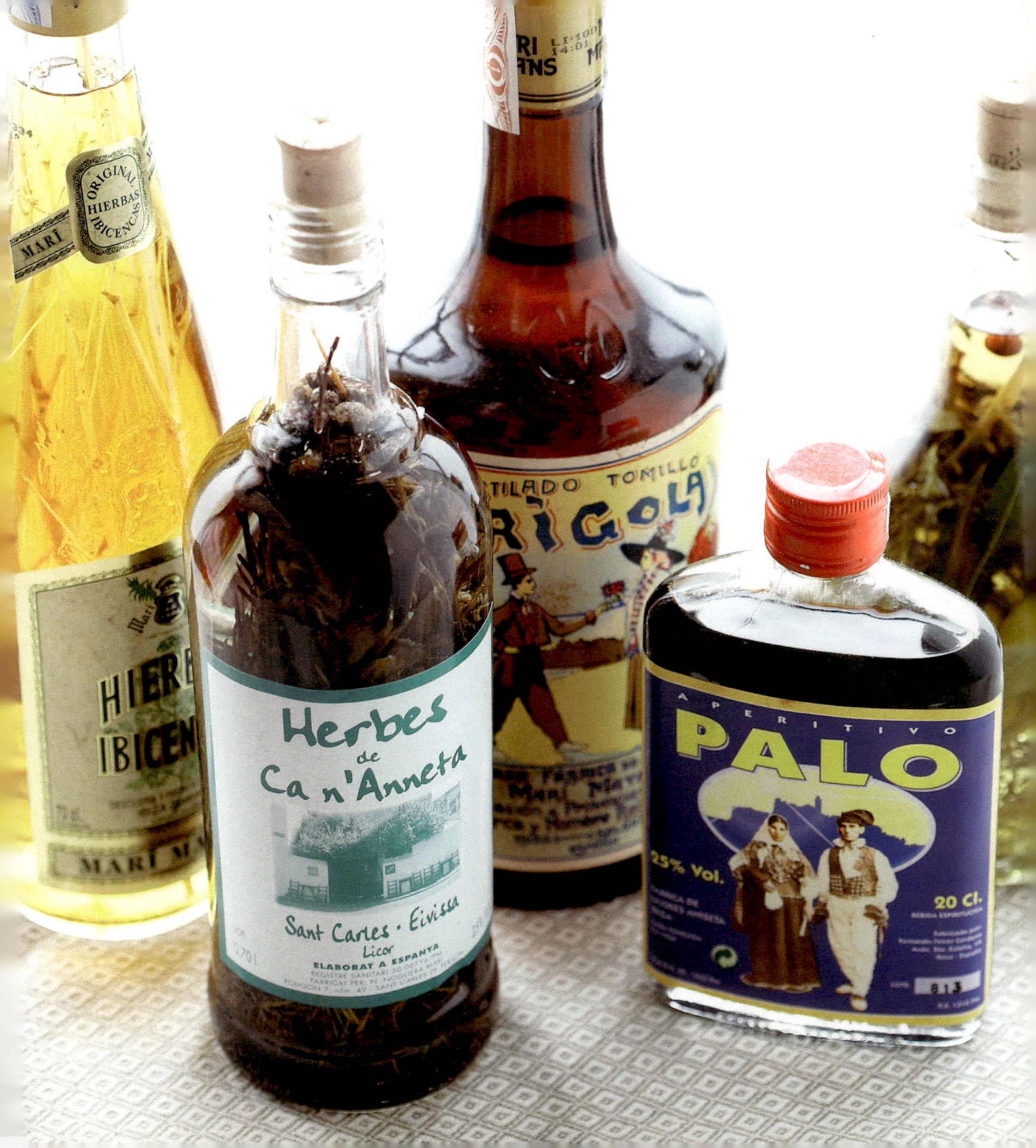

ORIGINAL
HIERBAS
IBICENCAS
MARÍ
TOMILLO
Herbes
de
Ca n'Anneta
Sant Carles · Eivissa
Licor
ELABORAT A ESPANYA
APERITIVO
PALO
25% Vol.
20 Cl.

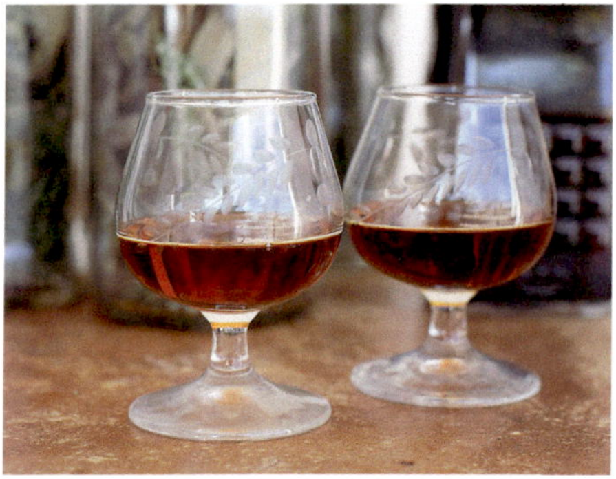

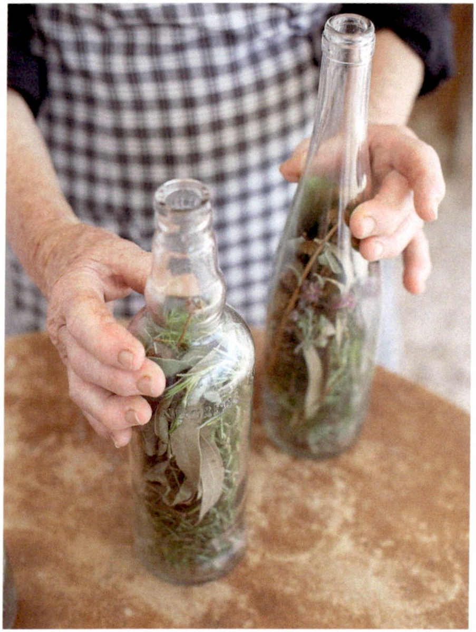

of production, among many others: rosemary, fennel, aniseed, lemon verbena, juniper, oregano, mint, leaves and lemon peel. Its manufacture includes the distillation processes in copper stills, maceration and infusion.

The herbs are often drunk after meals, on their own or with ice, and are available in all the bars in Ibiza and Formentera.

Frígola. Traditionally in the Pine Islands the flower of the thyme has had many uses, such as perfuming the dry figs (*xereques*) or snail stews, or for curing a stomach or neck ache. It contains very aromatic essential oils, with antiseptic, antibacterial and fungicidal properties. Moreover, it is the basic ingredient of the *frígola*, a medicinal liquor that is usually prepared with the distillation of the thyme flower in a still. Once the extract is obtained, a mixture of alcohol of molasses and sugar is added. The result is a sweet, orangey coloured liqueur and around 30° alcohol level. It is digestive and is usually drunk after meals, on its own or with ice.

Palo is also made, an aperitif obtained basically by the extraction of aromas from quinine and gentian and the addition of caramelised sugar, which gives it its characteristic dark

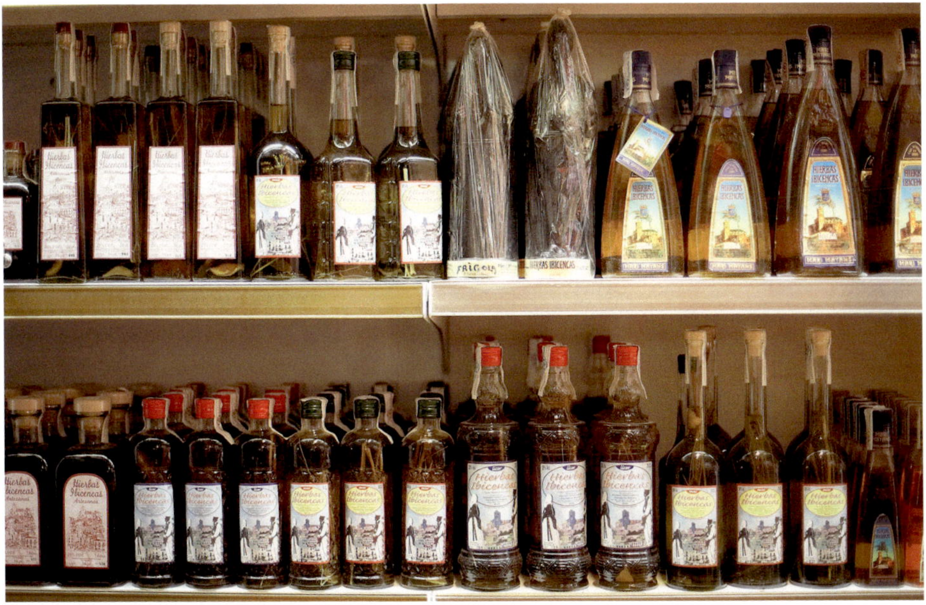

shade. It is usually drunk before meals, with a slice of lemon and ice.

In the mid-19th century the Pine Islands revitalised consumption of the mythical ***absinthe***, producing it in the factory in Formentera. It is made from distilling selected leaves and shoots of *Artemisia absinthium*, and the result is the unreal green-coloured liqueur. It was supposedly invented in 1792 by the French doctor Pierre Ordinaire as a remedy for some complaints; this virtue warranted the drink to be given the nickname "the green fairy". Due to its fame for causing hallucinations, at the beginning of the 20th century it was banned in the United States, Holland, Belgium, Brazil and France, among other countries, although it was still sold illegally.

The herbs, the *frígola* and the palo can be tasted in all the traditional bars in Ibiza and Formentera.

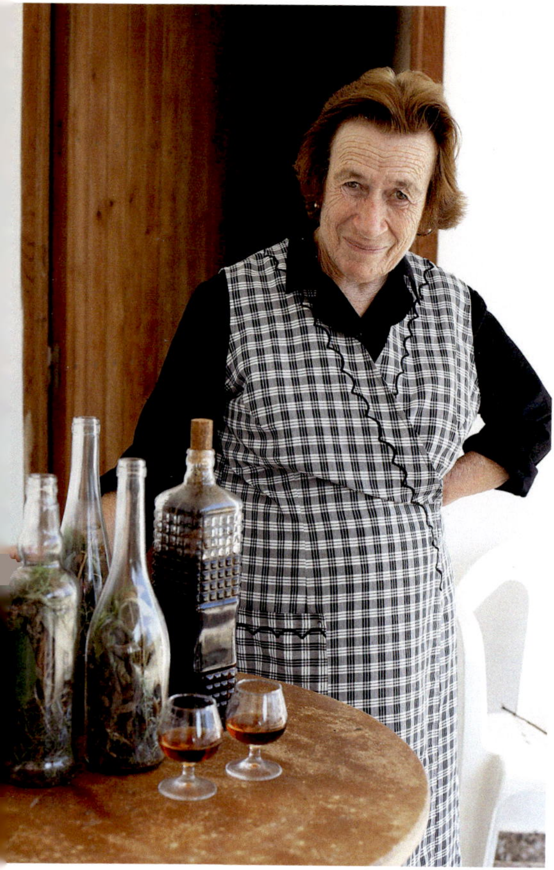

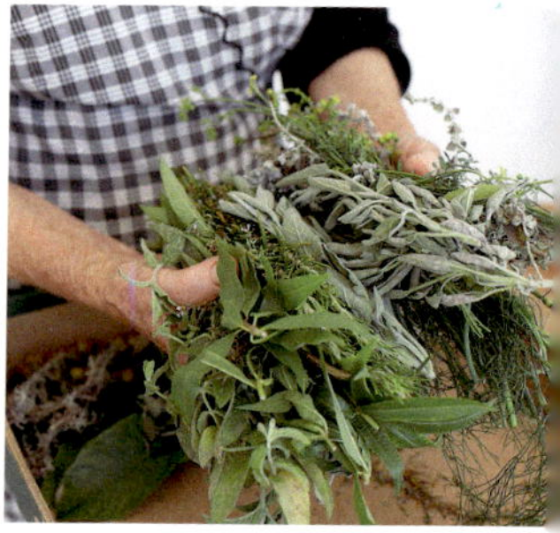

How to make good herbs

1 Picking and selection. The quantity and composition of the herbs varies according to the recipe of each home, but usually includes, among many others: rosemary, fennel, aniseed, lemon verbena, juniper, oregano and mint. They must be wild plants that are normally picked in the flowering months, between May and June. They are cut into small bunches so that they can be inserted into the bottles.

2 Inserting the herbs. Once ready, the herbs are inserted into the bottles, ensuring that in each one the composition is similar. It is a laborious task that requires a great deal of patience and skill.

3 Bottles ready. The bottles are now ready to be filled with sweet aniseed.

4 Adding the aniseed. The next stage is to add the aniseed with the help of a funnel. Some people also add a little dry aniseed. Every family and producer has their own secrets. There are no two herb liqueurs the same.

5 Maceration. The bottles are corked and left to macerate in a cool and dry spot for a minimum of three months. After this time, the herbs take on their characteristic colour and aroma.

2

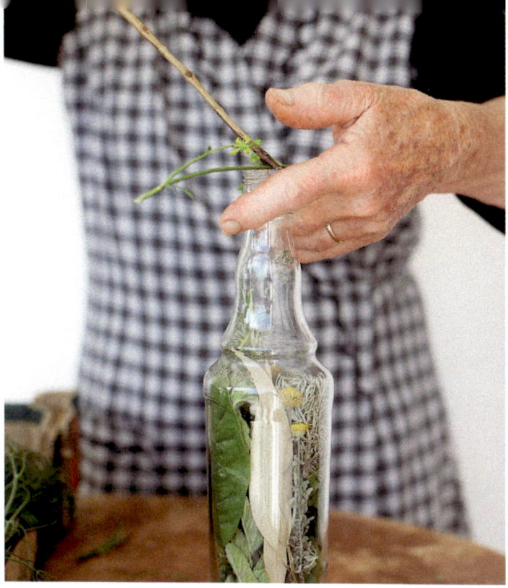

4

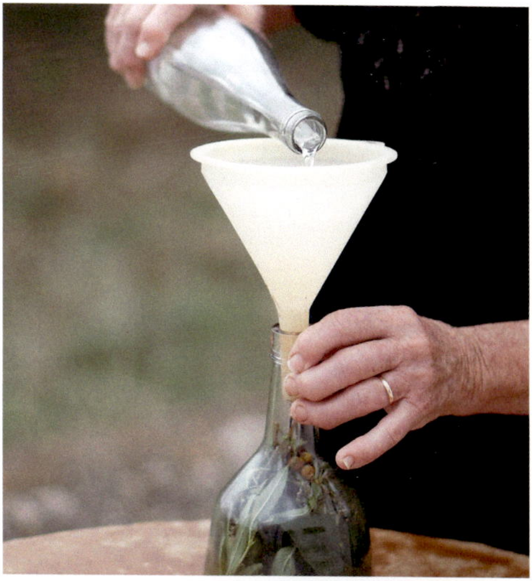

3

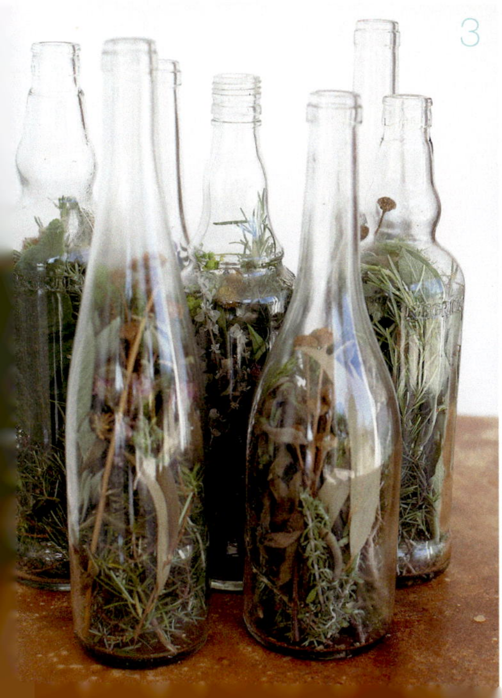

5

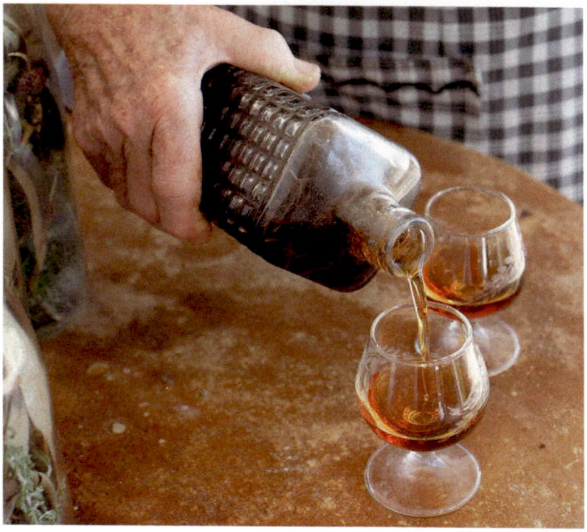

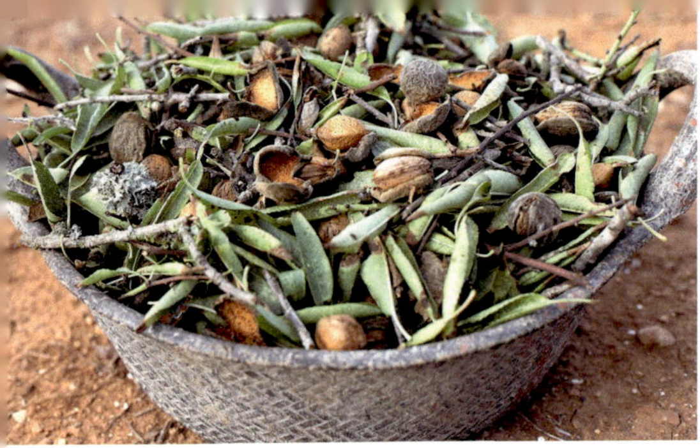

Almonds and other products

Along with the carob bean and the fig, the almond is one of the most representative trees of the dry region, Basic in the subsistence economy of the traditional agricultural world. In the 18th century, in Ibiza they began to plant large plantations of almond trees, which were increased in the 19th century after the vines were attacked by phyloxera and had to be pulled up. However, in the 20th century almond production fell into recession, above all because of the tourist boom, and was abandoned.

The almond tree, however, is still present in the landscape, above all in the Pla de Corona in Ibiza, where in January and February the flowering of the trees covers the landscape in a white cape of exquisite beauty. The use of the almond is also still alive: it appears in many sweet recipes and salads, especially in the sauces that give a definitive touch of flavour to fish and meat stews. They are also eaten raw or toasted to accompany, for example, dried figs.

However, if there is a dish in which the almond is the true star it is without doubt in the *salsa de Nadal*, the heavy star of the Pine Islands' Christmas festivities. It is only prepared once a year and eaten during the holiday period. In each area it is made in a particular way, which has caused —and continues to cause— passionate arguments about it, above all regarding some of the ingredients that make it up. It is made with toasted almonds, eggs and a stock of several meats, and the result is a more or less thick liquid sauce, with so many ingredients and so many ways of making it that it is almost impossible to come up with a single official recipe for this dessert. At Christmas, in the city of Ibiza a competition is held to reward the best sauce.

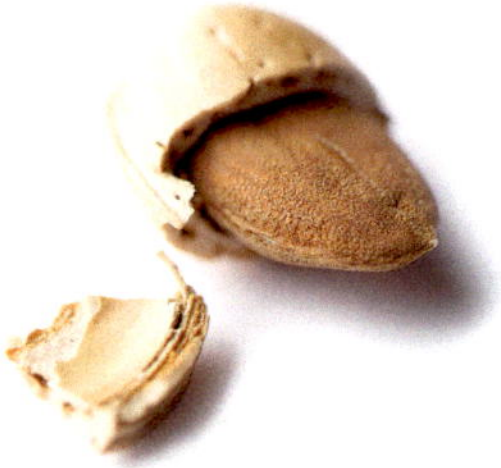

The almond tree forms part of the landscape of Ibiza, above all in the Pla de Corona, in the district of Sant Antoni de Portmany.

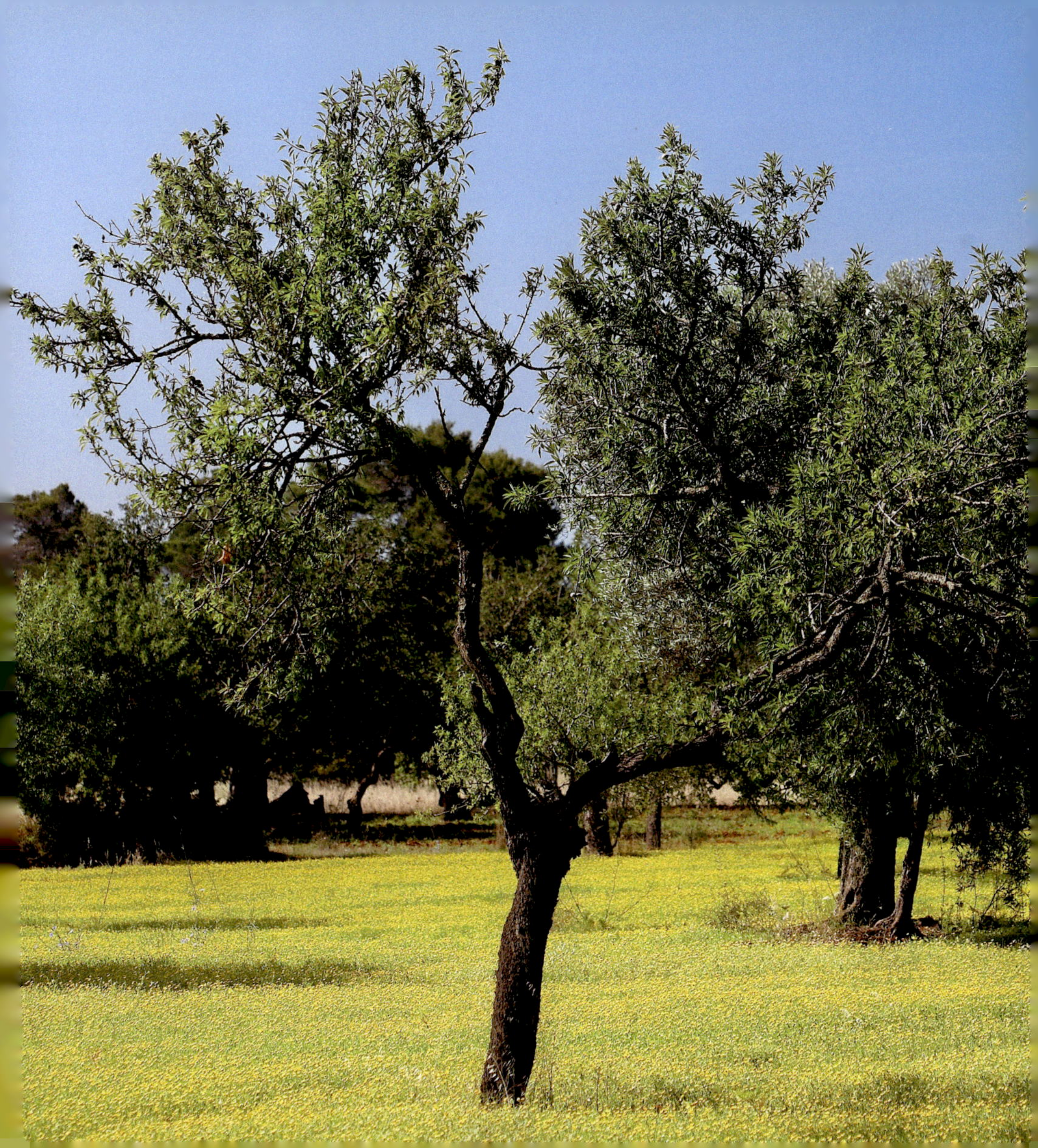

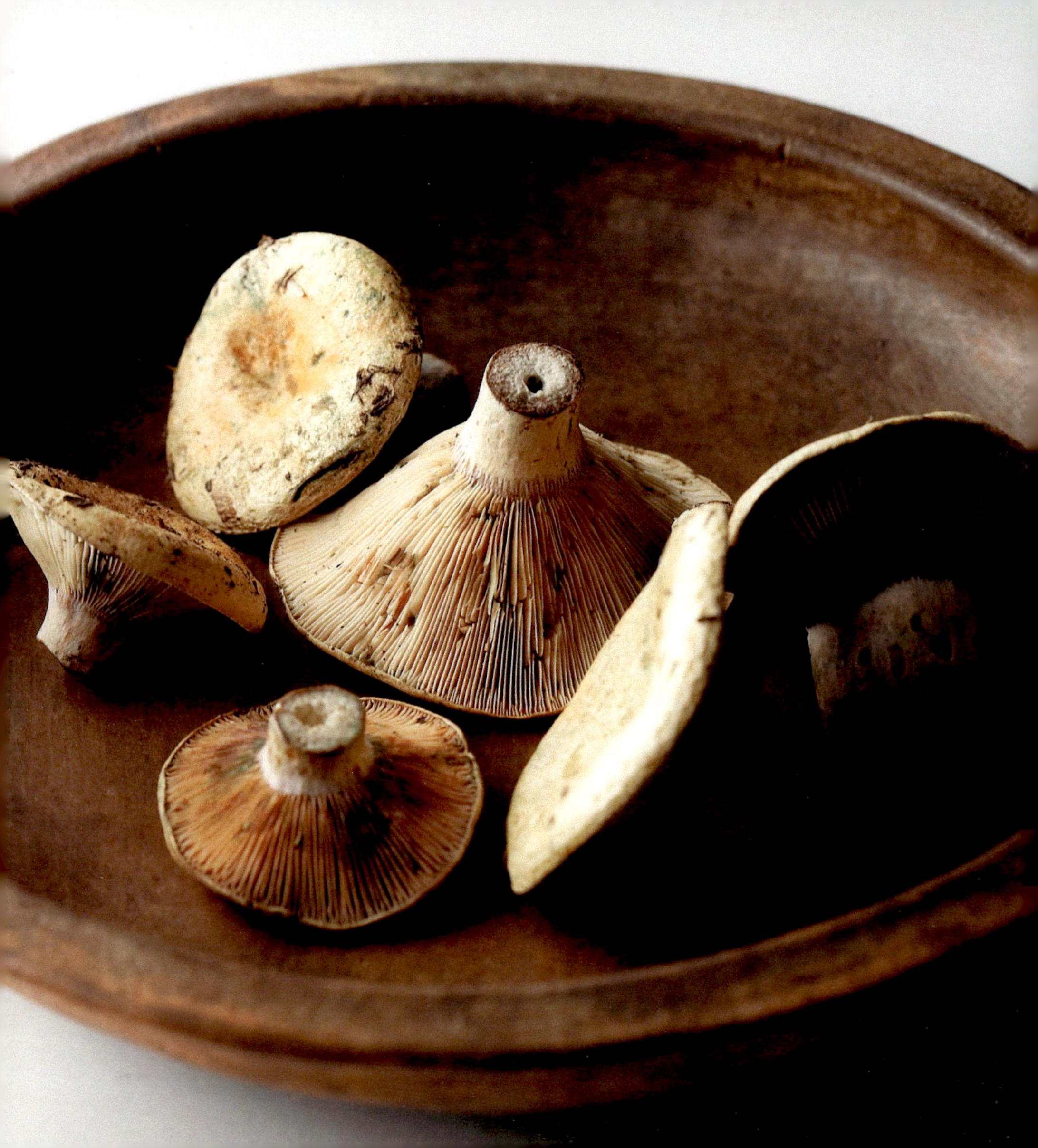

1 Milk mushrooms. The autumn rains result in the growth among the pine trees of the semi-hidden milk mushrooms (*pebrassos*), much sought-after for their strong flavour. They are usually small in size, and due to the high consumption of this product in autumn, milk mushrooms are usually imported from the peninsula, although considered to be of a lower quality. They are delicious cooked over the heat of the charcoal grill, sometimes accompanied by pieces of *sobrassada*, and sprayed with a good olive oil. They are also cooked in the oven with chunks of lean pork meat, and appear in rice dishes and autumn stews.

2 Snails. Until the 1970s, Ibiza exported snails to the Iberian Peninsula. In bygone times, going out to look for them after the first rains was a task for peasant women, who when they had enough would go to the city to sell them to shops that would export them. The snails from Ibiza are highly valued for their flavour, since they feed on a great variety of aromatic herbs. They are mainly cooked in stews and rice dishes, and the popular belief is that you should not eat them in a month without an "r" (May, June, July and August). It is important to clean them well before cooking.

3 Broad beans and *guixes*. The humble broad bean is very present in the cooking of Ibiza and Formentera, in dishes such as *faves cuinades*. They are also a food with many associated superstitions: they say that the fishermen from the islands go out to sea with half a dried broad bean, which sucks out the poison and calms the pain from a spider crab bite or other poisonous fish. *Guixes* (vetches) were eaten a lot in other times, and today they are a basic ingredient —along with the broad beans—, of the *cuinat*, a typical dish at Easter.

2

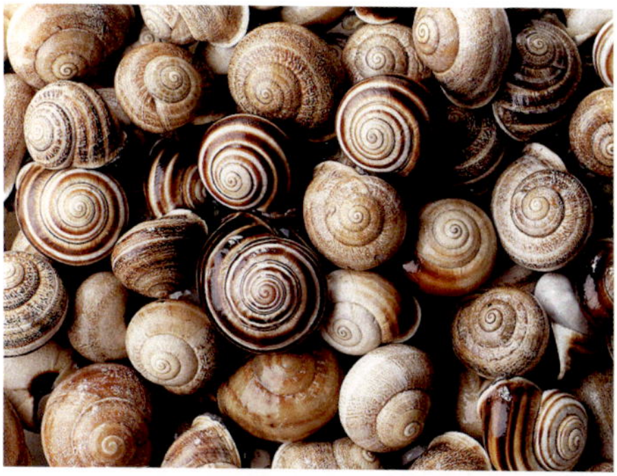

3

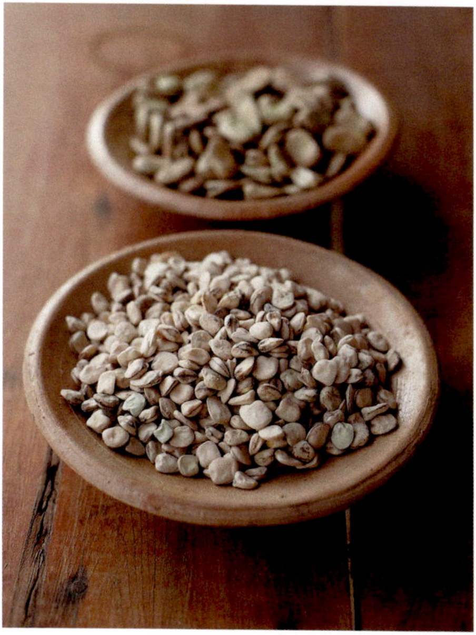

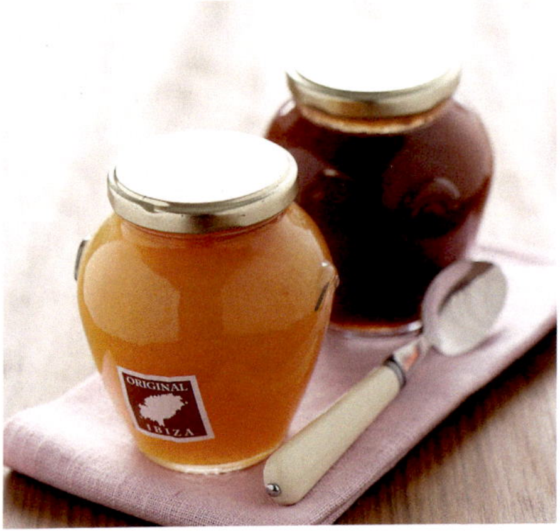

4

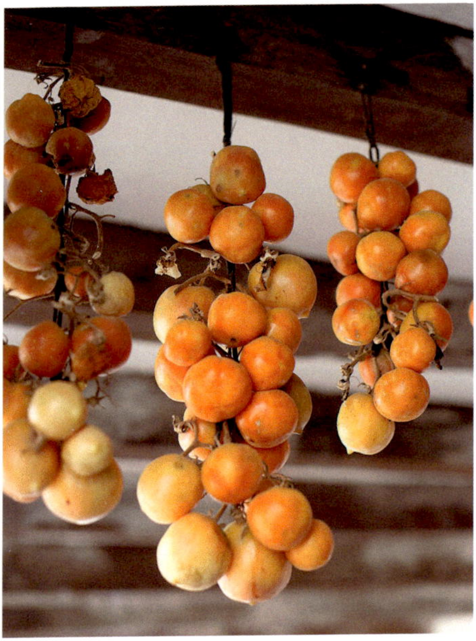

5

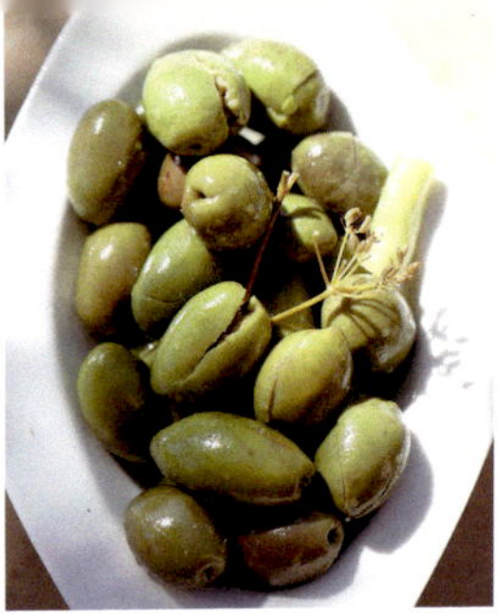

6

4 6 5

4 Preserves and jams. Since yesteryear, the surplus fruit has been used to make preserves and jams, with fruits such as figs, oranges, plums or apricots, perfumed with cinnamon and grated lemon.

5 Tomatoes *de penjar*. In rural houses it is common to produce tomatoes *de penjar*, which are hung on strings or in bunches in dry spots, not too warm of humid, so that they are conserved fresh for a long time. The most characteristic variety is the ramellet tomato, with a tough, resistant skin, and a balanced and highly appreciated flavour.

6 Olives. Olives are ever-present in aperitifs and salads, and they are still prepared in some rural houses, in diverse degrees of maturation. The most common ones are the *trencades* (open) —green olives that are given a bang one by one with a wooden mallet, preserved in brine— and whole salted ones, almost ripe olives that that take more time than the open ones to be ready to eat.

7 *Ñoras*. *Ñoras* (small spicy red peppers) are indispensable in dishes such as stewed snails, the cuinat or rice with pork. In the Pine Islands they are grown in small allotments or gardens for personal consumption; they are picked at the end of summer and left to dry hanging in the sun.

7

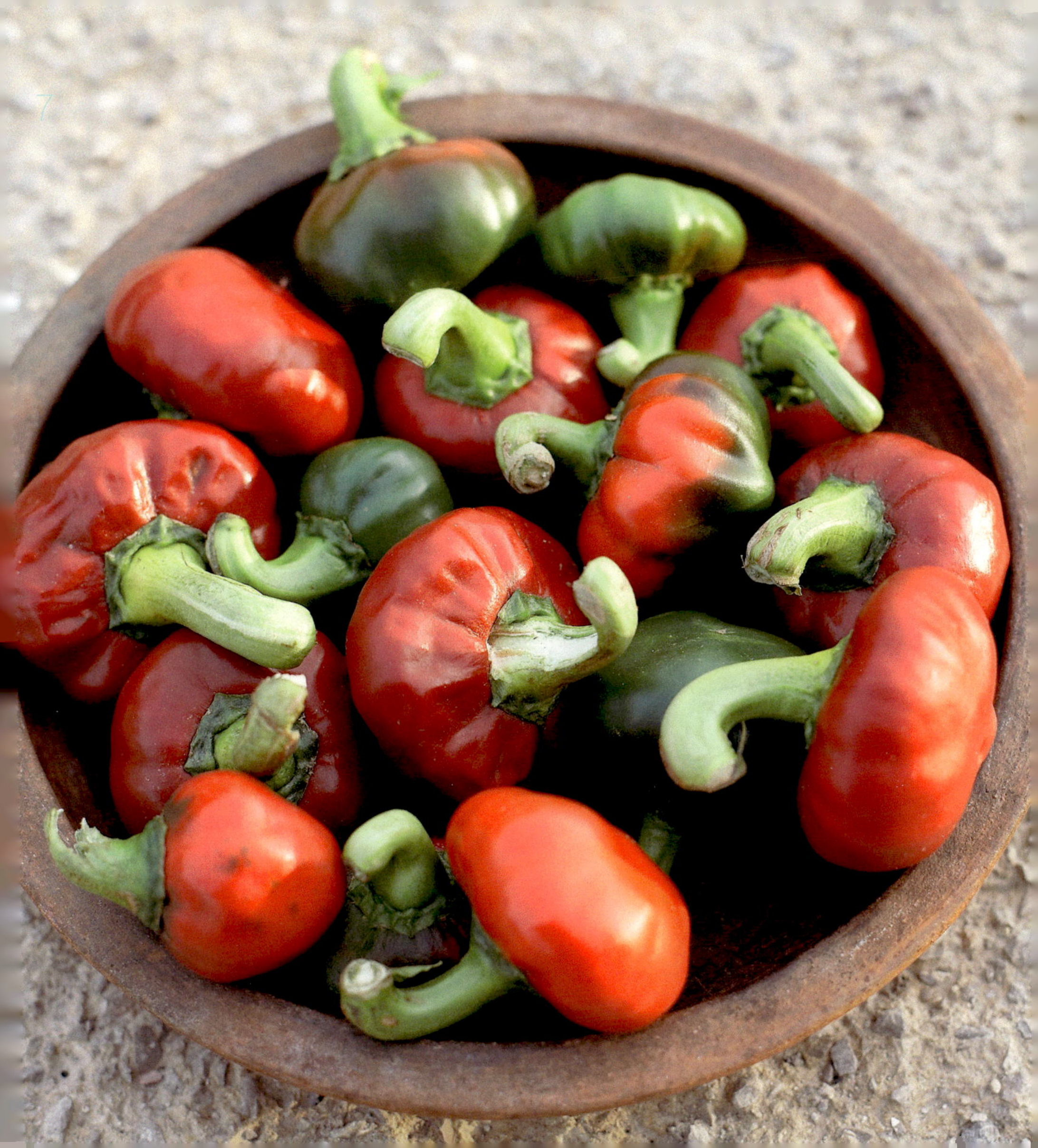

Fruits

Fruit trees are sprinkled all over the countryside, be they small fields of orange, apple or apricot trees, or some pomegranate, fig or quince tree standing alone. In summer, honeydew melons and watermelons are also grown. Primarily fruit is eaten fresh, but figs are also dried, apricots added to sweet flat breads, preserves are made —for example marmalade with oranges— and sweet quince jelly. Pomegranate seeds are often eaten with wine and sugar.

1

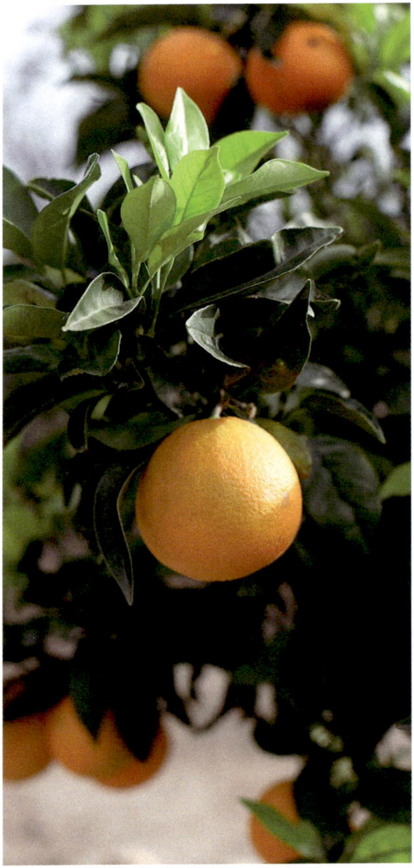

2

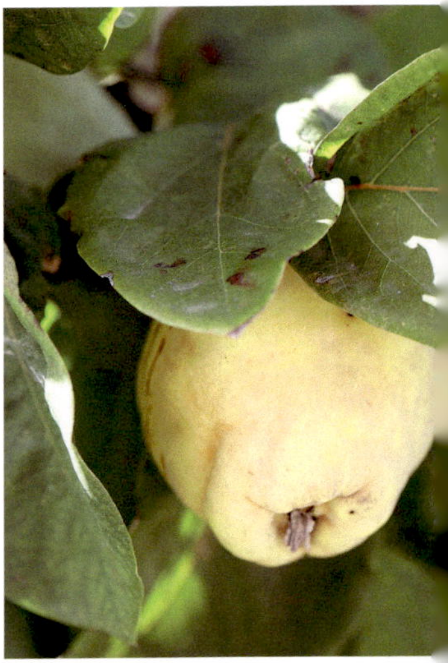

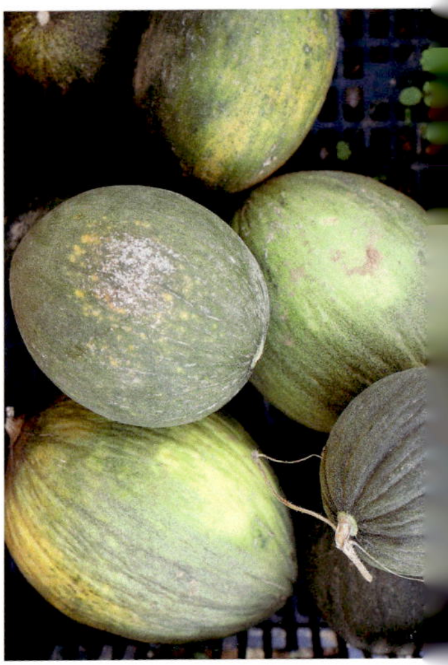

3

6

4

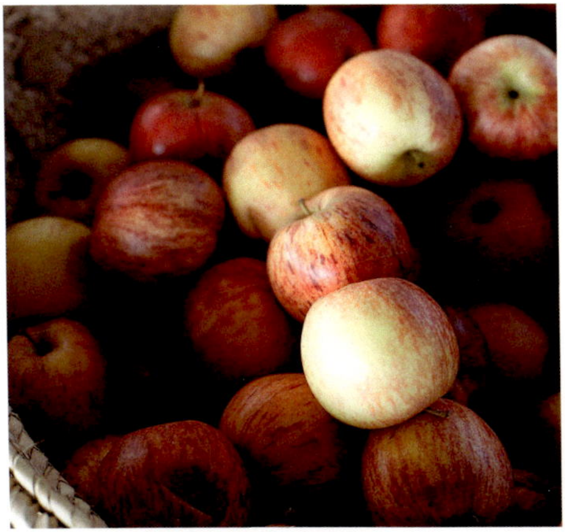

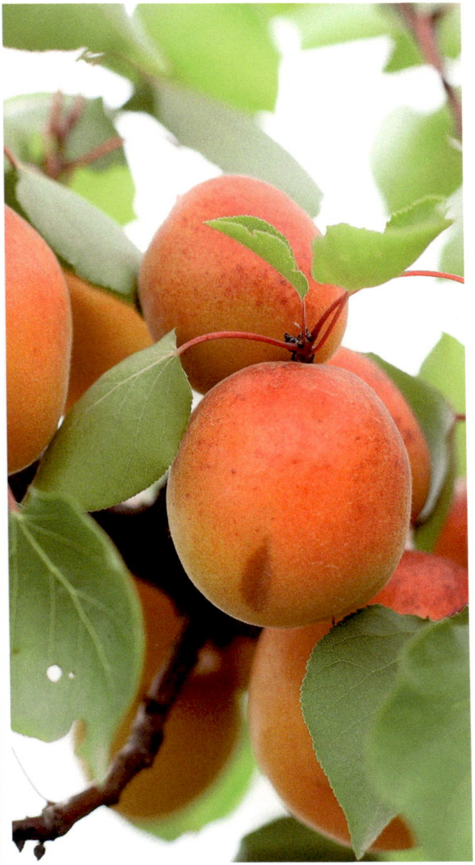

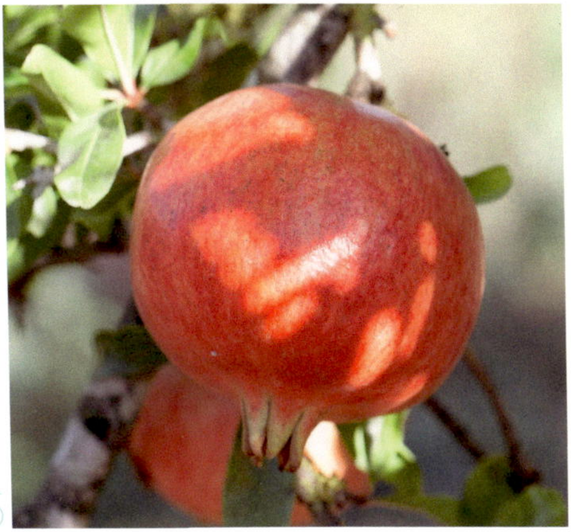

5

1 Oranges **2** Quince **3** Melons **4** Apples **5** Pomegranate **6** Apricots

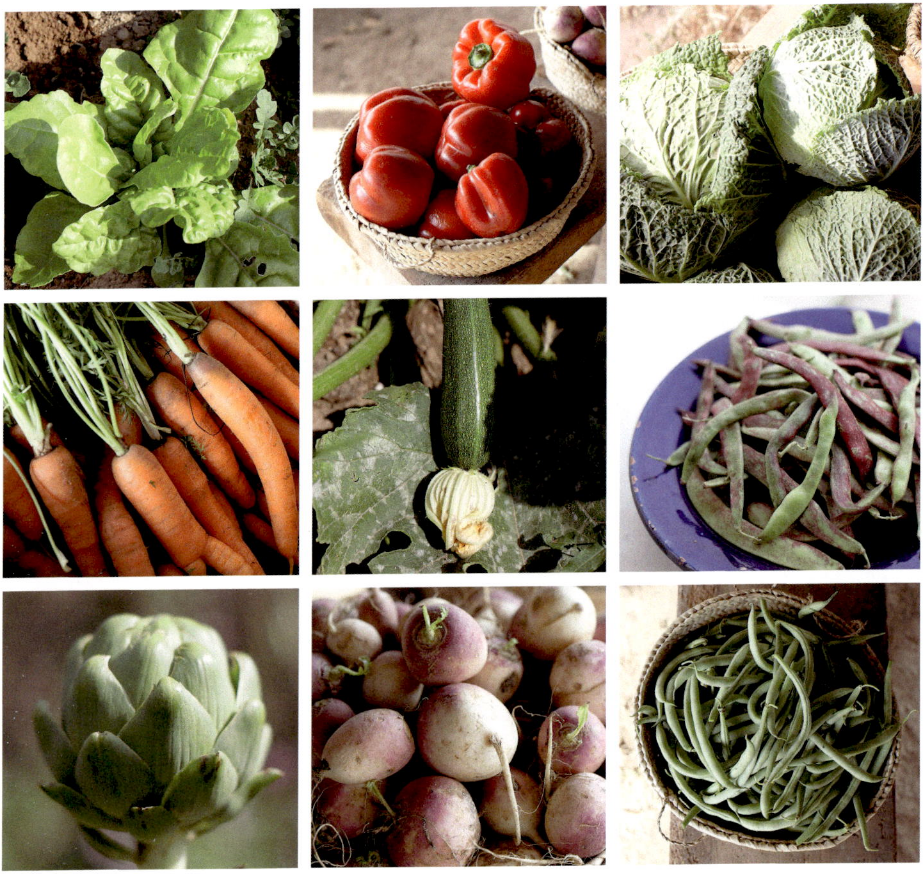

Top to bottom, left to right: **1** Swiss chard **2** Peppers **3** Cabbages **4** Carrots **5** Courgettes **6** Vetches (*guixes*) **7** Artichokes **8** Turnips **9** Green beans

Garden produce

The orchards produce all kinds of fruit and vegetables typical of the Mediterranean diet: green beans, peas, artichokes, cauliflower, cabbage, Swiss chard, spinach, carrots, aubergines, courgettes, red and green peppers... All of them appear in many recipes for both meat and fish, or in rice dishes or those such as sautéed cauliflower, sautéed spinach, stuffed aubergines and peppers, hotpot, to mention just a few. Also grown are excellent tomatoes and lettuces, present in salads. And potatoes, which are cooked with or without skin, featuring in the *cassoleta de patates* (casserole of potatoes). The presence of local produce grown on smallholdings that have opted for organic agriculture is gradually increasing.

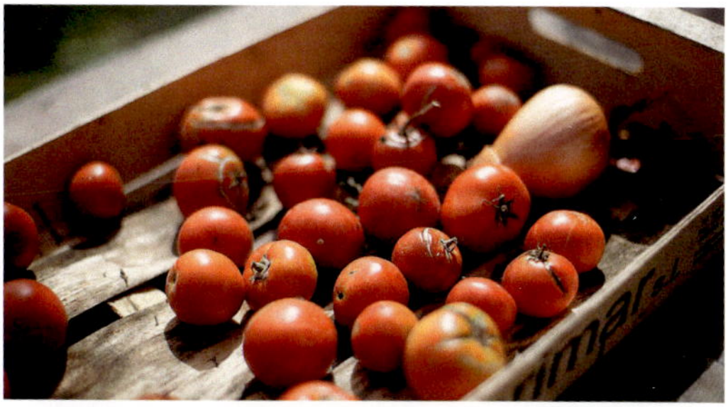

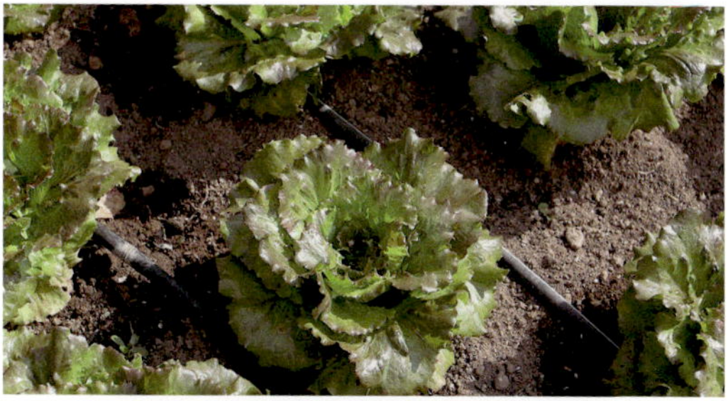

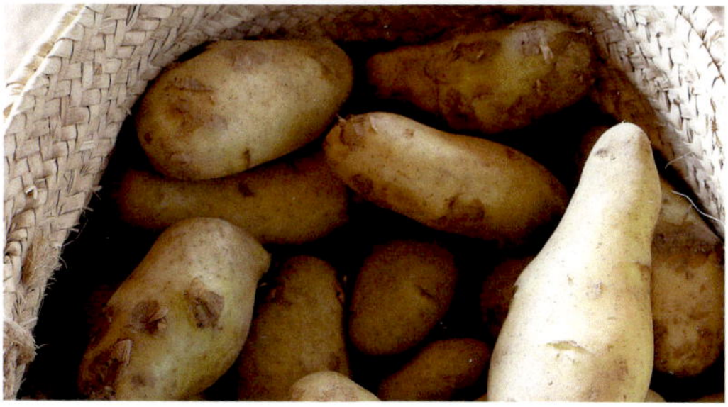

1 In Ibiza and Formentera different varieties of tomatoes are grown, among them *de penjar*, which conserve for a long time. **2** A large variety of lettuces are also grown and eaten a lot. **3** Potatoes, greatly appreciated for their good quality.

01

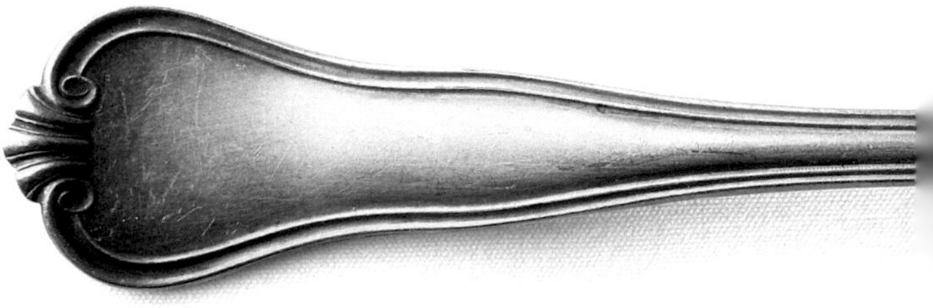

Starters recipes

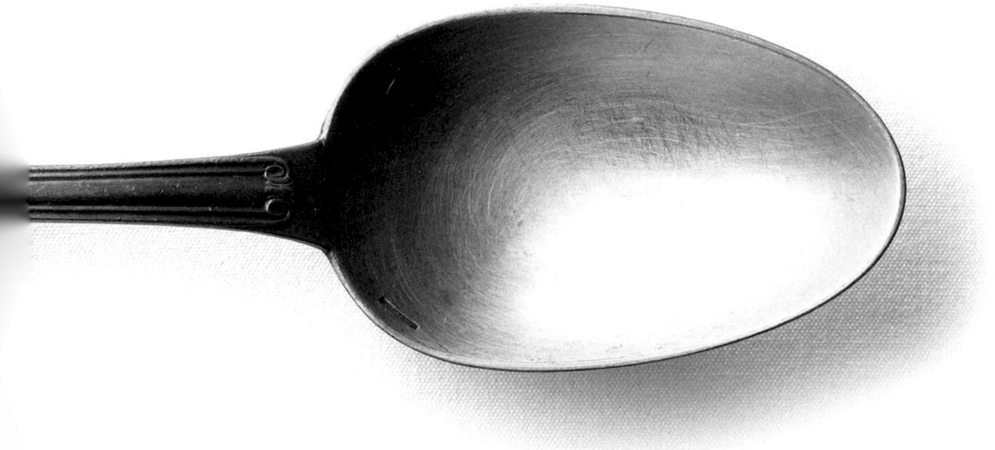

S'enciam

S'enciam

For 4 people:

* 1 large onion * 2 salad tomatoes * 2 green peppers * 1 garlic clove
* 4 spoonfuls of olive oil * 1 spoonful of vinegar * salt

1. Peel the onion removing the outer layers and cut it into very thin slices. Salt it and place it in a salad bowl or soup bowl for a few minutes so it releases its strong juice. Next, rinse it twice through fresh water, dry it and season it with a pinch of salt.
2. Wash the tomatoes and cut them into segments of the same size. Wash the peppers and break them up by hand. Peel and crush the garlic clove.
3. Place the onion in a salad bowl (*enciamera*) and cover with the tomatoes and peppers. Salt lightly, sprinkle with the crushed garlic and season with vinegar and olive oil. Toss well and serve.

This recipe is one of the most popular in Ibiza cuisine in summer. It is often combined with other vegetables and completed with capers and olives.
Ibiza salads are traditionally served with *crostes de bescuit*: slices of dry bread re-baked in the oven and seasoned with olive oil, tomato, dried fish...
The peppers are always broken by hand because popular wisdom states that metal gives them a bad flavour.

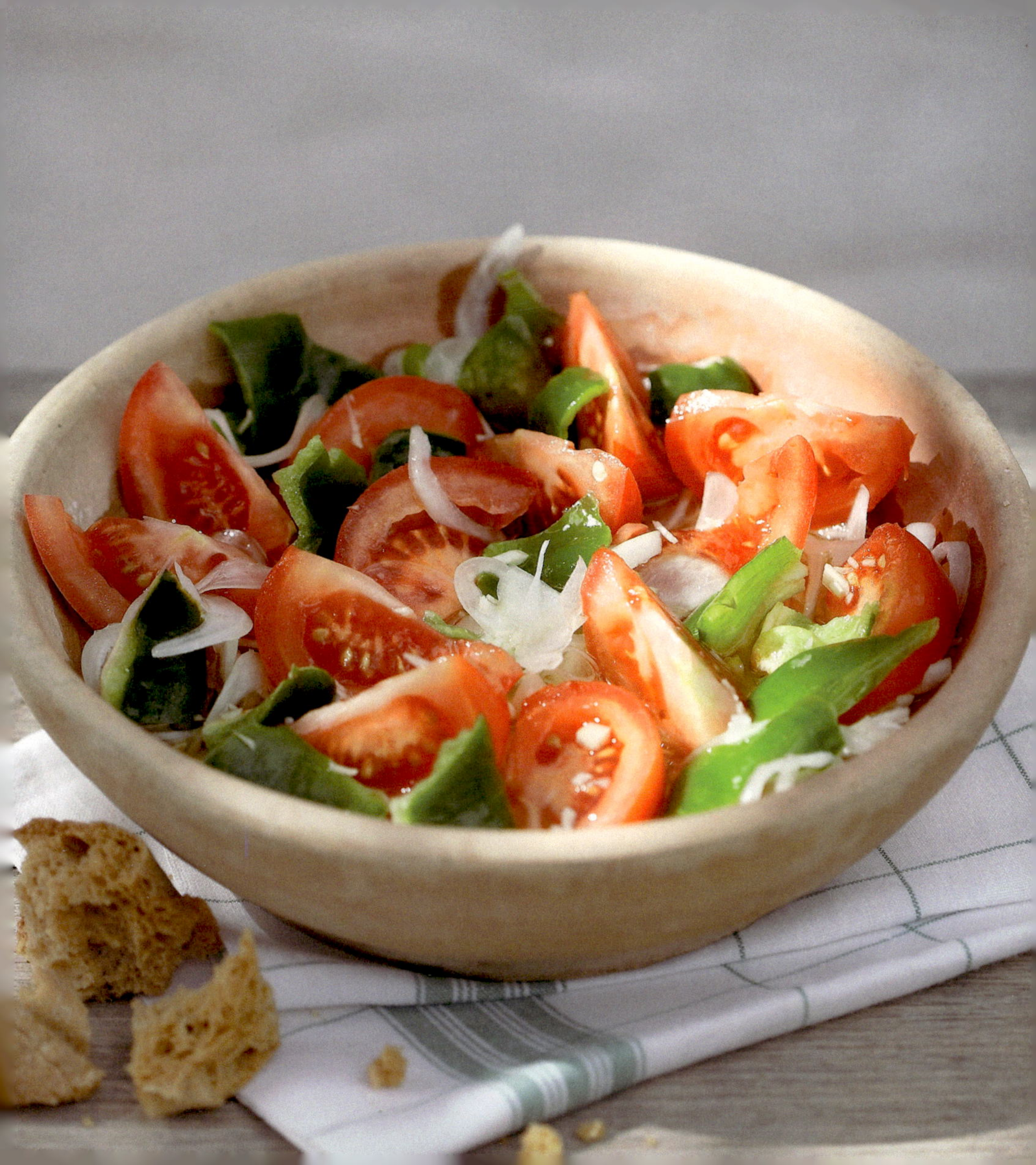

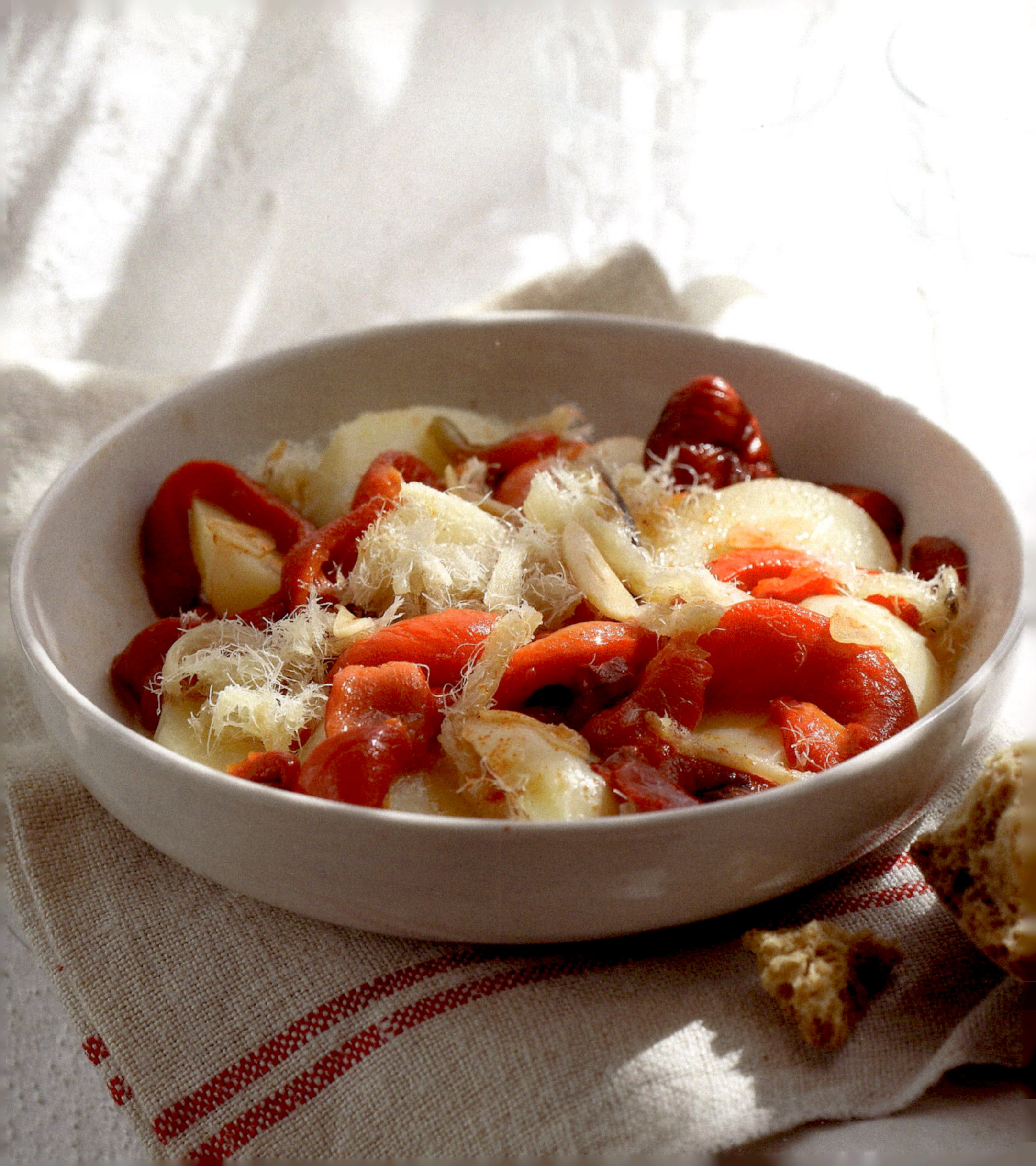

Amanida de peix sec de Formentera

Dried fish salad from Formentera

For 4 people

* 3 red peppers * 3 large potatoes * 150 g of dried fish * 1 clove of garlic
* 4 spoonfuls of olive oil * 1 teaspoon of paprika * salt

1. Wash the peppers and bake them for 45 minutes in the oven at 200° C. Remove them, wrap them in a clean kitchen cloth and leave them to cool a little so they can be easily peeled. Remove the stalks and seeds inside and cut them into strips. Put to one side.
2. Cook the potatoes in their skin for 25 minutes in a pot with a lot of salted water. Drain them and leave them to cool. Then peel them and cut them into slices.
3. Peel the clove of garlic and cut it into very thin slices. Sauté it in a pan with one spoonful of oil without letting it brown. Add the strips of baked pepper, sauté with the garlic for 2 minutes so they soak up the flavour and salt lightly. Remove from the flame and leave to cool.
4. Place the slices of potato on the bottom of a plate. Salt them lightly and sprinkle them with a pinch of paprika. Cover with the baked pepper strips now fried. Add the crumbled dried fish, dress with the remaining olive oil and serve.

This salad and its many variants is traditionally made on the island of Formentera with autochthonous fish: tuna, bonito, mackerel, dogfish (*gató*) or skate, among others.

Cuinat
Cuinat

For 8 people

⁎ 200 g of dried broad beans ⁎ 200 g of vetches (*guixes*), chickpeas or other pulse ⁎ 1 kg of campion (*verdura*) or spinach ⁎ 1 bunch of Swiss chard ⁎ 3 spring onions ⁎ 4 cloves of garlic ⁎ 2 young garlics ⁎ 2 *ñoras* (spicy red peppers) ⁎ paprika ⁎ olive oil ⁎ 1 lemon ⁎ 1 small bunch of mint ⁎ salt

1. The night before, leave the dried broad beans and the *guixes* to soak in water.
2. Wash the Swiss chard and chop it. Wash the *verdura*, using only the leaves. Cook both ingredients in a pot with salted water for 5 minutes. Drain and put aside.
3. Peel and chop the cloves of garlic, spring onions and young garlic. Wash the mint and chop the leaves.
4. Place the dried broad beans and the *guixes* in a pot with cold water, add the vegetables and cook for 20 minutes. Add the chopped garlic and spring onions, the chopped spicy red peppers and mint. Add salt to taste, add 2 spoonfuls of oil and a teaspoonful of paprika and continue cooking until the broad beans are tender.
5. When serving, season each plate with a few drops of lemon juice, olive oil and a pinch of paprika.

Verdura, or campion as it is known in English, is a plant that grows spontaneously in the fields of Ibiza. In some areas of Almería is is called "gypsy grass" and is very popular prepared in the form of omelettes. It can be replaced with spinach. The *cuinat* is a very typical dish in the cuisine during Easter on the island.

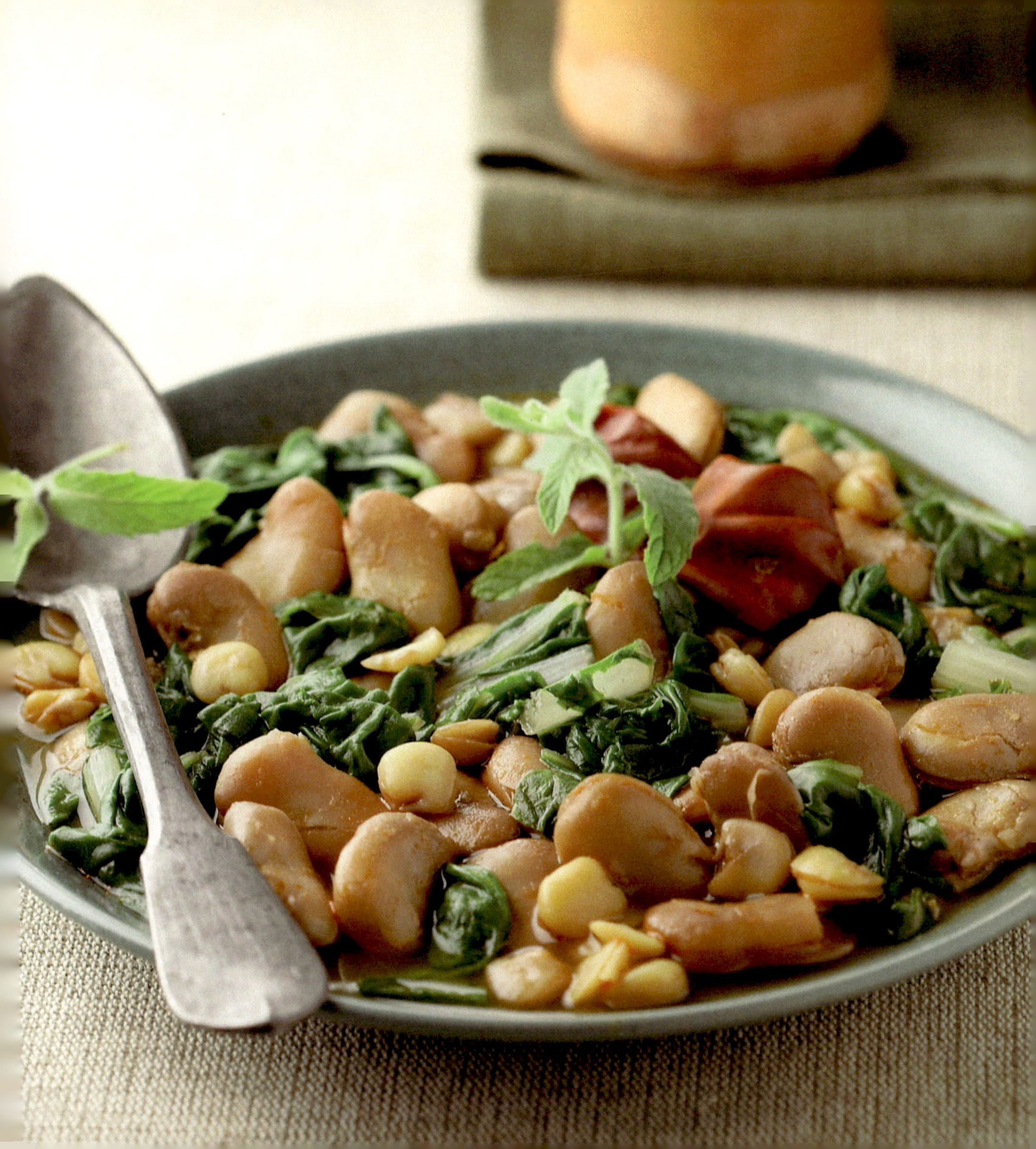

Olla podrida
Hotpot

For 4 people

* 1 onion * 1 tomato * 2 cloves of garlic * 100 g of *sobrassada* * 100 g of streaky bacon * 150 g of sausage * 4 medium-size potatoes * 200 g of green beans * 100 g of shelled young beans * 6 small pears * 3 spoonfuls of olive oil * a pinch of oregano * pepper * salt

1. Make a cut in the form of a cross at the base of the tomato, scald it for 2 minutes in boiling water, peel it and cut it into pieces. Peel and chop the onion and the cloves of garlic. Peel the potatoes and cut them in slices.
2. In a pot with 2 spoonfuls of olive oil brown the chopped sausage and the streaky bacon and remove them. Add another spoonful of oil and sauté the onion until it is transparent. Add the chopped garlic and tomato and cook for 5 more minutes. Add the *sobrassada* and the meats previously put to one side and cook for 10 minutes.
3. Add the potatoes in slices, the green and young beans and peeled and chopped pears. Cover with water and season with salt, pepper and oregano. Cook for some 35 minutes more and serve.

The *olla fresca* is the vegetarian version of this dish. The meats are replaced with dried broad beans, previously soaked, and it is seasoned with cinnamon, paprika and saffron.

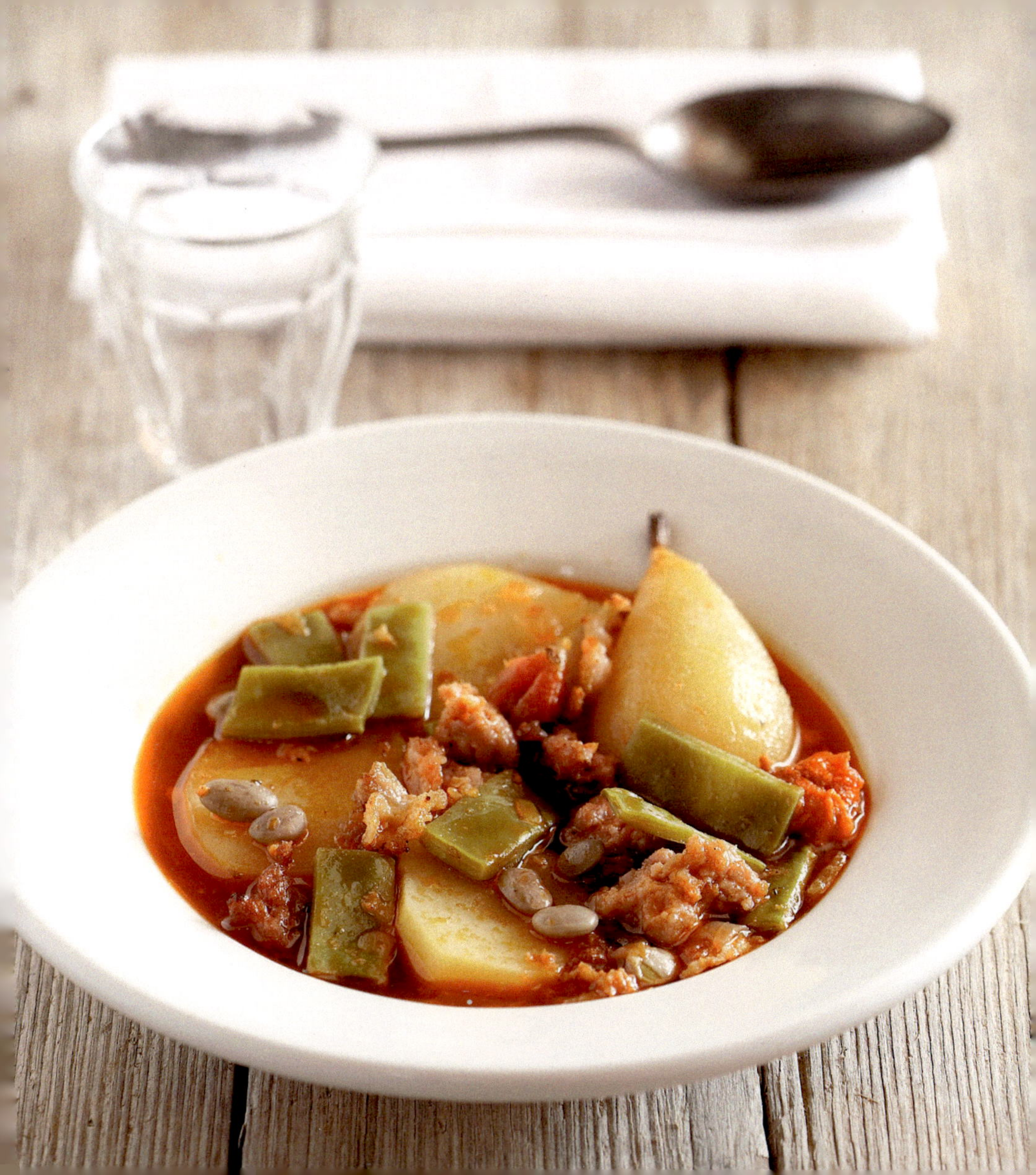

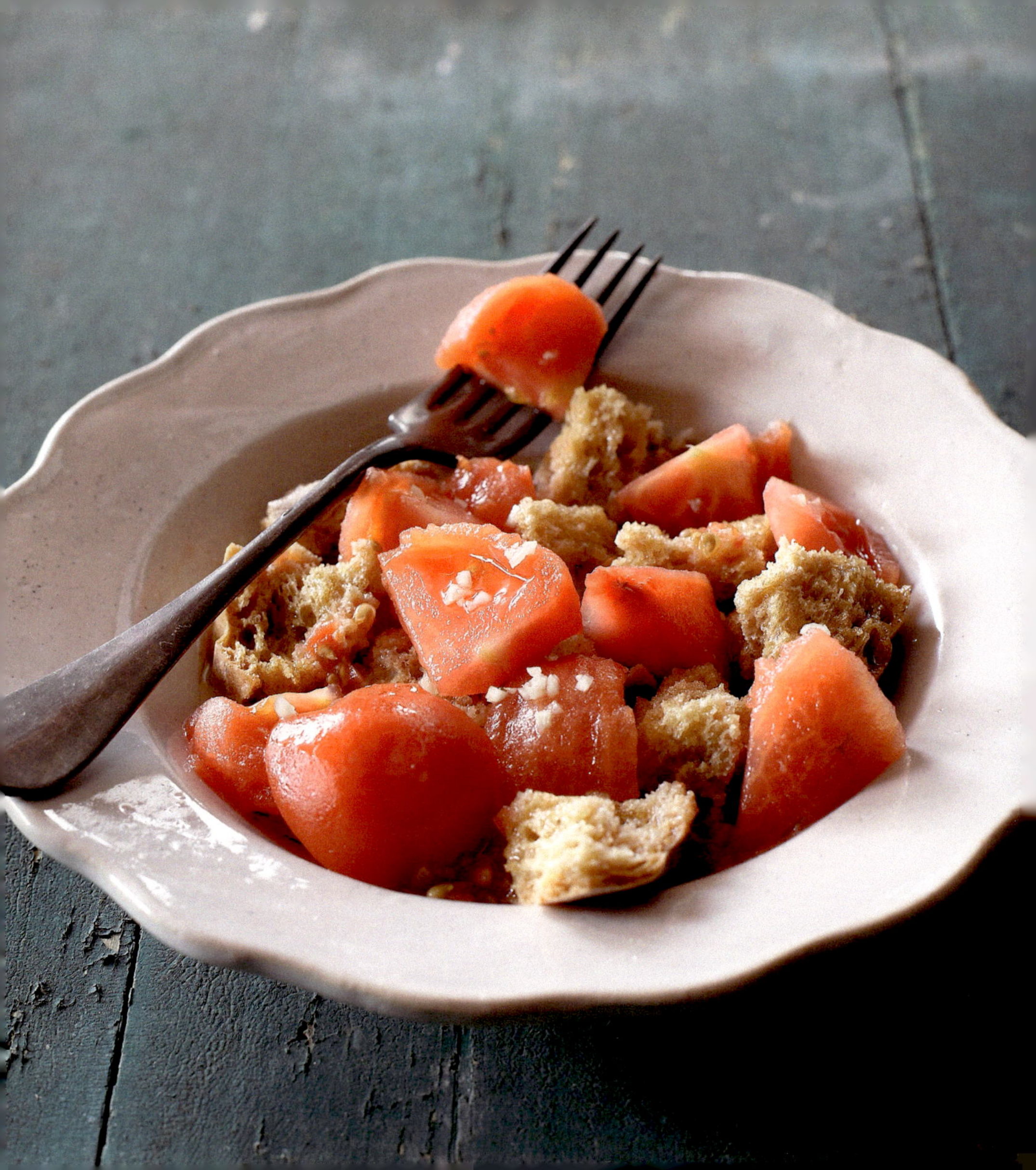

Sopes bòfegues
Bòfegues soups

For 4 people

* 400 g of *crostes de pa* (re-baked bread slices) * 4 ripe tomatoes * 2 cloves of garlic * olive oil

1. Crumble up the *crostes* into pieces but not too small. Sprinkle them with a little water so that they are humid and place them in a soup bowl. Peel and chop the cloves of garlic.
2. Make a cut in the form of a cross at the base of the tomatoes, scald them for 2 minutes in boiling water. Cool them under tap water and peel them. Cut them into small pieces.
3. Add the pieces of tomato over the *crostes*, salt and pepper lightly and sprinkle on the chopped garlic. Season with olive oil at the last moment and serve.

The *crostes de bescuit* are traditionally prepared with bread dough in the form of *cócs*, thick loaves that, once baked, are cut into slices and baked again so that they lose all their humidity and have a crispy biscuit-like texture. They could thus be conserved for a long time and eaten by sailors on their journeys.
This popular Ibiza dish can be served with crumbled dried fish. It is also often dressed with vinegar or lemon juice.

Sopa de salpes
Gilthead soup

For 4 people

* 800 g of gilthead * 1 large onion * 2 tomatoes * 2 cloves of garlic * 1 bunch of parsley * 3 spoonfuls of oil * lemon juice * a pinch of paprika * pepper * salt

1. Remove the scales from the giltheads and clean them thoroughly, totally removing the black velum on the lower part of the belly. Scrub them well with salt, cut them into pieces and leave them to macerate with lemon juice for 1 hour. Wash the parsley and chop it finely.
2. Peel and chop the onion and the garlic. Scald the tomato in boiling water for 2 minutes, peel it, remove the pips and chop it. In a *greixonera* or ceramic casserole with 3 spoonfuls of oil, sauté the onion until it is transparent. Add the chopped garlic and cook 3 more minutes. Add the chopped tomato, salt and pepper, season with paprika and lots of chopped parsley, and cook for another 10 minutes on a low flame until the sauce is thick like jam.
3. Drain the fish from the maceration, wash it briefly under the tap and add it to the casserole. Cover with water and cook for 25 minutes.
4. Leave to rest for 10 minutes and serve the soup on scalding slices of toasted bread (*sopes*) previously placed on each of the individual soup bowls.

The gilthead is considered a fish of very poor quality since, due to the fact that it feeds on algae, generally gives off a very strong odour in its ventral part. However, if cleaned well or this part removed, if forms a very tasty and economic dish. This recipe can also be presented with the fish served on a separate plate and accompanied by an *all i oli* sauce (egg yolk, garlic and oil). Another very popular sauce for this dish can be made by grounding in the mortar a clove of garlic with lots of parsley, a pinch of paprika, lemon juice and a few spoonfuls of the fish soup.

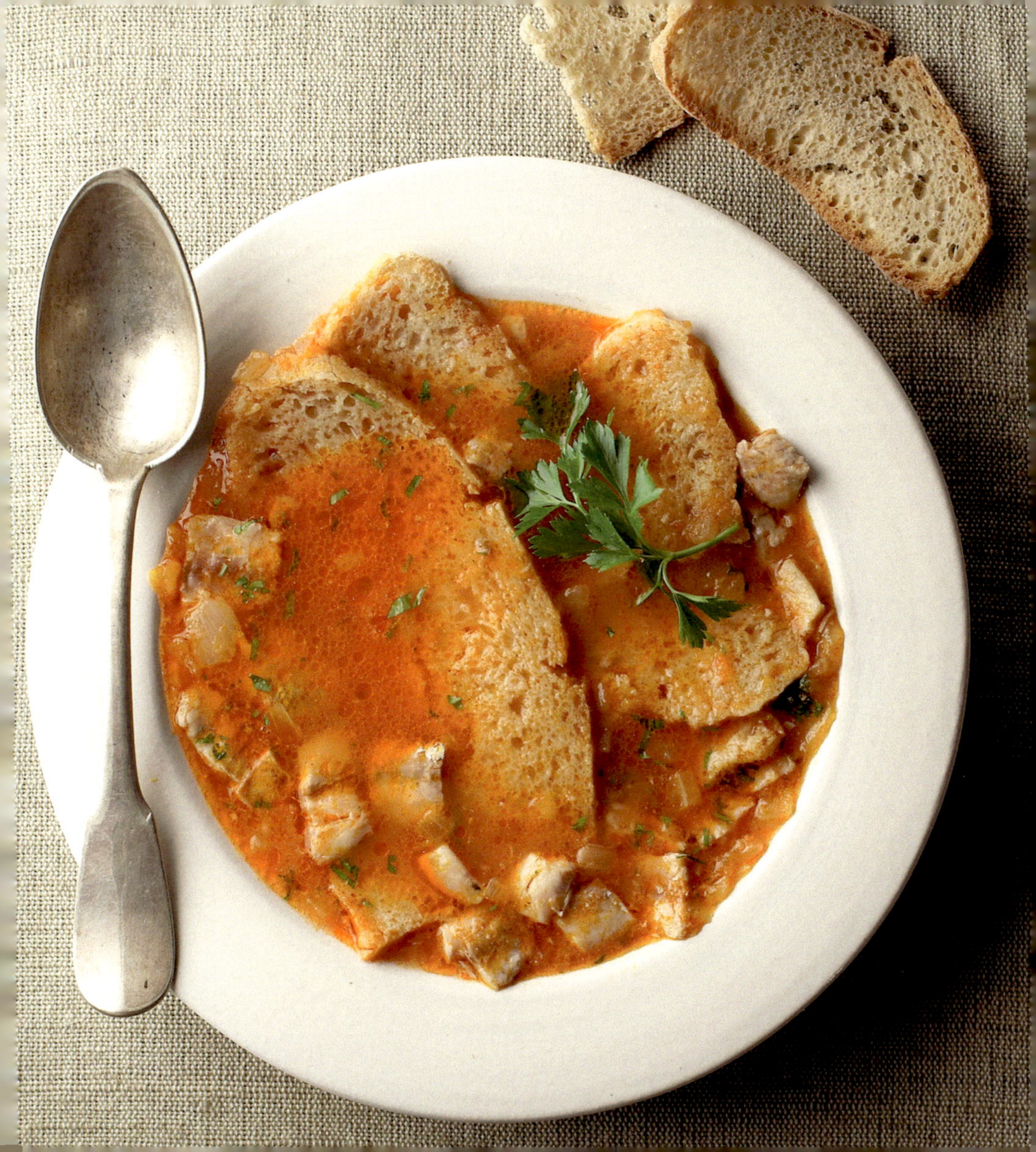

Pebreres farcides d'anfós
Peppers stuffed with grouper

For 4 people

* 8 medium-size red peppers * 4 slices of grouper * 2 large onions * 2 cloves of garlic * 1 small bunch of parsley * 4 spoonfuls of olive oil * a pinch of paprika * pepper * salt

1. Wash the peppers and dry them with a clean cloth. Peel and chop the onions and garlic. Wash the parsley and chop it finely.
2. In a pan with 2 spoonfuls of oil, brown the slices of fish for 2 minutes on each side. Add salt and pepper, leave them to cool and break them up, removing the bones and skins. Put to one side.
3. Add 1 spoonful of oil to the pan and sauté the chopped onion until it is transparent. Add the chopped garlic and cook for 3 more minutes. Add the pieces of fish, with salt and pepper, season with a pinch of paprika and sprinkle it with lots of chopped parsley. Cook for 2 more minutes and remove from the cooker.
4. Cut the upper part of the peppers as if it were a top and remove the filaments and seeds from inside. Fill them with the prepared stuffing and cover them again with the upper top, attaching it, if you want, with the help of two toothpicks. Pre-heat the oven to 200° C.
5. Coat a ceramic casserole or oven dish with the remaining olive oil, place the filled peppers in it and bake at 200° C for 35 minutes. Remove from the oven, leave to cool and serve.

This recipe can be made by cutting the peppers longitudinally.
You can use any type of white fish with few bones, traditionally amberjack or dentex.

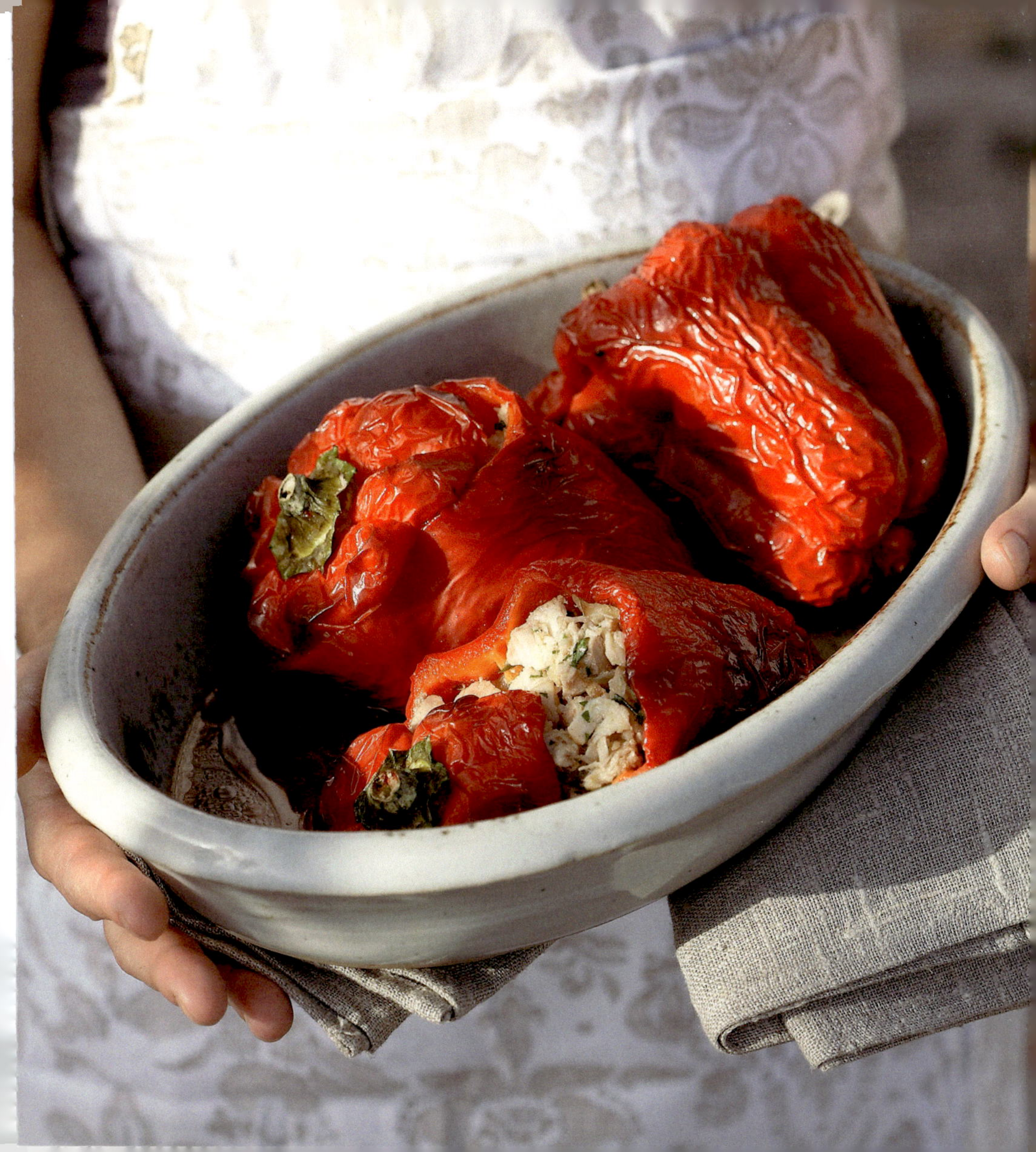

Cassoleta de patates
Potato casserole

For 4 people

* 800 g of potatoes * 1 onion * 3 tomatoes * 3 cloves of garlic * 2 eggs * 4 spoonfuls of olive oil
* 1 small bunch of parsley * 1 teaspoonful of paprika * a pinch of cinnamon * pepper * salt

1. Peel the potatoes and cut them into pieces the same size. Peel and chop the onion and the garlic. Cut a cross in the base of the tomatoes and scald them for 2 minutes in a casserole with boiling water. Cool them under the coldwater tap, remove the pips and cut them into pieces.
2. Sauté the onion in a casserole with 3 spoonfuls of oil until it is transparent. Add the garlic and the tomato and cook for 10 more minutes, until the fry mixture has the consistency of jam.
3. Add the potatoes, season with paprika, cinnamon, and add salt and pepper. Cover with water and cook for 20 minutes. After this time add the beaten eggs with a pinch of salt and stir. Cook for 5 more minutes for the sauce to thicken, sprinkle with lots of chopped parsley and serve.

In Ibiza's cuisine potatoes combine with practically any ingredient according to season. They are popular with Swiss chard and carrots, dressed with vinegar and chopped garlic. They are also often stewed with cabbage, cauliflower, green beans, peas, artichokes or broad beans.
To serve as an accompaniment they can be prepared *en casaca*. The potatoes are boiled in their skins, later peeled and cut into thick slices. Finally, they are coated with firstly flour, then beaten egg and breadcrumbs and fried in a generous amount of hot oil.

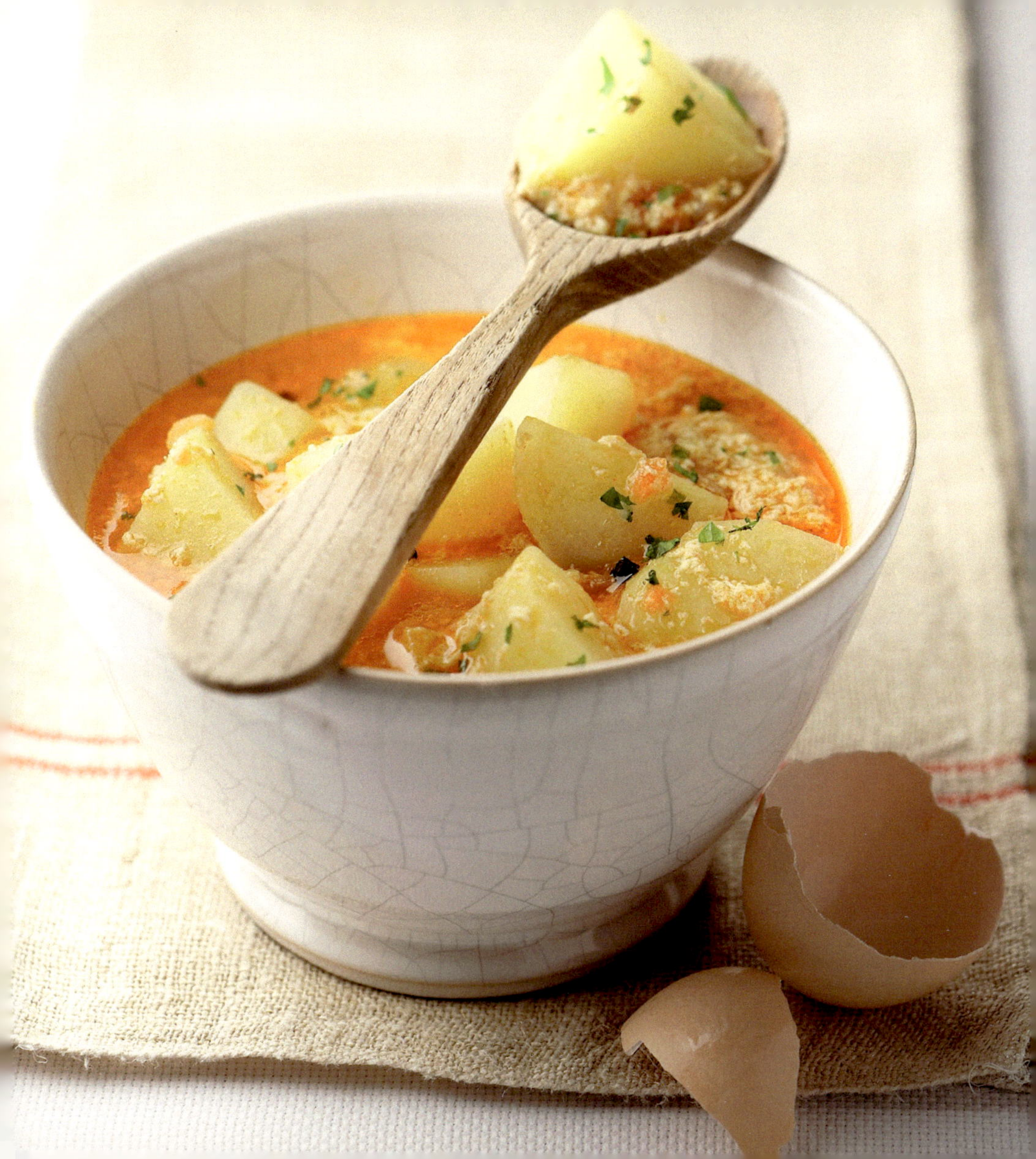

Faves cuinades
Broad bean stew

For 4 people

* 1.5 kg of broad beans * 150 g of green beans * 1 large onion * 2 ripe tomatoes * 1 head of garlic * 100 g of *sobrassada* * 100 g of bacon * 1 teaspoonful of paprika * a splash of vinegar * oil * salt

1. Peel and chop the onion. Wash the tomatoes and cut them in pieces. Cut the *sobrassada* and bacon into pieces. Clean the green beans, remove the ends and side filaments and cut them up.
2. Heat 3 spoonfuls of oil in a ceramic casserole and sauté the chopped onion until it is transparent. Add the tomato and cubes of bacon, and cook for about 10 minutes. Then add salt and pepper, season with paprika and add the *sobrassada*, the head of garlic, broad beans and green beans.
3. Pour in a splash of vinegar, leave it to evaporate for a minute on a high flame and cover with water. Add salt, cover and cook for 30 minutes. Leave to rest for 5 minutes before serving.

The *fava pelada* is a popular dish made in a very similar way to peeled dried broad beans. At the end of the cooking, noodles and a generous sprinkling of chopped mint are added. This same recipe can be made also adding *botifarró*, raisins and pine nuts.
Another traditional dish is *faves envinagrades* (broad beans in vinegar). The first dried broad beans of the season are used, which are left to soak the night before and the following day are stewed in a fry-mix of tomato, onion, laurel and garlic with potatoes and green beans. It is often dressed with mint and thickened with a fried mix of garlic and toasted bread dissolved in some spoonfuls of vinegar and stock. The recipe for *olla fresca* is completed with pears and seasoned with cinnamon and saffron.

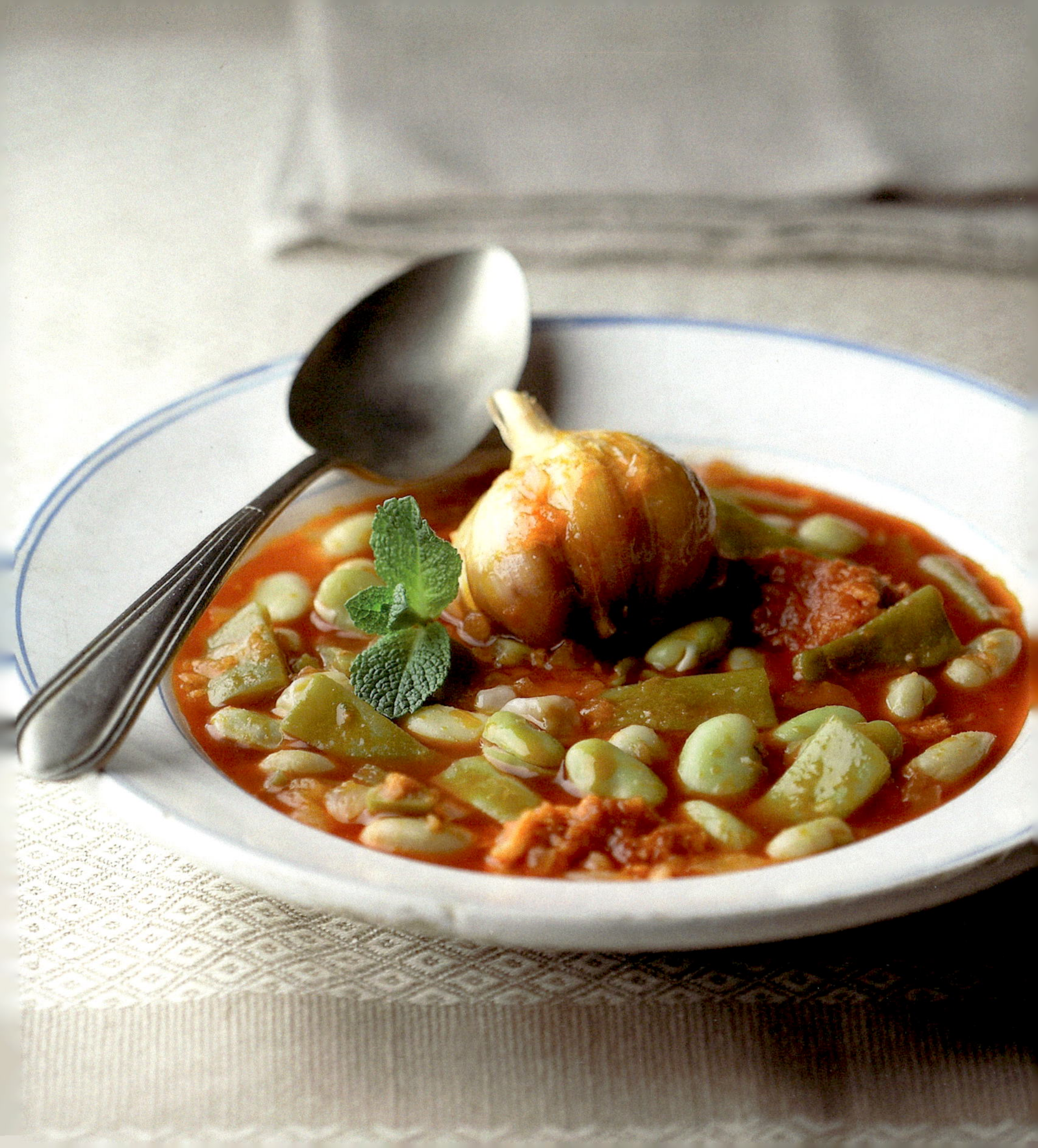

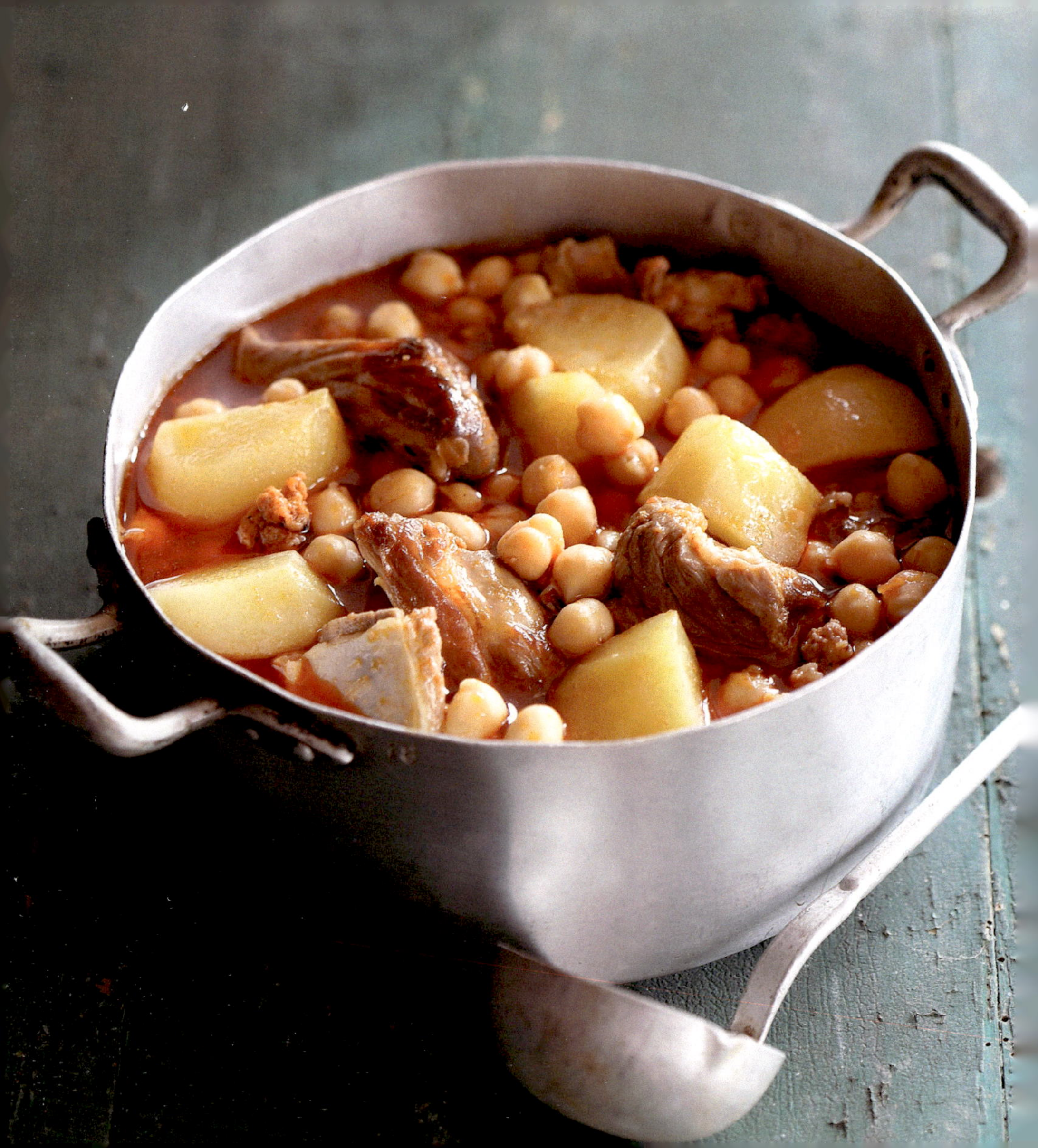

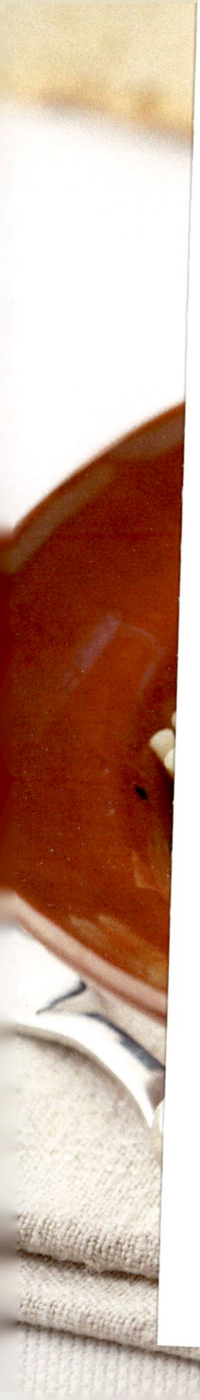

Ciurons amb sobrassada i botifarró

Chickpeas with *sobrassada* and *botifarró*

For 4 people

* 400 g of chickpeas * 1 large onion * 2 medium-size tomatoes * 2 cloves of garlic * 100 g of *sobrassada* * 100 g of *botifarró* * 50 g of streaky bacon * 150 g of pork rib * 4 medium-size potatoes * olive oil * salt

1. The evening before, leave the chickpeas to soak in water. Peel and chop the onion and the cloves of garlic. Cut a cross in the base of the tomatoes and scald them for 3 minutes in a casserole with boiling water. Cool them under the coldwater tap, peel them, remove the pips and cut them in pieces. Peel the potatoes and cut them into pieces.
2. In a casserole with 2 spoonfuls of oil, sauté the onion until it is transparent. Add the chopped garlic, tomato, the bacon cut into pieces, the pieces of rib, the *botifarró* and *sobrassada* crumbled. Cook for 10 minutes stirring continuously.
3. Add the drained chickpeas, stir so that they take in the flavour and cover with water. Add salt and leave to cook for about 2 hours, on a medium flame and covered, until the chickpeas are just about done.
4. Some 30 minutes before the 2 hours are up, add the potatoes. Leave to rest 10 minutes before serving.

In season, some cabbage leaves are often added to give the stew more flavour.
All the pulses (chickpeas, lentils, kidney beans, etc.) are also eaten simply cooked and dressed with a splash of olive oil, vinegar, salt and paprika to taste.
It was traditional to make the *sopa* or *bollit amb ossos de porc* (soup with pork bones). The salted pork bones were cooked (which were always available in the *aufabias* or large earthenware jars of the country houses) with vegetables such as cabbage, celery, potatoes and chickpeas. *Sobrassada*, *botifarró* and bacon is added and it is seasoned with salt, pepper, saffron and paprika. The resulting stock is used for soups and rice dishes.

Macarrons secs
Macaronis with mincemeat

For 4 people

* 350 g of macaronis * 2 onions * 4 ripe tomatoes * 2 cloves of garlic * 1 chicken or rabbit liver * 50 g of *sobrassada* * 50 g of bacon * 100 g de minced pork * olive oil * a pinch of oregano * 1 small bunch of parsley * pepper * salt

1. Cook the pasta in a casserole with lots of salted water for the time shown by the manufacturer. Drain, dress with a thread of oil and put to one side.
2. Peel and chop the onions, garlic and tomatoes. Cut the bacon in cubes. Wash the parsley and chop the leaves finely.
3. Heat 2 spoonfuls of oil in a casserole and fry the cubes of bacon and liver for 5 minutes. Remove and, in the same oil, sauté for 5 minutes the mincemeat. Remove and put to one side. Chop the liver.
4. Add 2 more spoonfuls of oil to the pan and sauté the onion until it is transparent. Add the chopped garlic and cook for 2 more minutes. Add the tomato and cook for some 10 minutes, until obtaining a sauce.
5. Add the *sobrassada* and cook for 2 more minutes. Then add all the meats again, add salt and pepper, sprinkle with oregano and the chopped parsley and continue cooking for another 10 minutes.
6. Add the macaronis, stir so that they get the flavour and cook for 4 more minutes before serving.

Traditionally pasta was made at home with wheat flour. This dish was made with both *canons* (macaronis) and *burbaies* (strips) or noodles.
Like many other traditional recipes, the sauce base can be prepared with lard.
This dish can also be made au gratin in the oven with breadcrumbs or cheese.

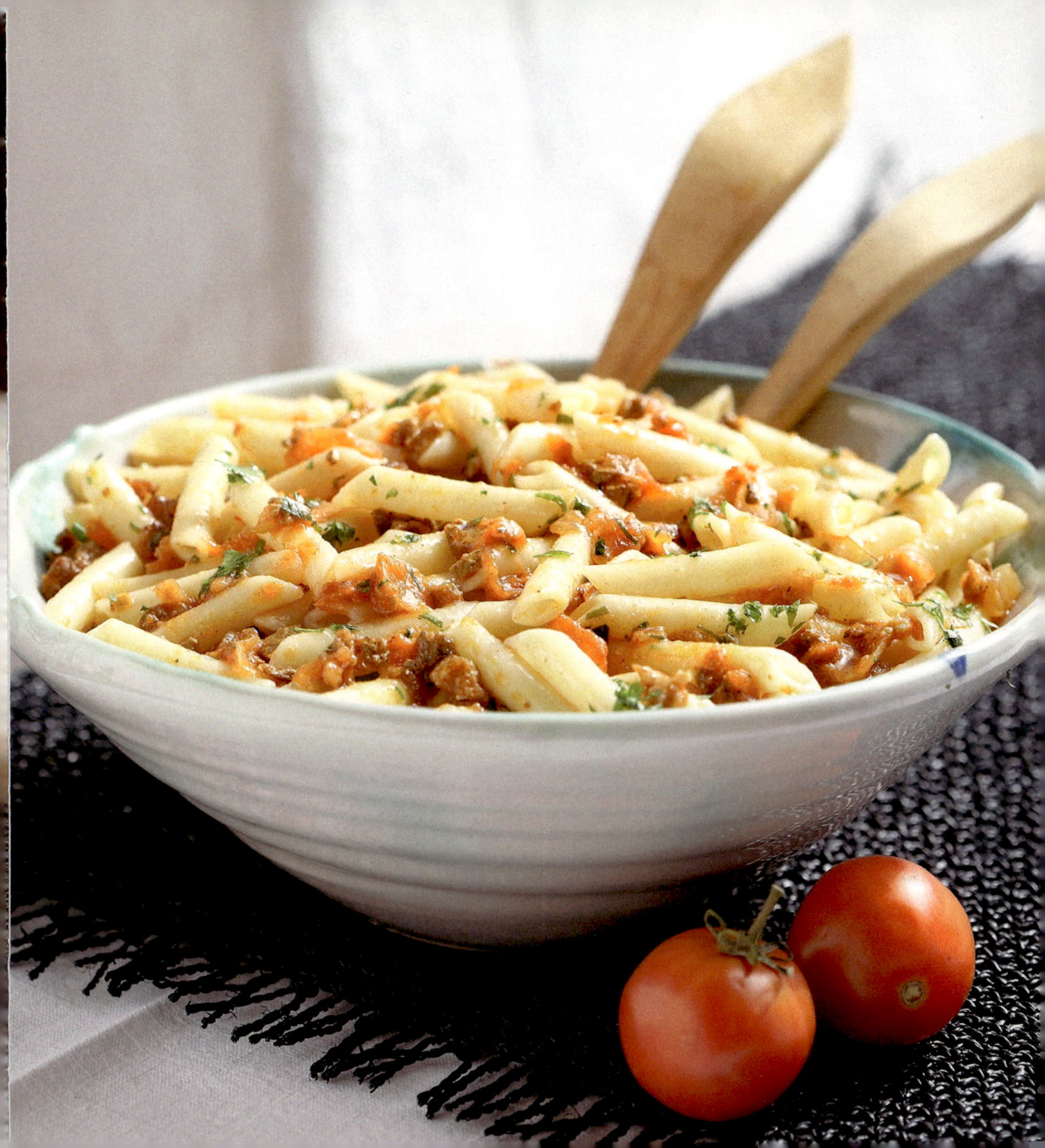

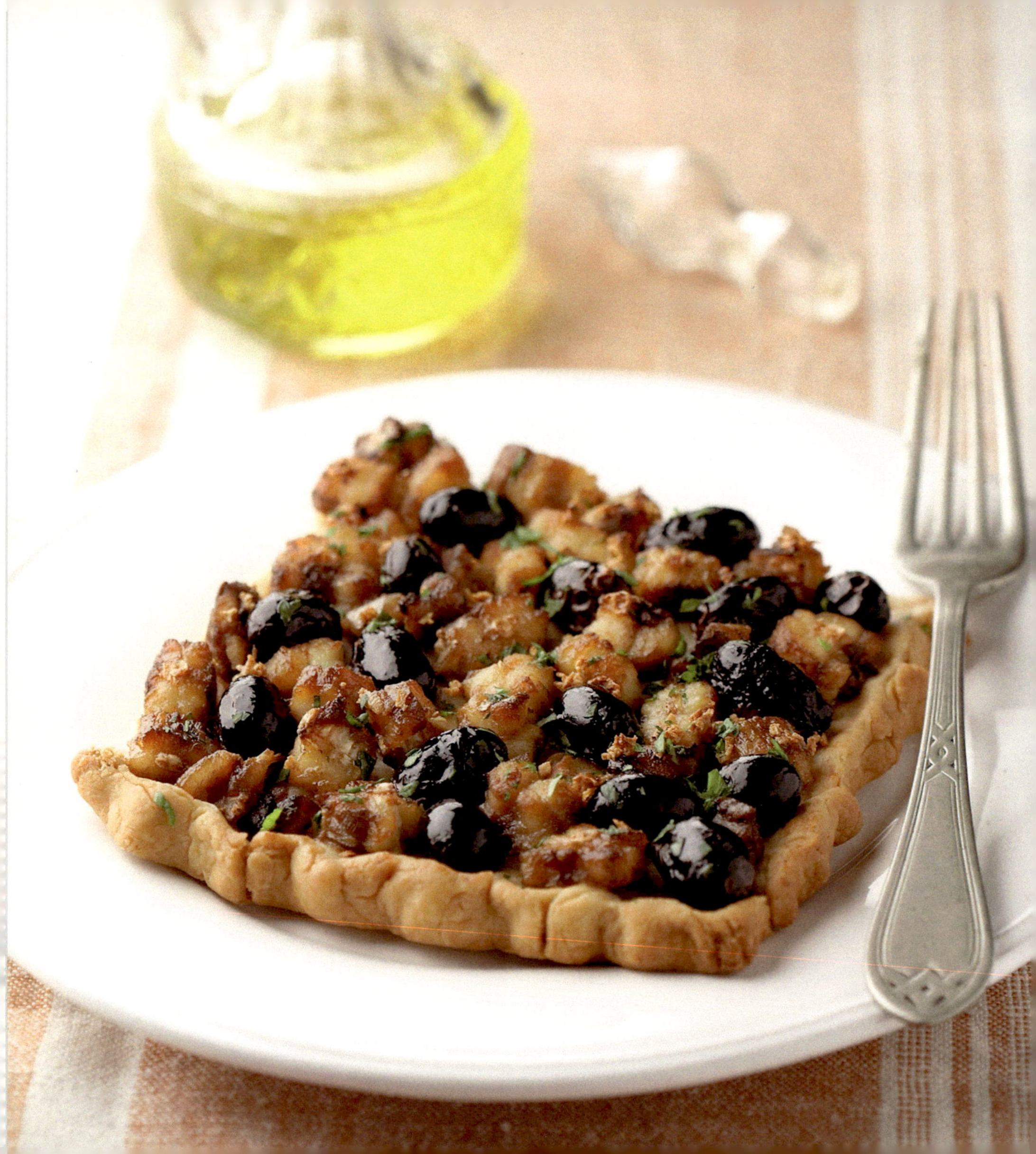

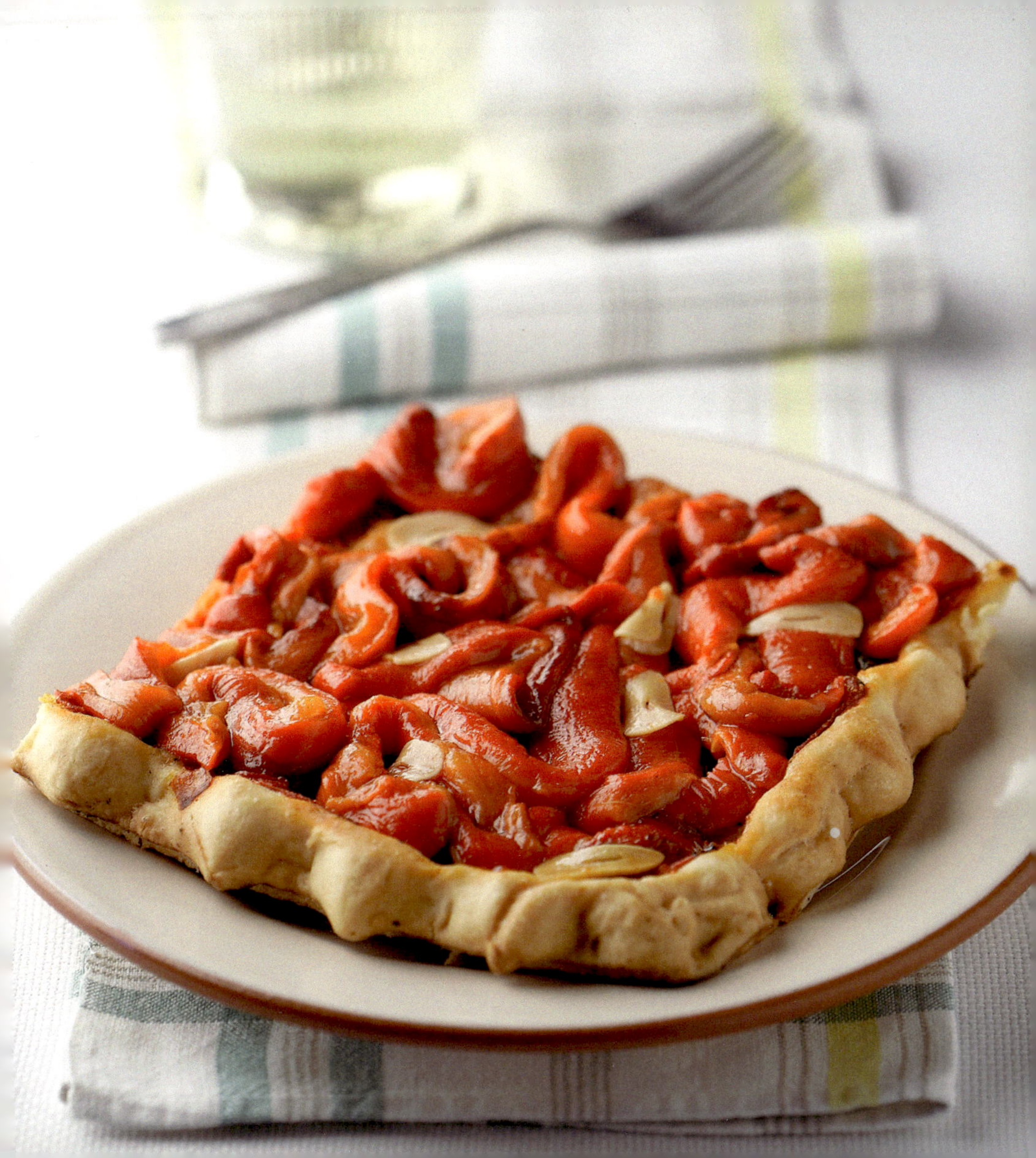

02

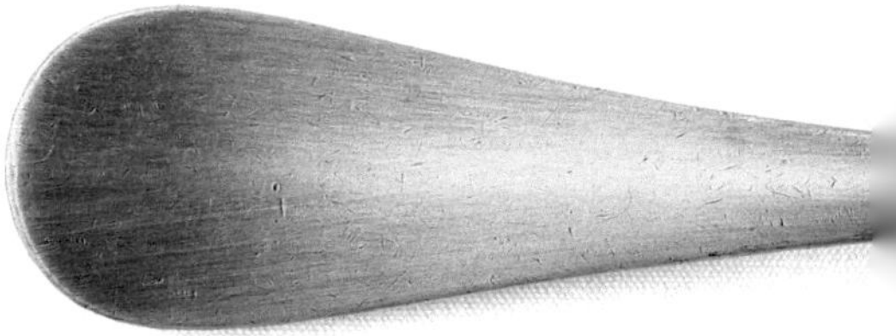

Meat and fish recipes

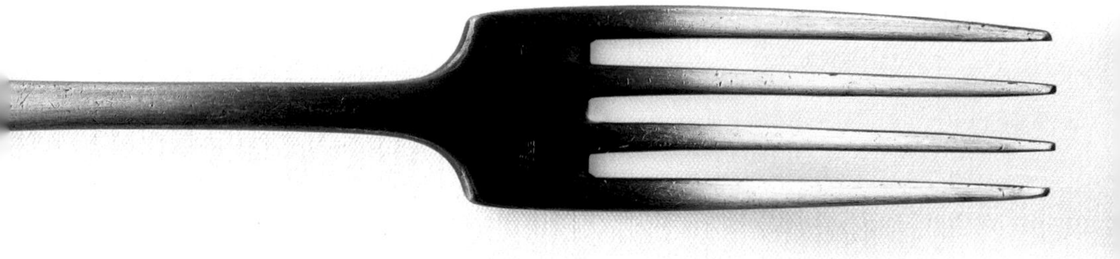

Borrida de rajada
Borrida of skate

For 4 people

* 1.5 kg of skate * 6 medium-size potatoes * 12 stalks of saffron * 1 lemon * a pinch of cinnamon * pepper * salt

For the sauce: * 100 g of toasted, peeled almonds * 1 small bunch of parsley * 1 small bunch of mint * 1 clove of garlic * 2 eggs

1. Clean the skate and cut it into pieces. Leave it to macerate with a pinch of salt and a little lemon juice for 30 minutes in the fridge, so that it loses its strong smell. Then wash the pieces of fish under the tap.
2. Peel the potatoes, cut them in slices and cook them for 12 minutes in a casserole with slightly salted water. They must be almost cooked. Drain and keep the cooking water.
3. Boil for 4 minutes the pieces of fish in a casserole with a little salted water. Drain them and place to one side.
4. Prepare a sauce base with the almonds, clove of garlic and aromatic herbs. Add 2 beaten eggs and mix.
5. Place the slices of potato in a ceramic pot and, on top, the pieces of fish. Add salt and pepper, season with the saffron and a pinch of cinnamon and cover with a little of the stock kept from the cooking of the potatoes. Add the sauce base and cook on a low flame for 7-8 minutes until it thickens. Serve immediately.

This recipe has very many variants. Some people prefer to place the fish with the potatoes forming layers and sprinkling the stew with a mix of onion, tomato and peppers in order to finally, once cooked, thicken the sauce with a base made from Inca biscuits, chopped hard-boiled egg or even with the skate's liver, previously boiled.

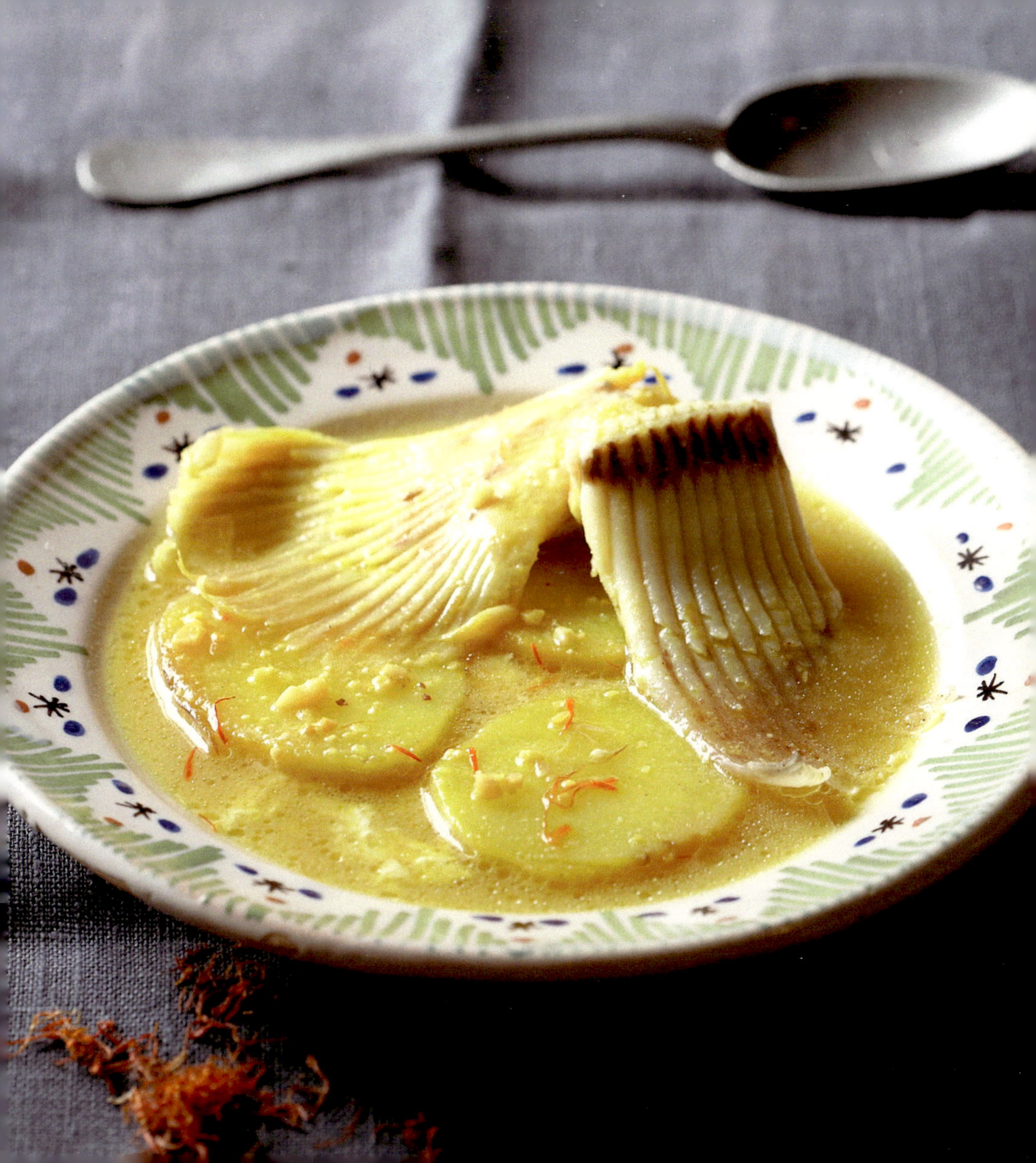

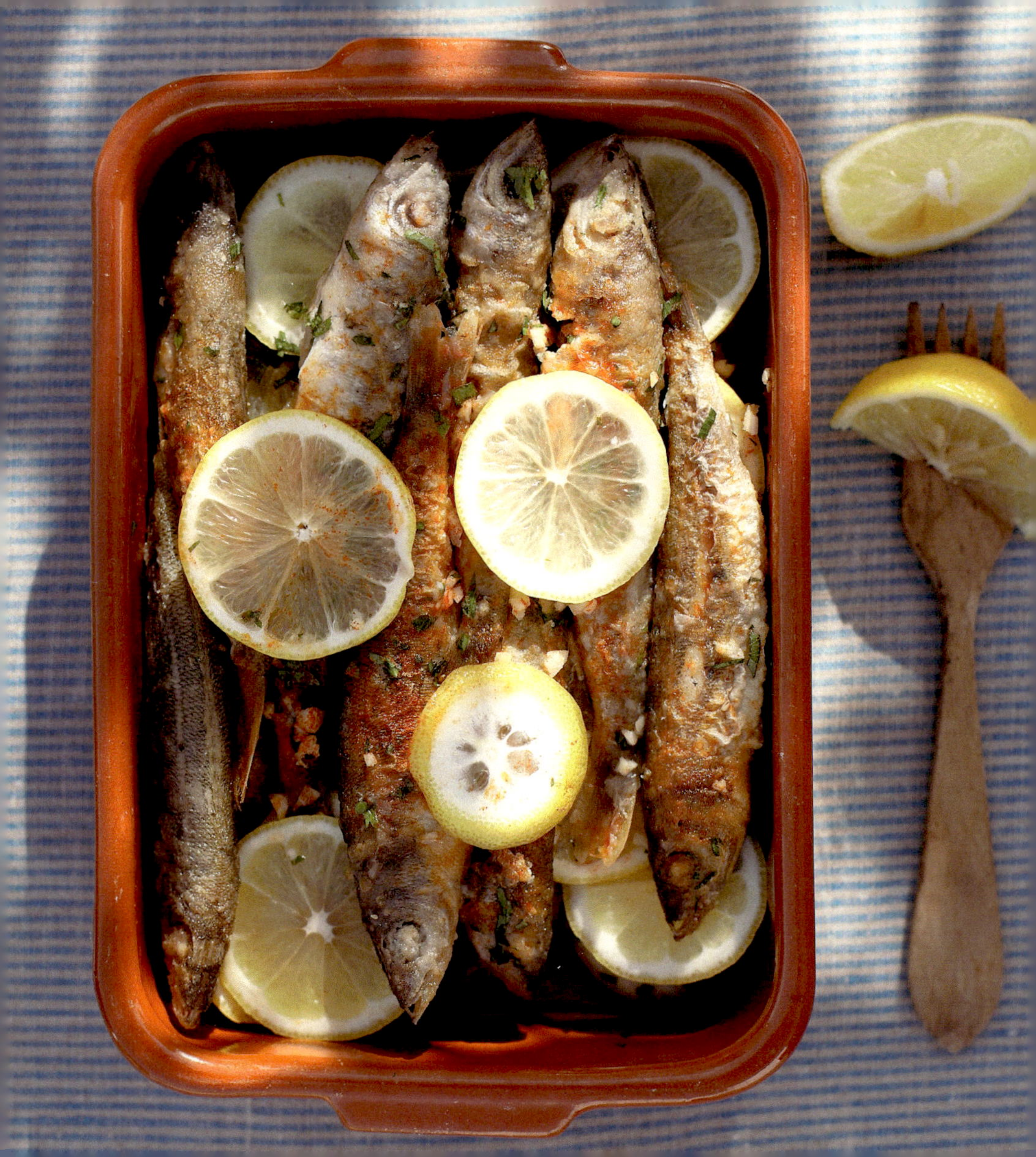

Gerret a la matança
Sardines *a la matança* (pig slaughter day)

For 6 people

* 1 kg of sardines (*gerrets*) * 4 lemons * 3 cloves of garlic * 1 small bunch of parsley * 3 spoonfuls of paprika * 1 cup of flour * olive oil

1. Wash the lemons under the tap, dry them with a cloth. Squeeze the lemon juice from two of them and cut the other two into thin slices. Wash and chop the parsley finely. Peel and chop the cloves of garlic.
2. Clean the fish of innards and scales, and coat them lightly with flour. Heat a generous amount of oil in a pan and fry the fish in batches.
3. Once fried, drain the fish and then place them in a ceramic casserole or platter in layers. Sprinkle each layer with the mixture of garlic and parsley, a pinch of paprika and a little lemon juice. Spread slices of lemon between each layer of fish, and leave to macerate in the fridge overnight.

This original dish is traditionally prepared as breakfast for the day when the pig is slaughtered.
The *gerret* or sardine is a highly appreciated fish on the island. It is also eaten in pickle sauce (*escambetxat*) or just grilled over the barbecue on trips to the country or *moregades*.

Guisat de calamars amb panses i pinyons
Squid stew with raisins and pine nuts

For 4 people

* 4 medium-size squid * 1 onion * 3 potatoes * 1 spoonful of raisins * 2 spoonfuls of pine nuts * 1/2 glass of matured wine or a splash of Jerez sherry * 1 laurel leaf * a pinch of nutmeg * 1/2 teaspoonful of ground cinnamon * 1 teaspoonful of sugar * olive oil * pepper * salt

1. Clean the squids removing the innards, cuttlebone, eyes and beak. Cut the body into slices and the tentacles into two or three pieces.
2. Peel and chop the onion. Soak the raisins in warm water (you can also use tea, white wine or spirit). Cut the potatoes into thin slices.
3. Heat eight spoonfuls of oil in a casserole and sauté the potatoes on a very low flame for 10 minutes, until they are almost cooked. Remove them from the oil, pour away half and add the chopped onion. Sauté on a very low flame for 15 minutes, until it is crystallised and has the appearance of dark jam. Add the slices of squid. Soak with the wine, leave to reduce for a moment on a high flame and add the laurel, pine nuts and drained raisins.
4. Replace the potatoes in the casserole, add salt and pepper and season with the cinnamon and nutmeg. Add a teaspoonful of sugar and cover with a little water. Cook on a low flame for 10 more minutes and serve.

If you want, you can thicken the stew with a mixture of almonds, garlic and parsley.
In season you can replace the potatoes with yams.
Other very popular dishes with squid on the island are *calamars amb sutja* (in their ink), *farcits* (stuffed) or *a la pagesa* (coated, fried and seasoned with a mixture of garlic, parsley and paprika, and conserved in oil to be served cold).

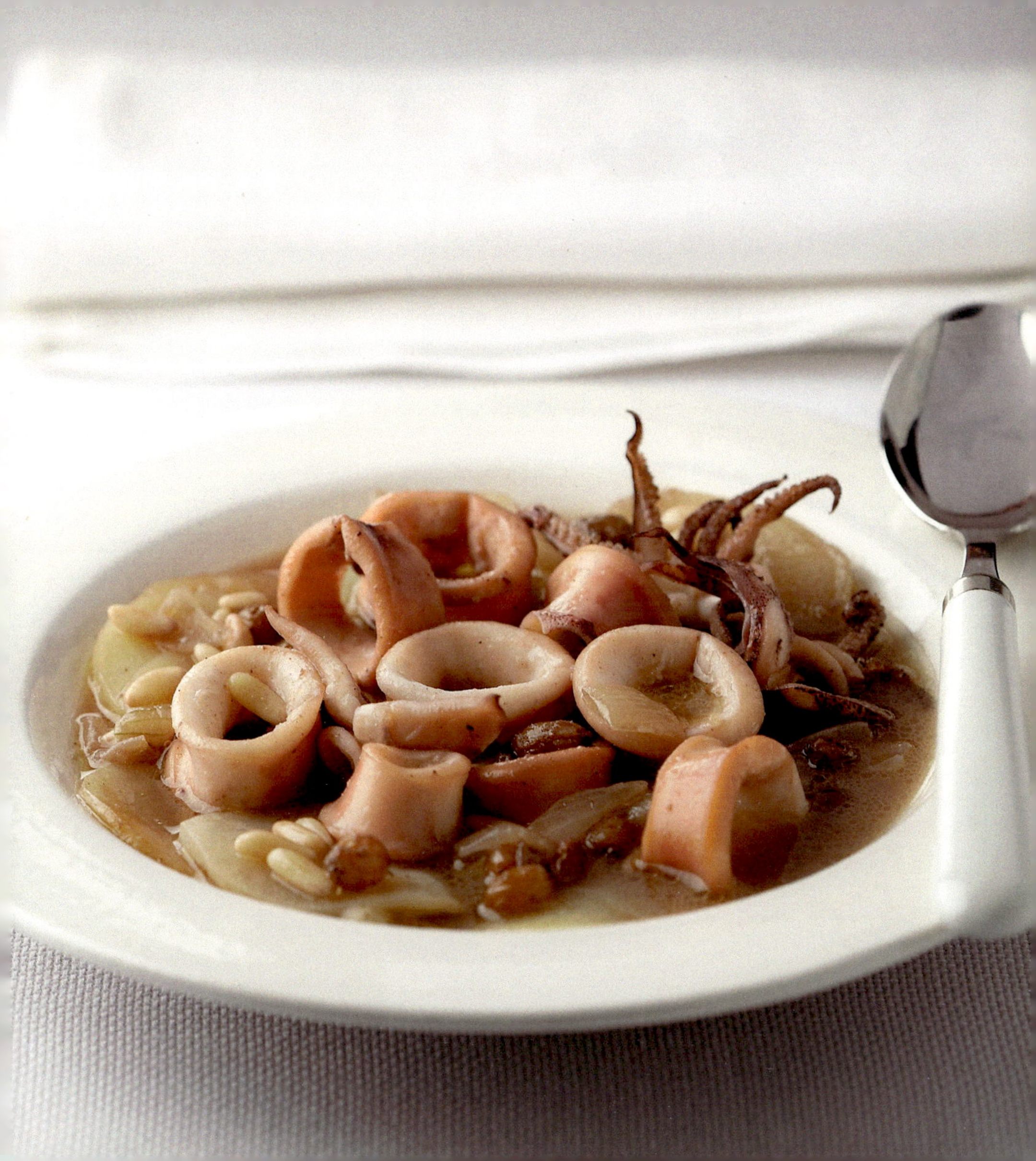

Guisat de peix
Fish stew

For 4 people

* 1.5 kg of rock fish * 1 onion * 2 tomatoes * 3 cloves of garlic * 6 medium-size potatoes * some stalks of saffron * a pinch of cinnamon * 1 small bunch of parsley * olive oil * salt

1. Clean and remove the scales from the fish and cut it into pieces. Peel and cut the potatoes. Peel and chop the onion and the cloves of garlic.
2. Heat four spoonfuls of oil in a large and flat ceramic casserole, and sauté the chopped onion until it is transparent. Add half of the chopped garlic and tomato cut into pieces, and cook for about 10 minutes, until obtaining a sauce. Add the cut potatoes and season with the salt, cinnamon and saffron (previously toasted, if you want). Sprinkle half of the chopped parsley, sauté one minute and cover slightly with water. Cook for some 15 minutes on a very low flame.
3. Place the cut fish over the stew, and add a little water if necessary. Cook everything together for 10 more minutes.
4. Grind the remaining garlic and parsley in a mortar. Dissolve this mixture in a little stock and pour it over stew at the last moment.

For this recipe rock fish specific to the island are used: the *roja*, spider crab, Atlantic stargazer... green or red pepper can also be added to the fry mixture.
It can be served accompanied by an *all i oli* sauce apart. A rice dish would be made with the remaining sauce or stock.

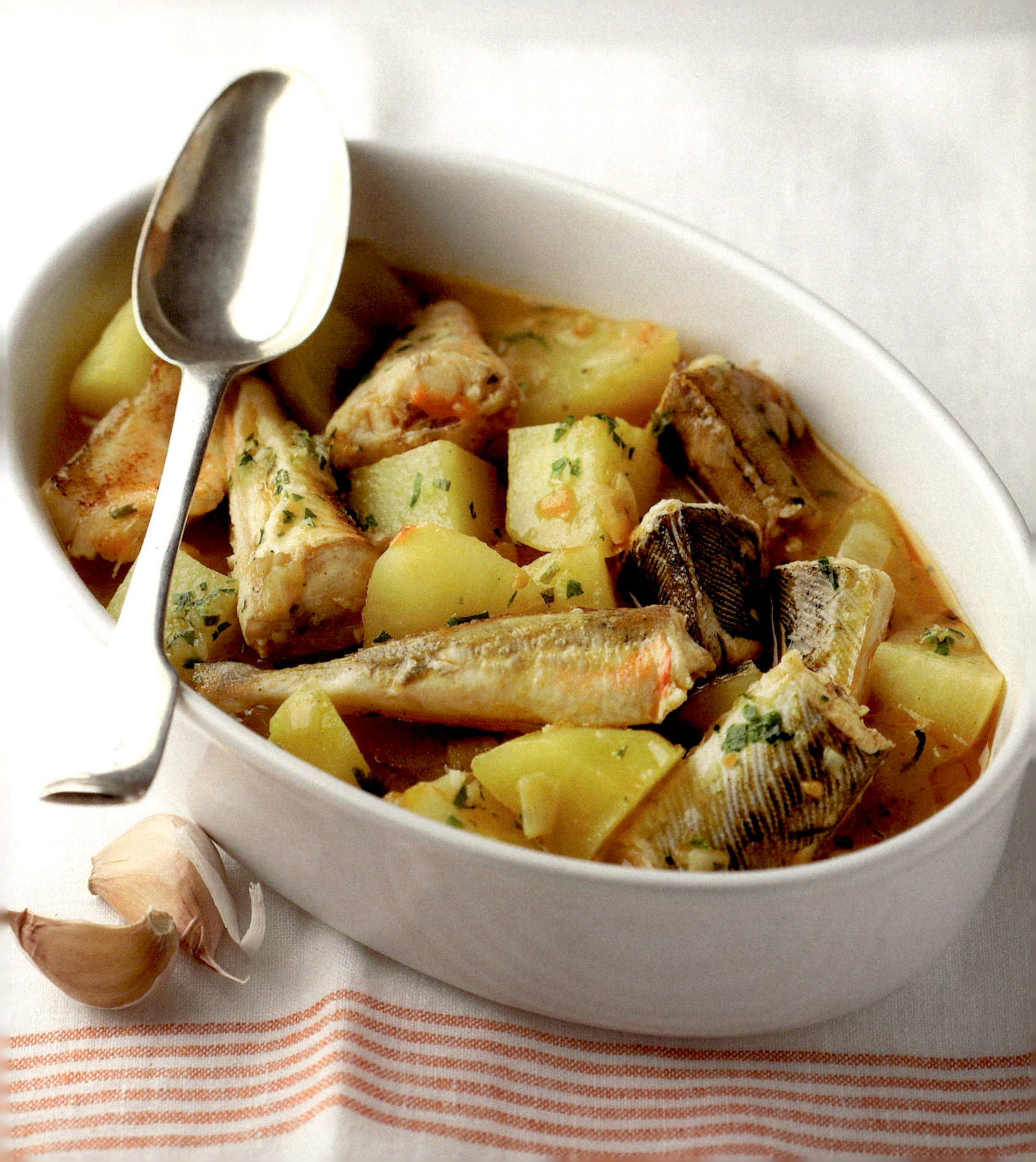

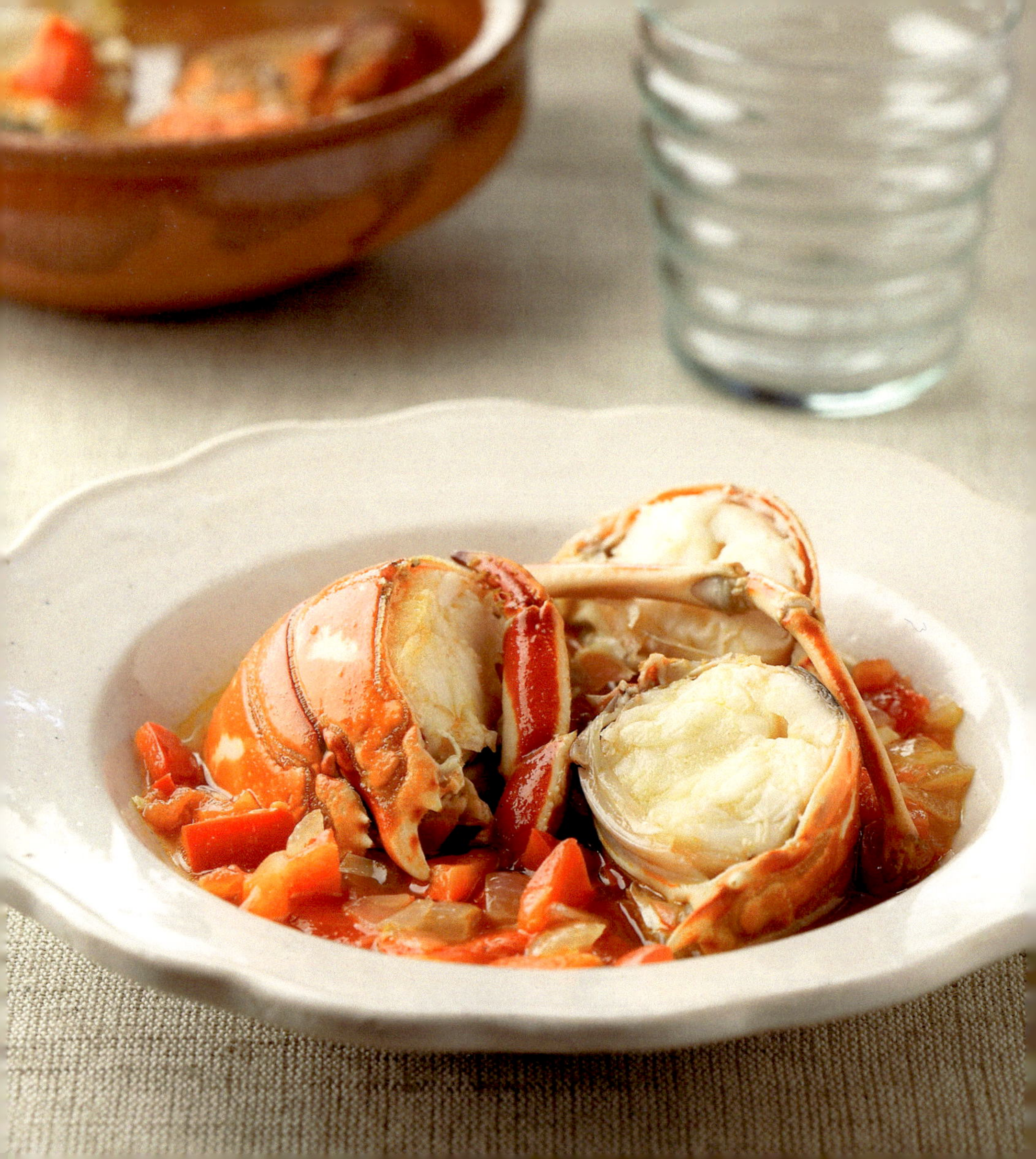

Llagosta a la marinera
Fisherman's lobster

For 4 people

* 2 medium-size lobsters * 1 onion * 1 large tomato * 1 red pepper * a loose bunch of aromatic herbs * 2 cloves of garlic * 1 clove * a pinch of nutmeg * a pinch of paprika * pepper * salt
For the stock: * 1 tomato * 1 onion * 2 cloves of garlic * 1 small bunch of parsley * a pinch of paprika * salt

1. Preparation of the stock: peel and chop the onion and the cloves of garlic. Sauté the onion in a pot with 3 spoonfuls of oil. When it is transparent, add the chopped garlic and tomato cut into pieces. Add salt and pepper, season with a pinch of paprika and sprinkle with chopped parsley. Cook for about 10 minutes and then cover with water, add the lobsters and bring to the boil. Cook for 15 minutes.
2. Remove the lobsters from the stock and leave them to cool. Place them on a worktop. Separate the heads from the bodies. Split the heads and cut the tails into thick slices without removing the shells. Keep all the juices that they give off on cutting them.
3. Peel and chop the remaining onion and the cloves of garlic. Wash the pepper and chop it finely. Heat three spoonfuls of oil in a ceramic casserole and sauté the onion until it is transparent. Add the chopped garlic, tomato and red pepper. Add salt and pepper and season with a pinch of paprika, nutmeg, a clove and the small bunch of aromatic herbs. Soak this preparation with two ladles of the stock, add the cut lobster and juices, and cook it all together for 4 more minutes. Serve immediately.

The remaining stock, seasoned with a little more garlic and a fried *ñora*, a spicy red pepper, is perfect for preparing rice dishes.
Another very popular preparation is Ibiza-style lobster (*llagosta a l'eivissenca*), with stewed onion and a short thick stock with a sauce made of pine nuts, garlic, toasted almonds, paprika, parsley and saffron.

Lluç a la marinera
Fisherman's hake

For 4 people

* 800 g of hake cut into slices * 2 ripe tomatoes * 1 onion * 4 potatoes * 1 garlic clove * 1 small bunch of parsley * 1 teaspoonful of paprika * olive oil * pepper * salt

For the sauce: * 1 garlic clove * 1 spoonful of lemon juice * 2 spoonfuls of olive oil * paprika * nutmeg * salt

1. Peel and chop the onion and clove of garlic. Heat 4 spoonfuls of oil in a casserole and sauté the onion until it is transparent. Add the chopped garlic, sauté 1 minute without letting it brown and add the tomato cut into pieces. Cook for 12 minutes until obtaining a sauce-like consistency. Add salt and pepper and season with a teaspoonful of paprika and lots of chopped parsley.
2. Peel the potatoes, cut them into slices and add them to the casserole. Sauté for 2 minutes in the sauce and cover them with water. Add salt to taste and cook for 15 minutes on a low flame. After this time, add the slices of salted and peppered hake, cover and leave to cook for 5 more minutes.
3. In a mortar, prepare a sauce grinding 1 clove of garlic with a lot of chopped parsley, a pinch of salt, paprika and nutmeg. Dissolve with a spoonful of lemon juice, 2 spoonfuls of oil and 6 of stock from the casserole, until obtaining a sauce.
4. Place the slices of potato on a service dish with the slices of hake on top. Pour on the sauce and serve immediately.

Cooking the hake just right is a delicate task. It is better to cook the potatoes first in the stock and, once these are cooked, add the slices of hake, cover and cook briefly until the fish has browned in colour and is very lightly cooked. This recipe can also be served with an *all i oli* sauce or a mayonnaise aromatised to taste.

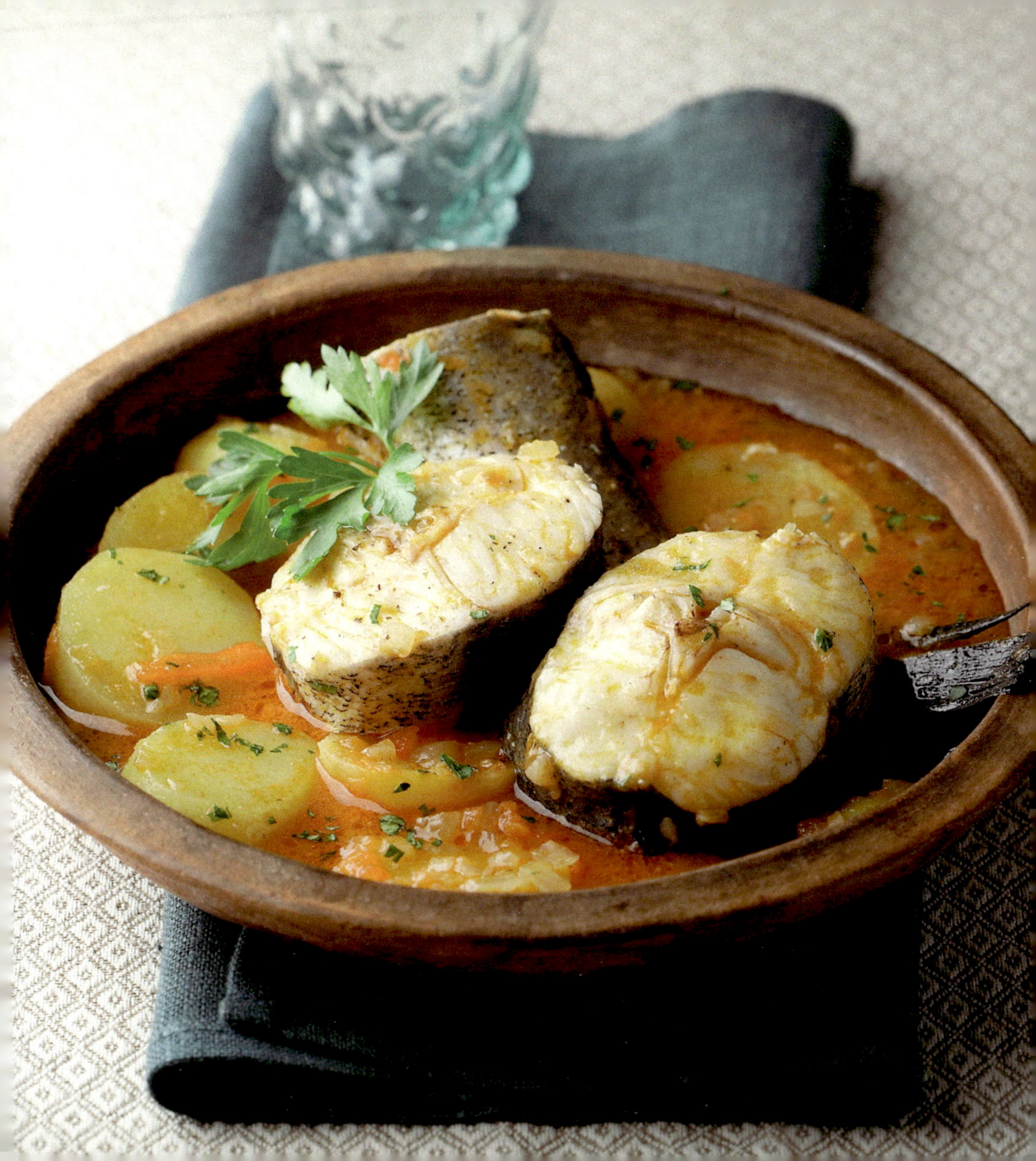

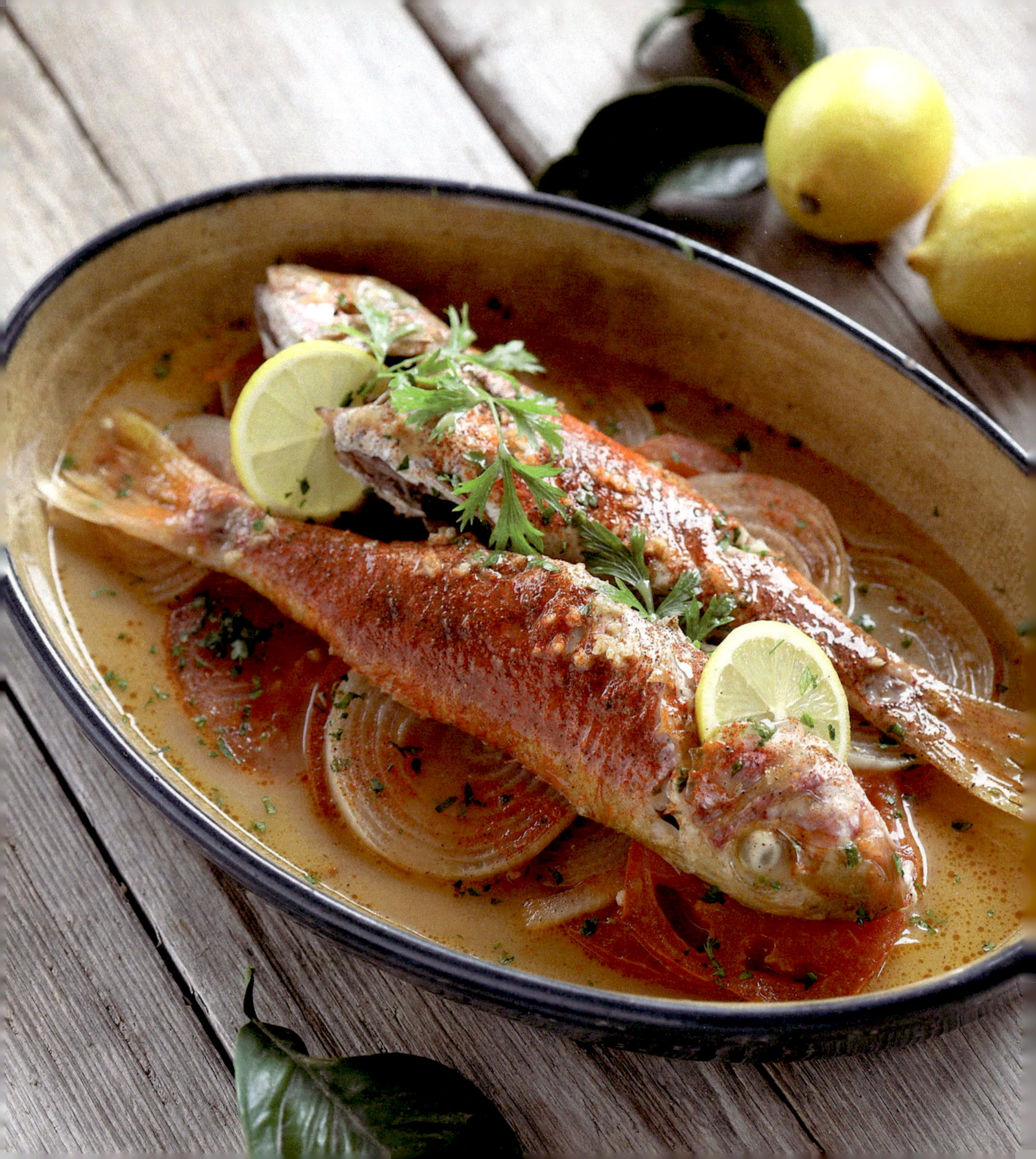

Molls a la greixonera
Casseroled red mullet

For 4 people

* 8 large red mullets * 1 onion * 1 tomato * 1 clove of garlic * 1 small bunch of parsley * 1 teaspoonful of paprika * 2 spoonfuls of ground salted biscuit * 1 small bunch of aromatic herbs: laurel, rosemary and marjorum * 1 spoonful of lemon juice * olive oil * pepper * salt

1. Wash the tomato and cut it into very thin slices. Peel the onion and also cut it into thin slices. Peel and chop the clove of garlic and the parsley. Descale the red mullets, remove the innards, dry them lightly with kitchen paper and add salt and pepper.
2. Pour 2 spoonfuls of oil in a ceramic casserole and spread the slices of tomato and onion forming layers. Salt and pepper each layer and place the red mullets on top. Season with the mixture of garlic and parsley, sprinkle over the ground biscuit and aromatise with the paprika and the aromatic herbs.
3. Pour four spoonfuls of water and a spoonful of lemon juice, cover the casserole and cook on a very low flame for 12 minutes. Serve immediately.

This recipe can also be prepared in the oven, calculating about 10 minutes at 200° C.

The livers of the red mullets can be ground with a little chilli, paprika and garlic to obtain delicious sauce base.

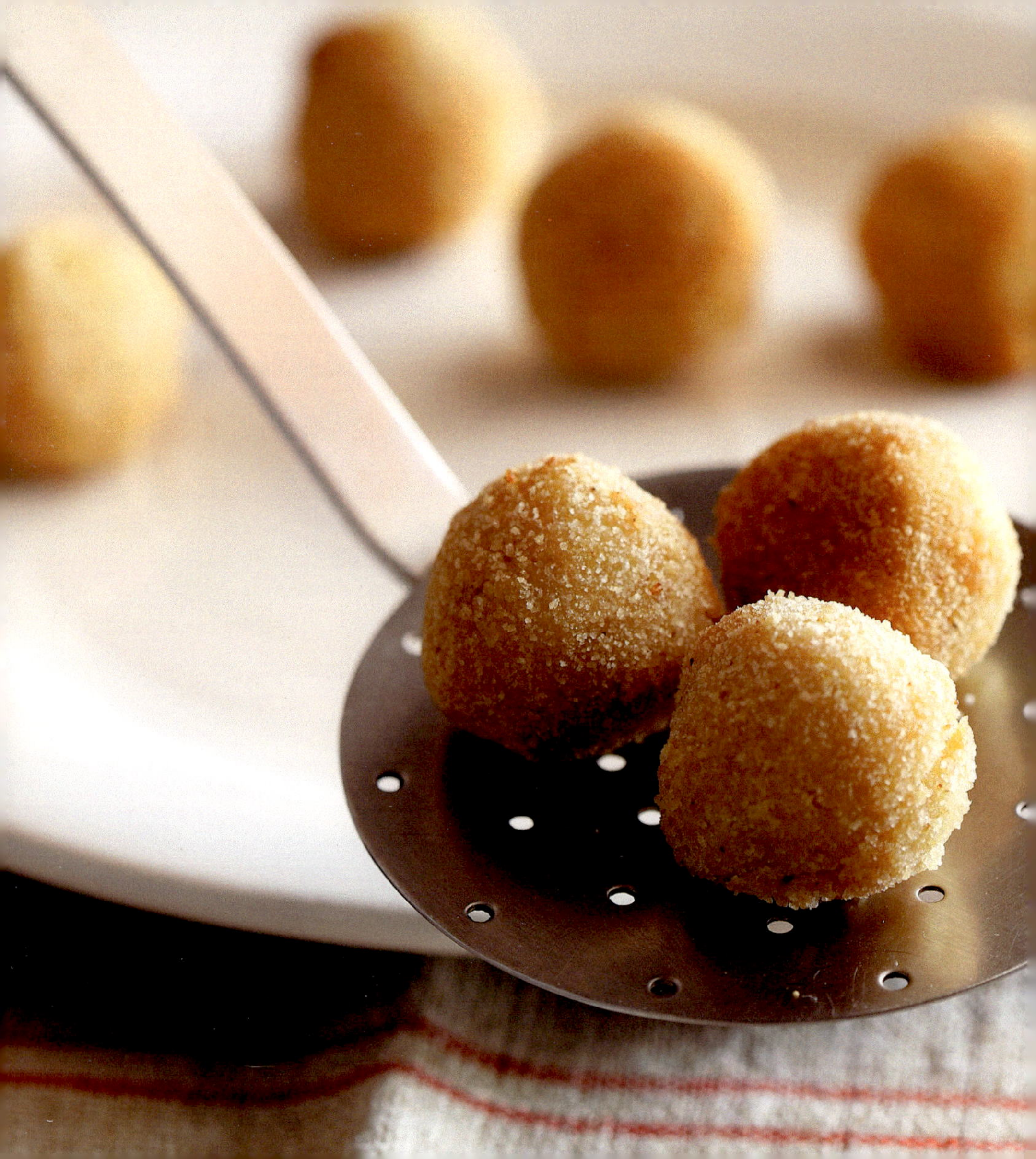

Pilotes de gató
Dogfish meatballs

For 4 people

* 4 potatoes * 600 g of dogfish, already chopped, skinned and clean * 1 clove of garlic * 1 small bunch of parsley * 2 eggs * 1 cup of breadcrumbs or ground salted biscuit

For the béchamel: * 1/2 l of milk * 50 g of flour * 50 g of butter * 1 egg yolk * a pinch of nutmeg * pepper * salt

For the dressing: * 4 spoonfuls of lemon juice * 1 spoonful of oil * 1 splash of vinegar

1. Leave the pieces to fish to marinate in the dressing in the fridge for a minimum of one hour. Peel and chop the clove of garlic and parsley finely.
2. Cook the potatoes in their skins in a casserole with a lot of salted water boiling for 25 minutes. Drain them, leave them to cool and peel them. Mash them with a fork until obtaining a purée texture.
3. Drain the fish from the dressing and cook it for 7 minutes. Remove it, let it cool and crumble the meat, removing the bones. Mix it with the potato purée, aromatise with the mixture of garlic and parsley and salt and pepper lightly.
4. Prepare a béchamel sauce: heat the butter in a casserole, add the flour, cook for 3 minutes and pour the milk in, stirring continuously. Add salt and pepper, season with a pinch of nutmeg and cook on a slow flame until obtaining a thick béchamel sauce. Leave to go warm, mix with the egg yolk and add to the already prepared potato and fish. Stir well and spread the preparation on a flat service dish so that it cools.
5. Shape the mass into small balls with damp hands and pass them through beaten egg and breadcrumbs (or ground biscuit). Fry them briefly in a pan with lots of hot oil and serve them immediately.

With this recipe you can make meatballs from all the fish from the island: sardine (*gerret*), spider fish, grouper, hake, etc. Fish with tough skins such as the dogfish or skate are often left in a dressing before cooking them so that they lose their characteristic smell, rather ammonia-like.

Polps en greixonera
Casseroled octopus

For 4 people

* 1 kg of medium-size octopuses * 2 onions * 8 spoonfuls of fresh chopped tomato * 2 cloves of garlic * 4 medium-size potatoes * 1 teaspoonful of paprika * a pinch of nutmeg * 1 small glass of dry wine * 1 small bunch of parsley * olive oil * pepper * salt

1. Wash the octopuses and remove their innards, eyes and central beaks. Place them to cook in a pot with boiling salted water for 25 minutes. Leave them to cool a little in the cooking water, drain them, peel them and cut them into pieces of the same size.
2. Peel and chop the onions and cloves of garlic. Peel the potatoes and cut them into cubes. Heat 3 spoonfuls of oil in a ceramic casserole and sauté the onion until it is transparent. Add the chopped garlic, sauté one minute without letting it brown and add the chopped tomato. Cook for 15 minutes on a very low flame, until obtaining a thick sauce.
3. Add the potatoes to the casserole, season with salt, pepper, paprika and a pinch of nutmeg. Pour the wine, sauté 2 minutes and cover with a glass and a half of water or stock. Cook on a low flame for 20 minutes, adding the chopped octopus half way through the cooking time. Sprinkle with lots of chopped parsley and serve.

The island's traditional cuisine has many recipes with the eight-legged cephalopod as its star. We should highlight the octopus with onion (*polps amb ceba*), with green peppers (*amb pebreres*), with sauce (*amb salseta*) or, simply, baby octopuses grilled on the barbecue and dressed with garlic, parsley, paprika and lemon juice (*polps torrats*).

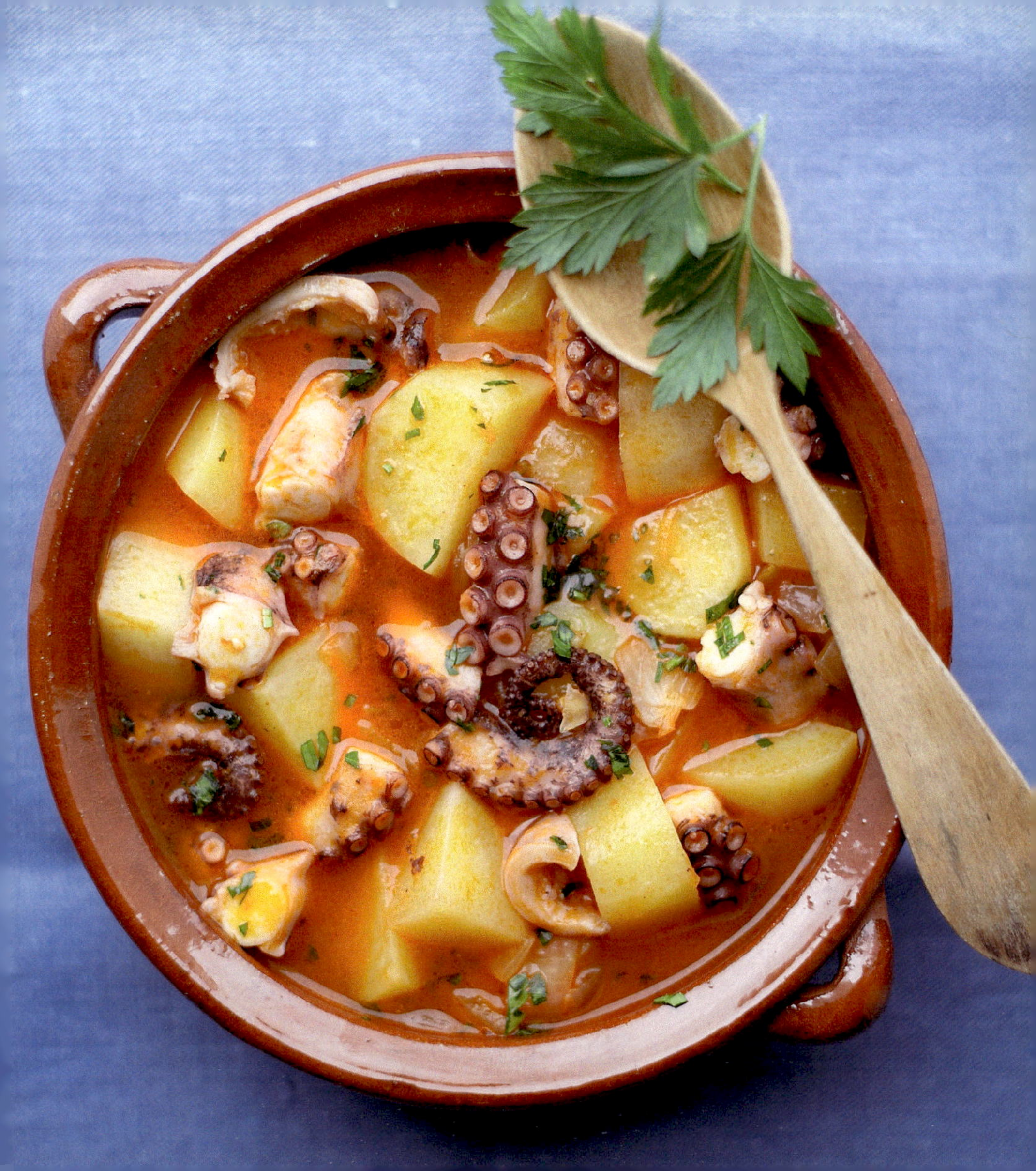

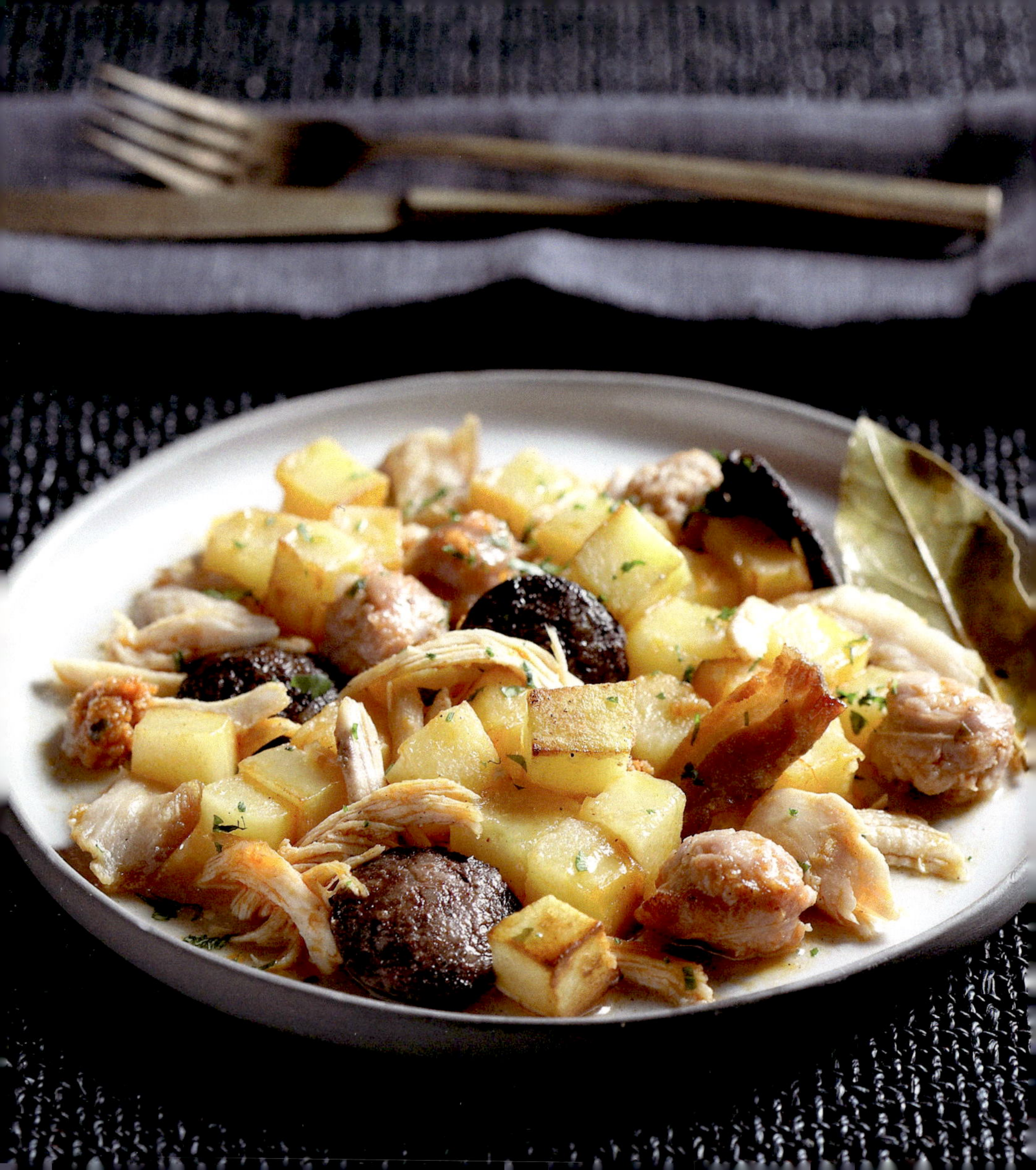

Sofrit pagès
Peasant fry-mix

For 4 people

* 1/2 chicken * 300 g of lamb * 100 g of streaky bacon * 50 g of *sobrassada* * 75 g of *botifarra* * 50 g of *botifarró* * 6 potatoes * 2 cloves of garlic * 1 laurel leaf * 1 small bunch of parsley * 3 spoonfuls of lard or oil * 2 cloves * a pinch of cinnamon * 8 threads of saffron * pepper * salt

1. Chop the chicken and lamb and boil them in a pot with lightly salted water. Cook for 45 minutes. Leave to cool a little, remove the meats and take out the bones. Keep the stock.
2. Peel and chop the cloves of garlic. Peel the potatoes and cut them into squares. Wash the parsley and chop it finely. Cut the streaky bacon into strips and the sausage and cured meats into slices.
3. Heat the lard or oil in a casserole and fry the streaky bacon and sausage for 5 minutes. Add the cubes of potato and cook for 5 more minutes, stirring continuously, until they are browned. Add the *sobrassada*, *botifarró* and the cooked meats and crumble up the chicken and lamb. Add the chopped garlic and sauté it all together for 2 minutes. Sprinkle with lots of chopped parsley and cover with stock.
4. Season the preparation with a pinch of cinnamon y pepper, the laurel leaf, the cloves and the saffron. Add salt to taste and cook for about 20 more minutes on a low flame, until the potatoes are just cooked and the stock has been reduced and is almost like a sauce.

The remaining stock is often used to condiment a rice dish which is served as a first course.
If you want, you can use cloves or whole heads of garlic. You can also prepare a sauce base in the mortar with the lightly fried chicken liver, toasted almonds, saffron, cumin and parsley. Add it to thicken the stock.

Llom amb pebrassos as forn

Baked pork with milk mushrooms

For 4 people

* 600 g of shoulder of pork * 700 g of milk mushrooms * 3 cloves of garlic * 1 small bunch of parsley * 1 teaspoonful of paprika * 1 small cup of breadcrumbs * 3 spoonfuls of olive oil * pepper * salt

1. Clean the mushrooms using a clean cloth or pass them briefly under the tap if necessary. Cut them into slices the same size, checking that they are in good condition. Pre-heat the oven to 220° C.
2. Cut the pork into eight slices, sprinkle them with a pinch of paprika and place them on a lightly oiled refractory dish. Peel and chop the cloves of garlic. Wash the parsley, dry it carefully with kitchen paper and chop it finely.
3. Spread the milk mushrooms over the pork and salt and pepper them. Add the chopped garlic and parsley and sprinkle with the breadcrumbs and paprika.
4. Pour on a thread of oil and bake at 220° C for 15 minutes. Serve immediately.

The *pebrassos* (*Lactarius sanguifluus* and *Lactarius deliciosus*) are known in other areas as *esclata-sangs* or *rovellons*. They have a very well deserved reputation in Ibiza cuisine, and feature in many recipes in autumn.
You can also add a little crumbled *sobrassada* to this dish to give it more flavour.

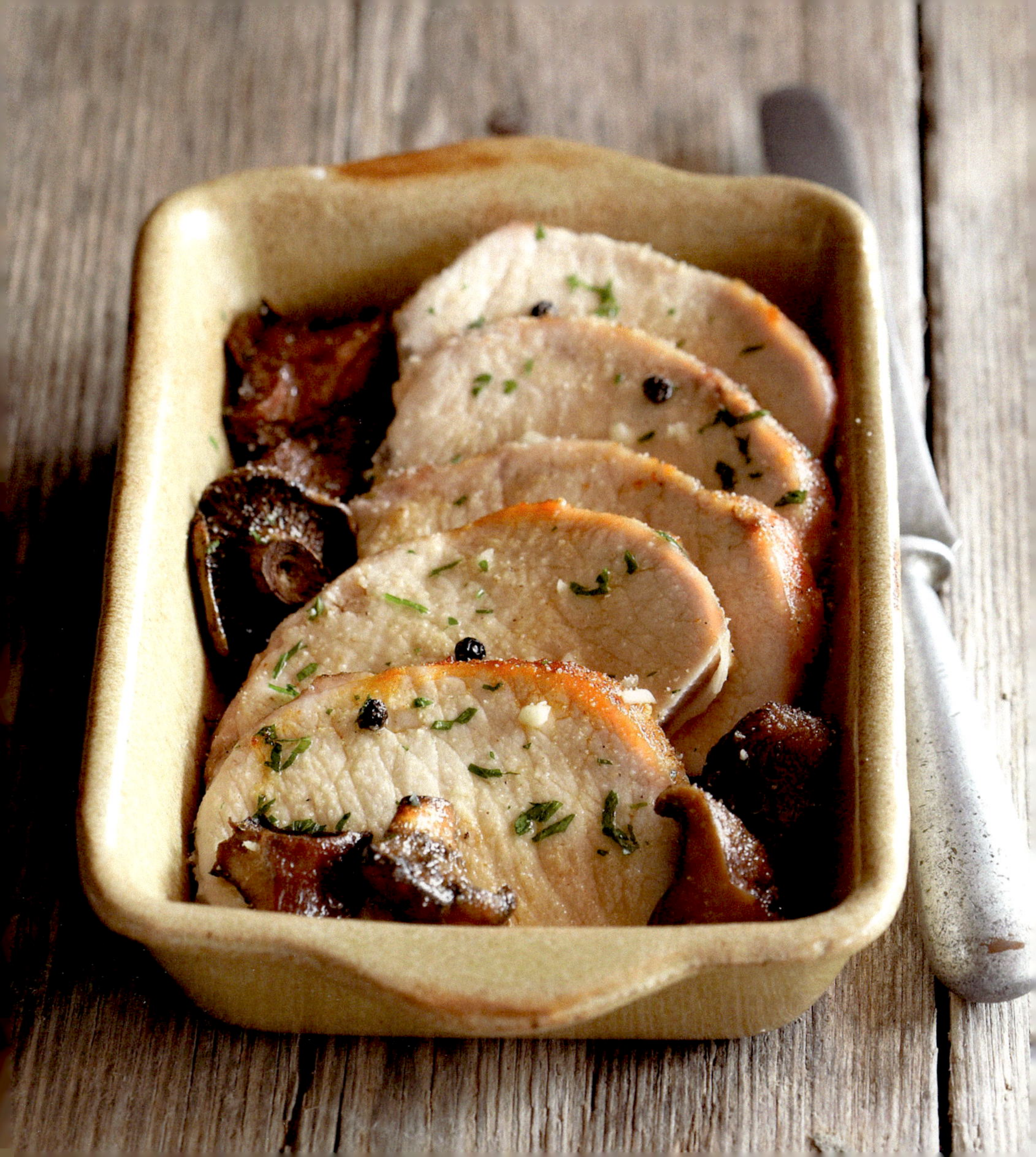

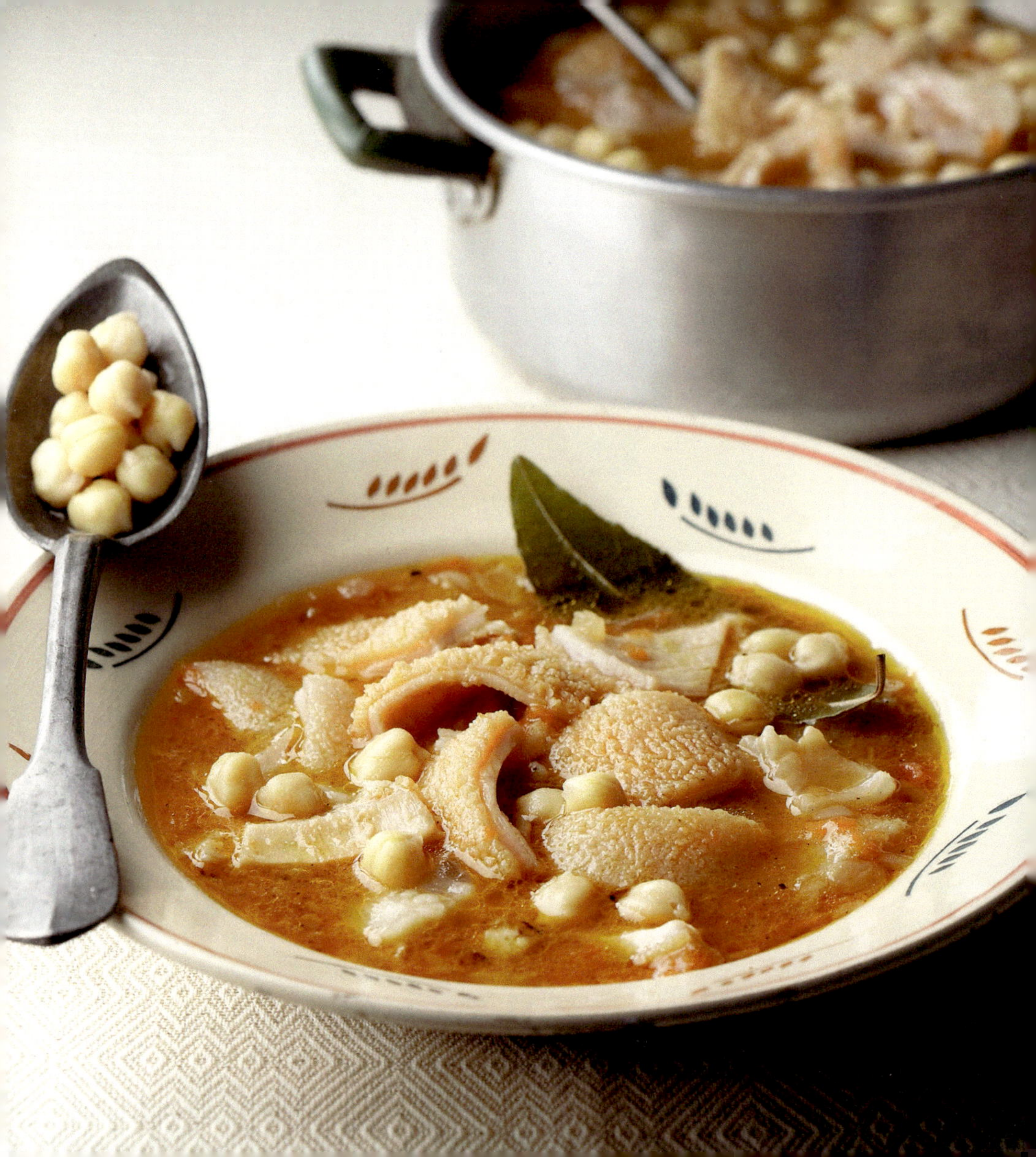

Tripa i pota
Ibiza-style tripe

For 4 people

* 600 g of veal tripe * 1 calf foot * 1 glass of white wine * 8 pepper seeds * 2 cloves * 1 laurel leaf * 1 onion * 2 tomatoes * 2 cloves of garlic * salt

For the sauce: * 2 cloves of garlic * a fistful of pine nuts * some marjorum leaves (*moraduix*) * a pinch of nutmeg

1. Scrape the tripe using a knife, cut off the edges and cut them into squares. Wash them thoroughly in a recipient with water and vinegar, and rinse them in lots of cold water. Cut the calf foot into four pieces.
2. Place the foot and the tripe in a casserole and cover with water. Bring to the boil and, after 5 minutes of boiling, change the water and add the salt, laurel, pepper seeds and cloves. Leave to cook on a low flame for some 4 hours. Drain the tripe and keep some of the cooking stock. Leave the tripe to cool a little out of the water.
3. Peel and chop the onion and the cloves of garlic. In a casserole with 4 spoonfuls of oil, sauté the onion until it is transparent. Add the chopped garlic and sauté 2 more minutes. Add the tomatoes cut into pieces and cook for 5 minutes. Soak with the wine and continue cooking for 10 minutes. Add the tripe, cover lightly with some ladles of stock kept by and cook for 30 minutes on a low flame.
4. For the sauce base: grind in a mortar the pine nuts with a pinch of cinnamon and pepper, the marjorum and 2 cloves of garlic. Add this mixture to the casserole when there are still 10 minutes of cooking remaining, and add salt to taste. Remove the casserole from the stove, leave to rest for 10 minutes and serve.

This recipe can be completed with stewed chickpeas or diced potatoes.
If you wish, you can replace the marjorum (*moraduix*) for a pinch of oregano.

Frita pagesa
Peasant fry-up

For 4 people

* 400 g of chopped pork chop * 250 g of sirloin pork * 200 g of pig's liver * 1/2 glass of white wine * 1 green pepper * 1 red pepper * 6 cloves of garlic * 1/2 kg of potatoes * 1 small bunch of parsley * olive oil * pepper * salt

1. Peel the potatoes and cut them into squares or strips. Wash the peppers and cut them into strips. Peel and chop the onion. Cut the sirloin pork and liver into small pieces the same size. Crush the garlic without peeling it, giving it a blow with the side of a knife. Wash and chop finely the parsley.
2. Heat 3 spoonfuls of oil in a pan and brown the meats in batches. Put them to one side and remove the fat from the cooking juices that have remained at the bottom of the pan with the white wine, stirring with a wooden spoon. Leave to reduce a little and put this juice to one side.
3. Add 3 spoonfuls of oil to the pan and sauté the onion until it is transparent. Add the crushed garlic, whole and without peeling, and sauté for 2 more minutes. Add the peppers and cook for 8 minutes stirring continuously, until they are soft.
4. Add the meats again to the pan with the juice that has been saved, add salt and pepper and cook all together for 5 minutes.
5. In a separate pan with a lot of olive oil, fry the diced potatoes until they are cooked. Drain them, salt them and add them to the pan with the fry-mix. Cook for 5 more minutes, sprinkle with chopped parsley and serve.

This dish was traditionally made with lard. In season chopped mushrooms would be added. Another very popular fry-mix (*frita*) on the island is made with lamb tripe (*freixura*).

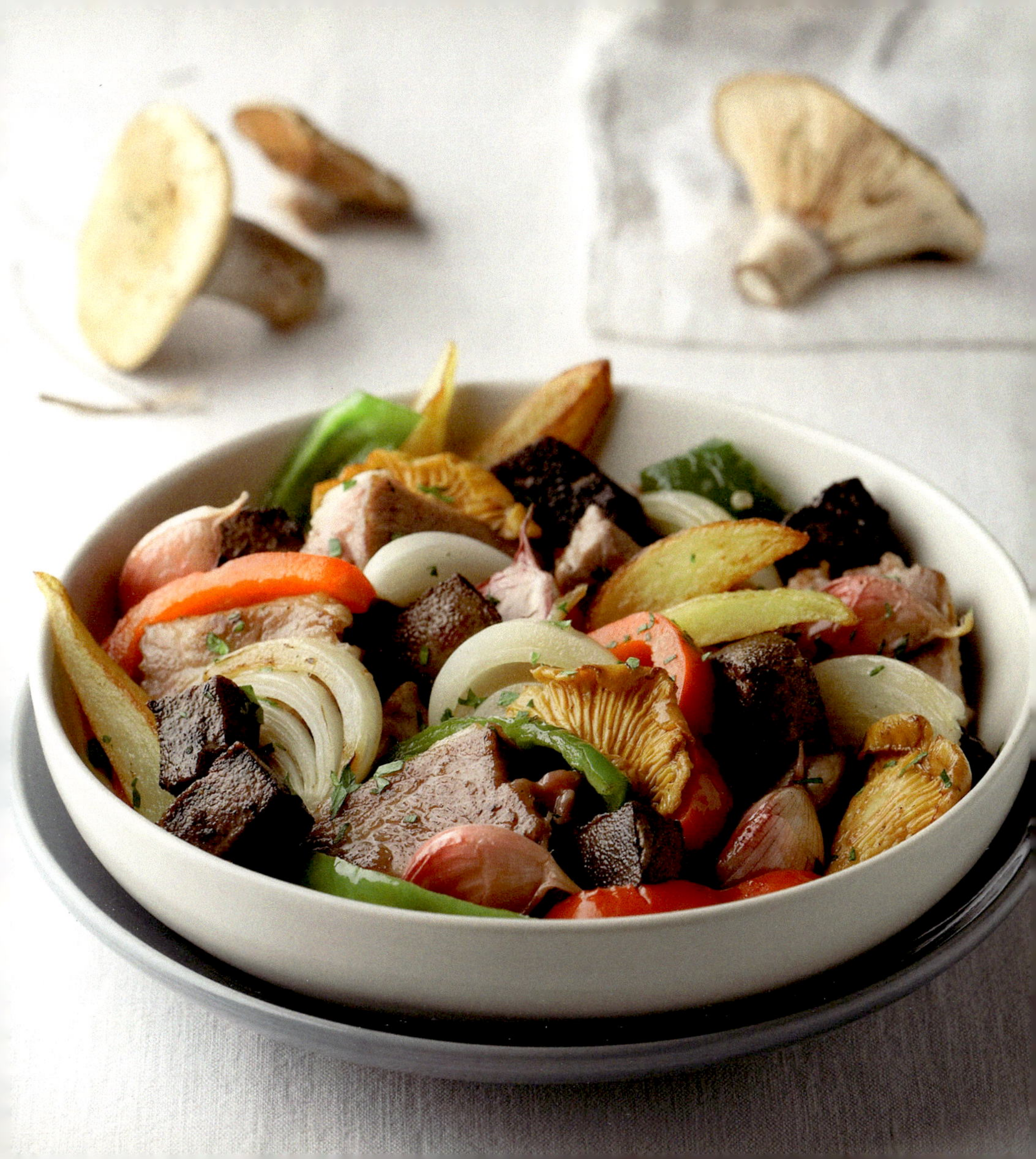

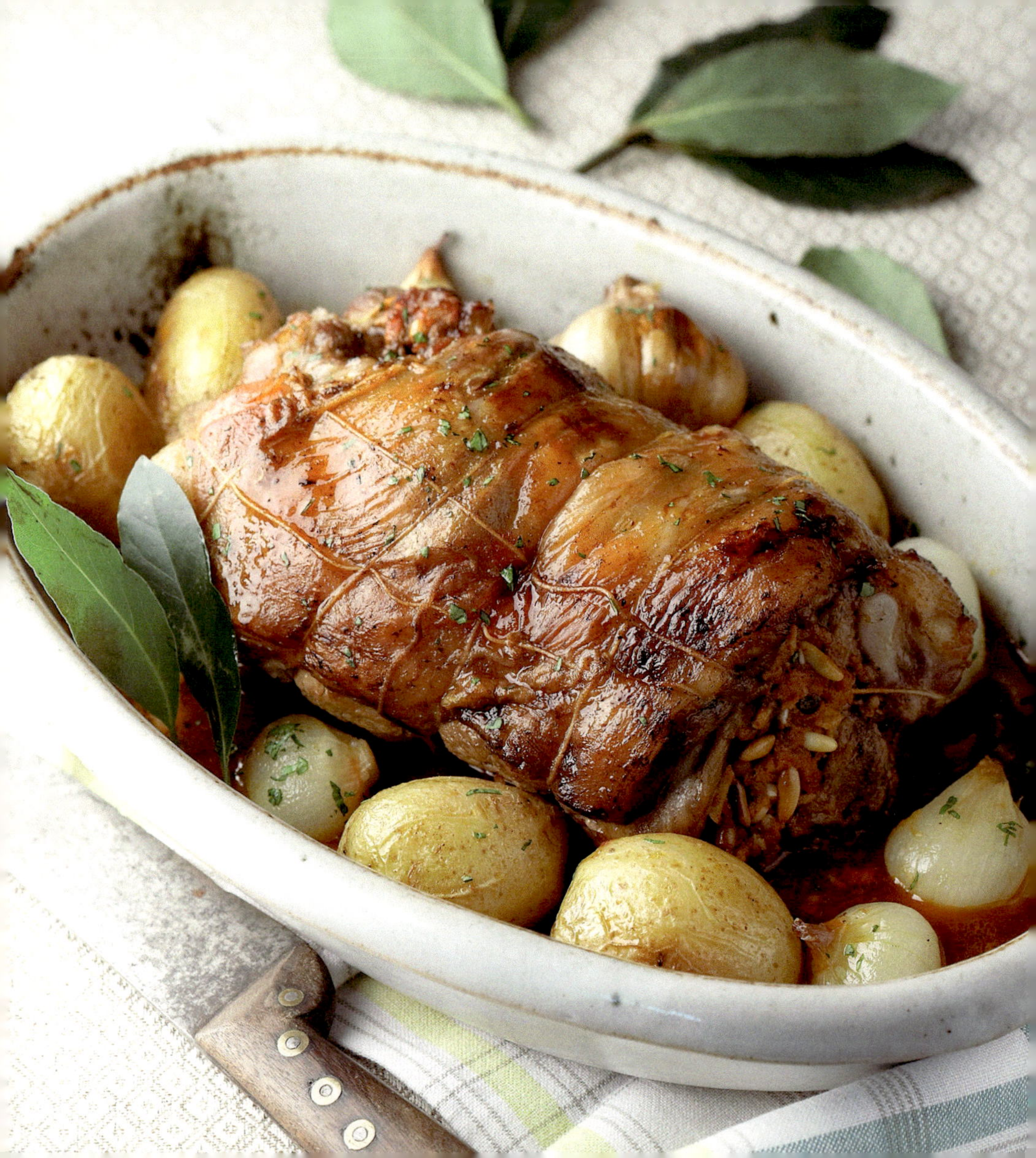

Cuixa de moltó farcida
Stuffed leg of lamb

For 6 people

* 1 deboned leg of lamb * 100 g of minced pork * 40 g of *sobrassada* * 1 spoonful of pine nuts * 2 cloves of garlic * 1 spoonful of lard * 1 lemon * 100 g of streaky bacon * 8 small potatoes (*patató*) * 3 small onion *1 laurel leaf * 1 head of garlic * 1 glass of white wine * 1 small branch of fennel * 1 small branch of thyme * 1 small branch of marjorum (*moraduix*) * a pinch of nutmeg * pepper * salt

1. Spread the meat over a worktop, so that it is flat and open like a book. Add salt and pepper on the two sides and season with a splash of lemon juice and a pinch of nutmeg.
2. Peel and chop 2 cloves of garlic. Brown the pine nuts lightly in a non-stick pan until they begin to brown. Add salt and pepper to the minced pork and mix it with the pine nuts, *sobrassada* and chopped garlic. Spread this mixture over the meat and roll it up forming a small package. Tie it with cooking string so that it is well closed, spread it with lard and place it on a refractory dish. Pre-heat the oven at 200° C.
3. Peel the onions and cut them in half. Wash the potatoes and leave them with their skin if they are small. Cut the streaky bacon into strips. Wash, dry and chop the parsley.
4. Place the onions, potatoes, garlic head and strips of streaky bacon around the meat. Add salt and pepper to the accompaniment, adding the aromatic herbs and laurel, and pouring over the white wine and a splash of water.
5. Roast at 200° C for 1 hour, covering with silver paper and leaving to cool for 10 minutes outside the oven so that the interior juices of the meat are spread out. Sprinkle the roast with lots of fresh parsley and cut into slices when serving.

If you wish, you can cook it in a casserole: first brown the surface of the meat in oil and lard, add the meat and the accompaniment and pour on white wine and water. Calculate a cooking time of around 45 minutes on a low flame and with the casserole well closed.

Greixonera de moltó amb carxofes

Lamb stew with artichokes

For 4 people

* 500 g of leg of lamb * 40 g of *sobrassada* * 1 onion * 1 tomato * 1 kg of potatoes * 6 artichokes * 100 g of peas * 1 head of garlic * 1 small bunch of parsley * paprika * pepper * salt

1. Peel and chop the onion. Peel the potatoes and cut them into small squares. Peel and chop the tomato. Cut the leg of lamb into cubes of the same size. Clean the artichokes removing the stalks, the outer leaves and the central threads. Cut them into four. Wash, dry and chop the parsley.
2. Brown the cubes of meat in a ceramic casserole with 2 spoonfuls of oil. Remove them and sauté the chopped onion until it is transparent. Add the head of garlic whole and the chopped tomato. Cook for 4 more minutes and add the crumbled *sobrassada*. Add the meat again and add the artichokes and peas. Add salt and pepper, season with a pinch of paprika and cover with water.
3. Add the potatoes to the casserole and stir. Cook for 25 minutes until the potatoes are just done. Sprinkle with the chopped parsley before serving.

This recipe can be made with a less tender part of the lamb, increasing the cooking time. If you wish, you can add a small bunch of aromatic herbs: thyme, marjorum and laurel.
For a thicker sauce, add a mixture of fried almonds or biscuits and a clove of garlic a few minutes before the cooking time is over.

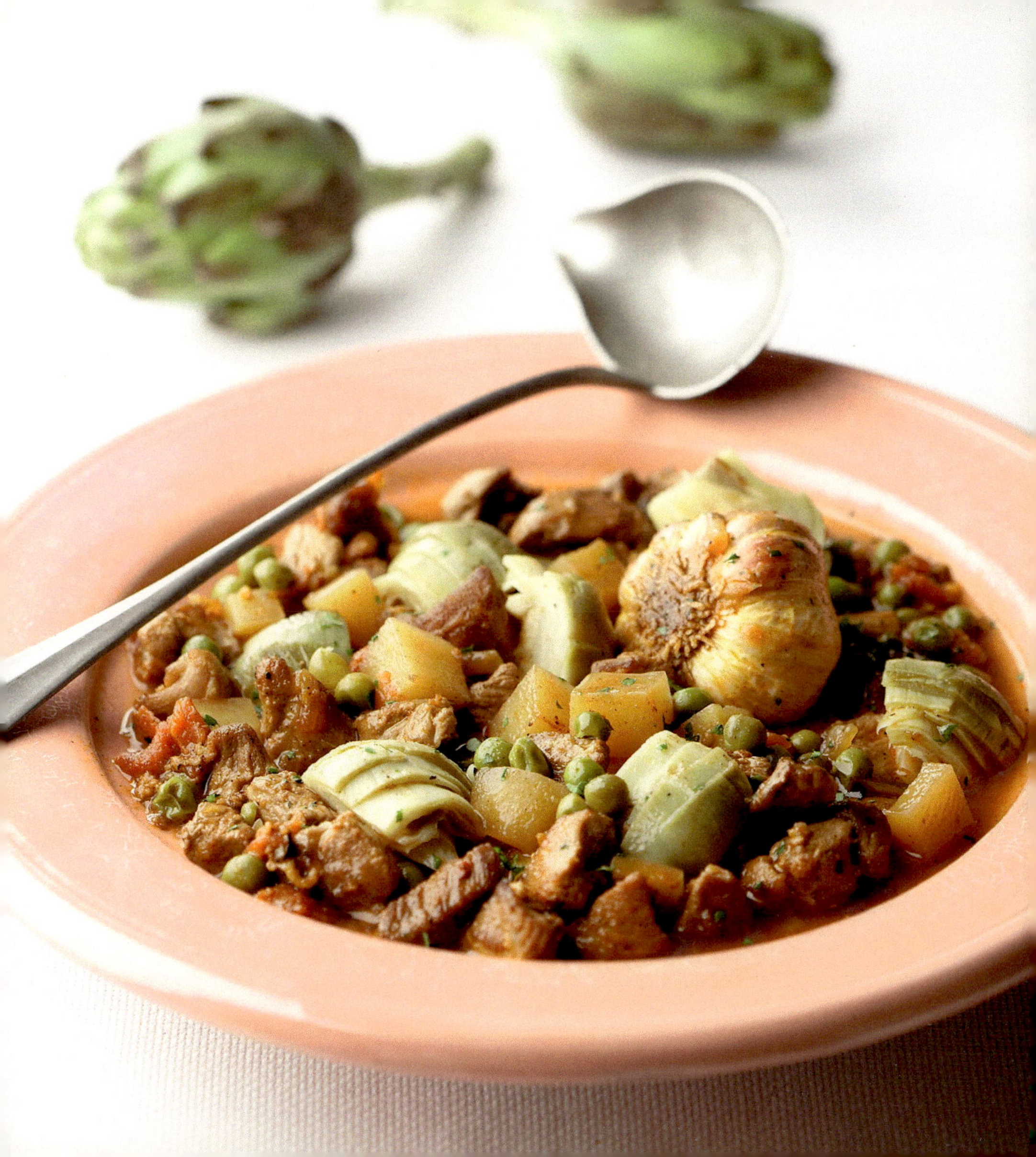

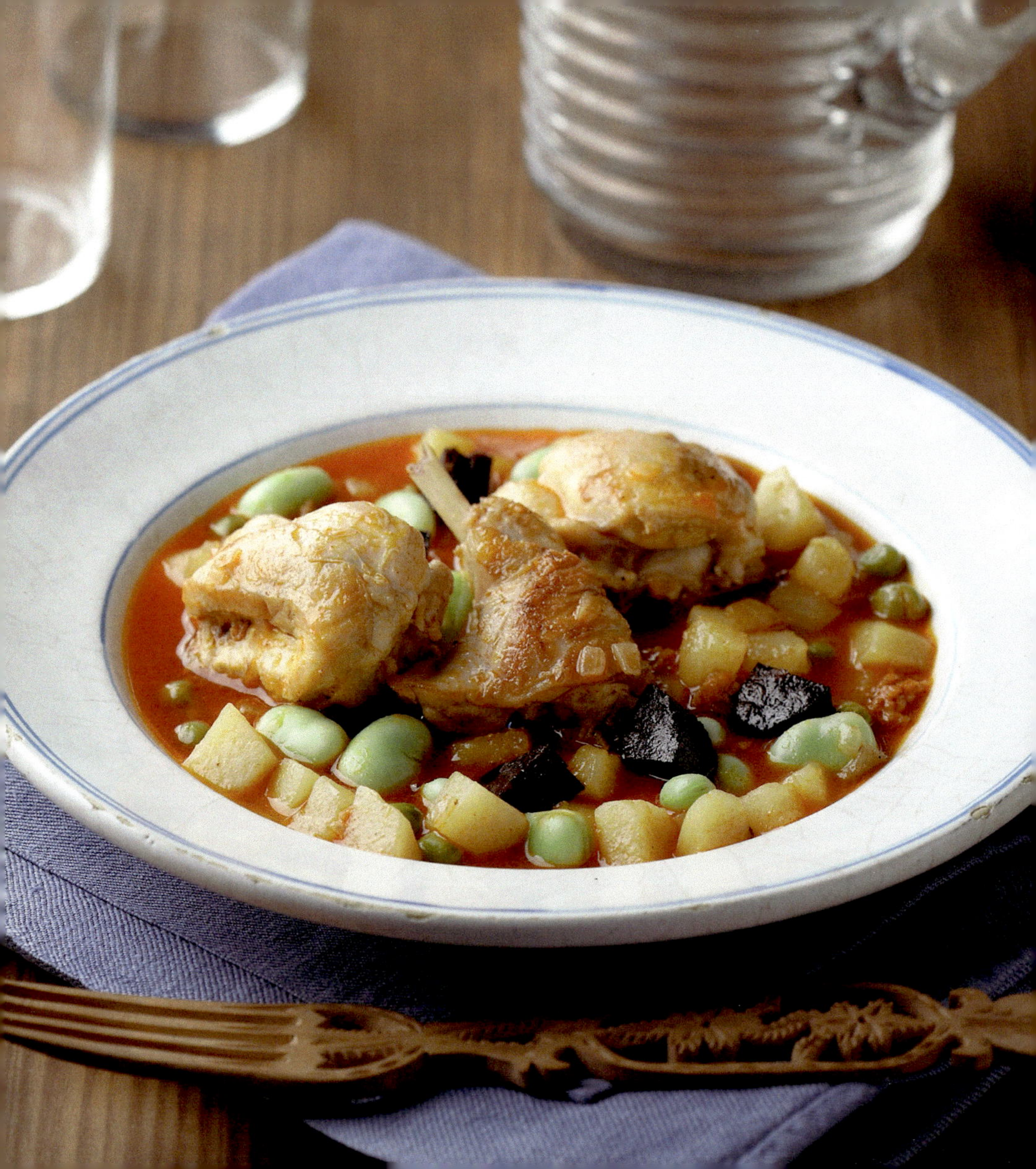

Coní amb pèsols
Rabbit with peas

For 4 people

* 1 rabbit * 50 g of *sobrassada* * 50 g of sausage * 100 g of peas * 50 g of young broad beans * 2 spring onions * 1 kg of potatoes * 1 laurel leaf * 1 small bunch of aromatic herbs: fennel, marjorum, thyme, etc. * 1 small bunch of parsley * 1/2 glass of matured wine or Jerez sherry * olive oil * a pinch of paprika * 1 clove * pepper * salt

1. Cut up the rabbit and leave it to macerate overnight with the matured wine (or sherry) and a pinch of pepper. Peel and chop the spring onions. Peel the potatoes and cut them into small squares. Shell the broad beans and peas if they are fresh. Cut the sausage into pieces the same size. Wash, dry and finely chop the parsley.
2. Remove the pieces of rabbit from the marinade and dry them carefully with absorbent paper. Heat two spoonfuls of oil in a ceramic casserole and brown the rabbit along with the pieces of sausage for 6 or 7 minutes. Add salt and pepper and place to one side.
3. In the same casserole, add two more spoonfuls of oil and sauté the chopped spring onion until it is transparent. Add the peas and the broad beans, add salt and pepper and season with a pinch of paprika and a clove.
4. Add the meats again to the casserole along with the *sobrassada*, the cubes of potato and the aromatic herbs. Cover with water and leave to cook on a low flame for 25 minutes. Remove from the stove and sprinkle with lots of chopped parsley before serving.

Lamb, game meat and poultry were usually left to marinate overnight with lemon juice, salt, pepper or matured wine. Moreover, it was a traditional practice to cover them with lettuce leaves so that they would be tenderer after cooking.

Perdius estofades
Stuffed partridges

For 4 people

* 4 partridges * 100 g of streaky bacon * 1 onion * 2 heads of garlic * 4 potatoes * 1 glass of matured wine or sherry * 1 small bunch of parsley * 1 laurel leaf * 1 small bunch of marjorum (*mo-raduix*) or oregano * a pinch of nutmeg * a pinch of cinnamon * 2 cloves * oil * pepper* salt

1. Peel and chop the onion and cloves of garlic finely. Wash the parsley, dry it with absorbent paper and chop it. Separate the partridges if they are big and salt and pepper them inside and out. Cut the streaky bacon into strips. Peel the potatoes and cut them in to small squares.
2. Heat 3 spoonfuls of oil in a casserole and brown the partridges for about 4 minutes on each side along with the streaky bacon. Remove everything from the casserole and, in the same oil, sauté the chopped onion until it is transparent.
3. Return the partridges and streaky bacon, add the chopped mixture of garlic and parsley and season with the nutmeg, cinnamon, cloves, laurel and aromatic herbs. Sauté for 2 minutes and pour in the matured wine (or sherry). Leave to reduce for a minute on a high flame and add 2 glasses of water or stock.
4. Add salt to taste, cover the casserole hermetically and leave to cook on a very low flame for approximately 35 minutes.
5. Fry the potatoes in a separate pan with a lot of hot oil. Drain them, add salt and pepper and add them to the stew. Cook them together for 5 more minutes and serve.

Partridges feature in other typical recipes of Ibiza cuisine. They are very popular served with cabbage (*perdius amb col*) or simply pickled.

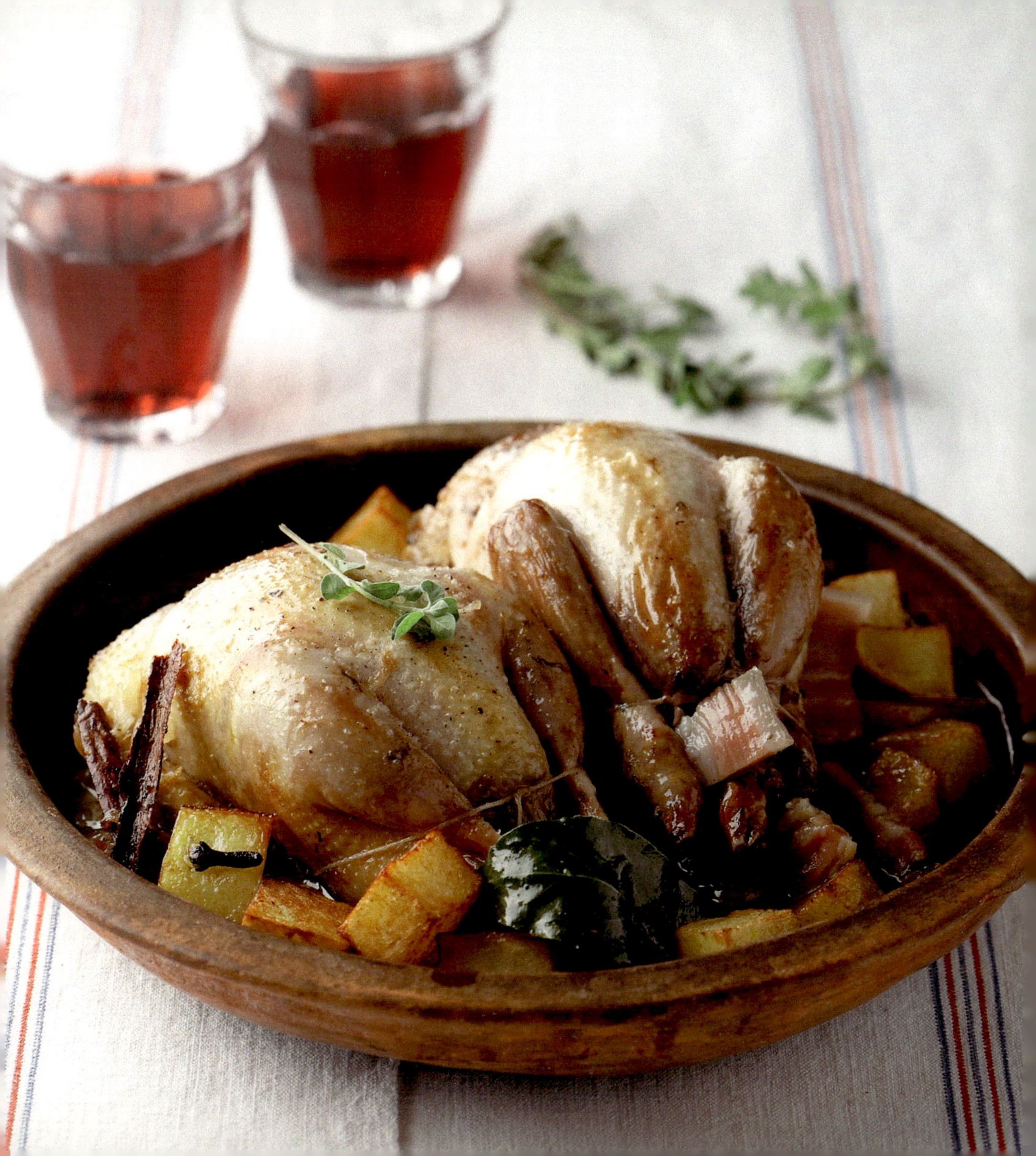

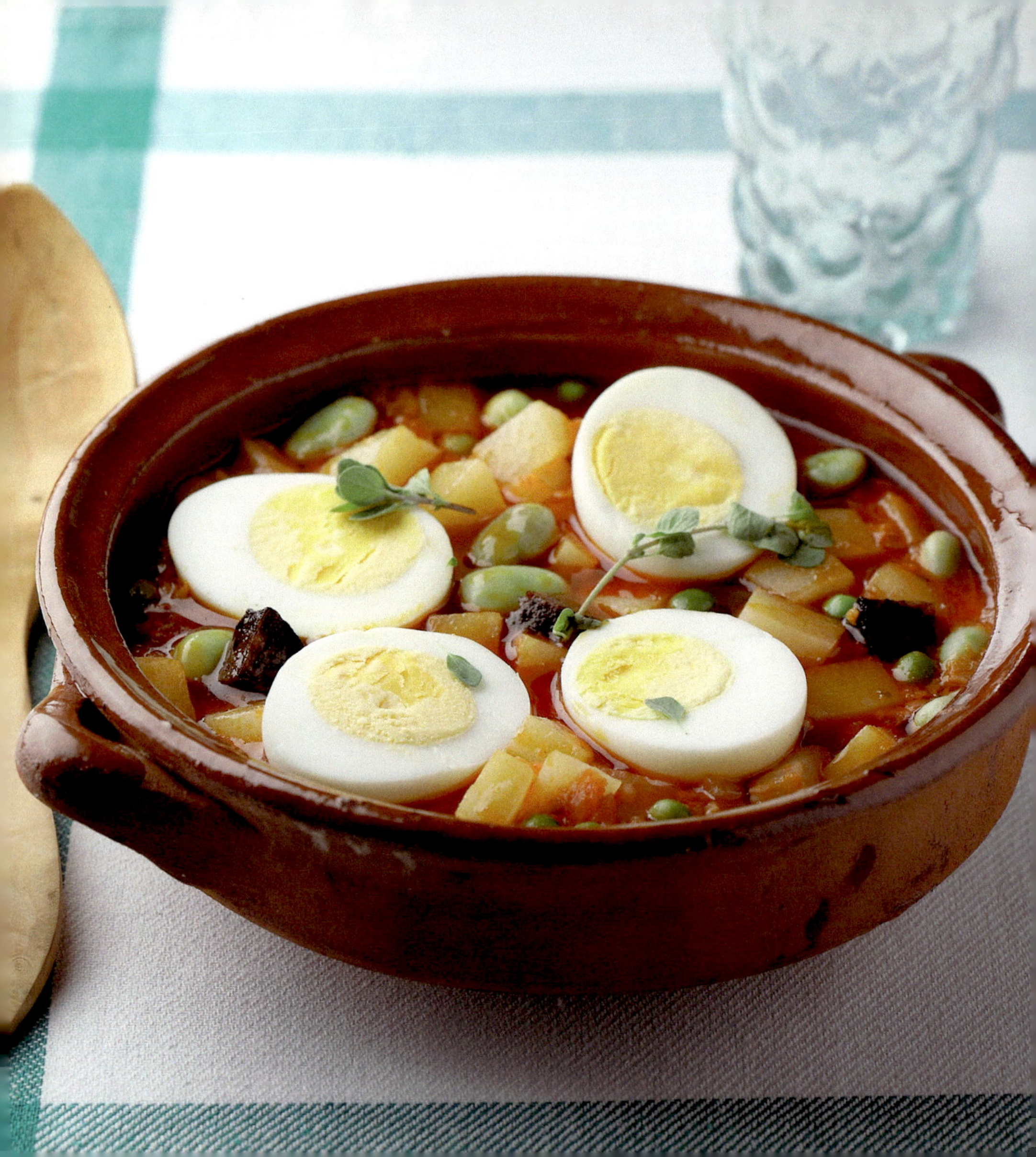

Guisat d'ous
Stewed eggs

For 4 people

* 4 eggs * 1 onion * 1 tomato * 150 g of sausage * 100 g of streaky bacon * 50 g of *sobrassada* * 4 potatoes * 50 g of young broad beans * 50 g of peas * a fistful of almonds or pine nuts * 1 small bunch of marjorum (*moraduix*) or oregano * olive oil

1. Peel the onion and chop it. Peel the potatoes and cut them into small squares. Cut the sausage into pieces the same size and the streaky bacon in strips.
2. Cook the eggs in a pot with boiling water for 10 minutes. Drain them, leave them to cool, peel them and cut them in half.
3. In another casserole with two spoonfuls of oil brown the sausage and the streaky bacon. When browned, add the chopped onion and sauté it all together for 5 more minutes, stirring continuously. Add the tomato cut into pieces and the *sobrassada*, and continue cooking 5 more minutes. Add the potatoes, broad beans and peas. Add salt and pepper and cover lightly with water. Leave to cook for 20 minutes on a very low flame.
4. Meanwhile, prepare a mixture in the mortar with the lightly toasted almonds (or pine nuts) and a few leaves of marjorum or oregano. Thin this mixture down with a little stock from the stew to obtain a type of sauce.
5. Add the hard-boiled eggs cut in half and the mortar sauce to the casserole. Add salt to taste and cook for 5 more minutes. Remove from the stove, leave to rest a few minutes and serve.

Eggs are a much-used resource in Ibiza's country cuisine in the most diverse preparations. Among them feature omelettes with all kinds of vegetables, the country omelette (with onion, peppers, tomatoes and potatoes), the *truitada* (a potato omelette with *sobrassada* and streaky bacon), the omelette with bread soaked in milk, fried eggs (seasoned with vinegar or chopped parsley), scrambled eggs or baked eggs with some slices of *sobrassada*.

Guisat de caragols
Stewed snails

For 4 people

* 1 kg of snails * 1 small bunch of aromatic herbs: fennel, mint, marjorum and fennel * 1 onion * 2 tomatoes * 2 cloves of garlic * 50 g of sausage * 75 g of streaky bacon * 50 g of *sobrassada* * 50 g of peas * 1 lettuce heart * 2 chilli peppers * 2 cloves * paprika * pepper * salt

For the spicy sauce: * a fistful of toasted almonds * 1 small bunch of parsley * 1 clove of garlic

1. Clean the snails well, washing them several times in water with salt and a splash of vinegar. Repeat the operation until the water passes through clean. Place them to cook in a pot with abundant water, salt, fennel, mint, marjorum and thyme. Cook them to start with on a very low flame and, when they have come out of their shells, increase the strength of the flame. Cook them for 45 minutes. Drain them and put them to one side.
2. Peel and chop the onion and the cloves of garlic. Cut the sausage into pieces the same size and the streaky bacon into strips. Wash the lettuce heart and cut finely au julienne. Wash the parsley, dry it and chop it finely.
3. In a casserole with two spoonfuls of oil lightly fry the streaky bacon and sausage until they are browned. Remove and put to one side. In the same oil, sauté the chopped onion until it is transparent. Add the chopped garlic and cook for 2 more minutes. Add the tomato cut into pieces and cook for 8 minutes, stirring continuously, to obtain a sauce.
4. Return the meats to the casserole, add the *sobrassada* and snails. Add salt and pepper and season with the chilli peppers, paprika and cloves. Add the lettuce au julienne and the peas, and cover with water. Leave to cook for 1 hour 30 minutes.
5. Prepare a spicy sauce mixture in a mortar with the toasted almonds and a clove of garlic, and add it to the casserole when there are 15 minutes of cooking time left.

The strength of the spiciness of this recipe can be altered adding or removing chilli peppers (*citrons*) to the fried sauce.

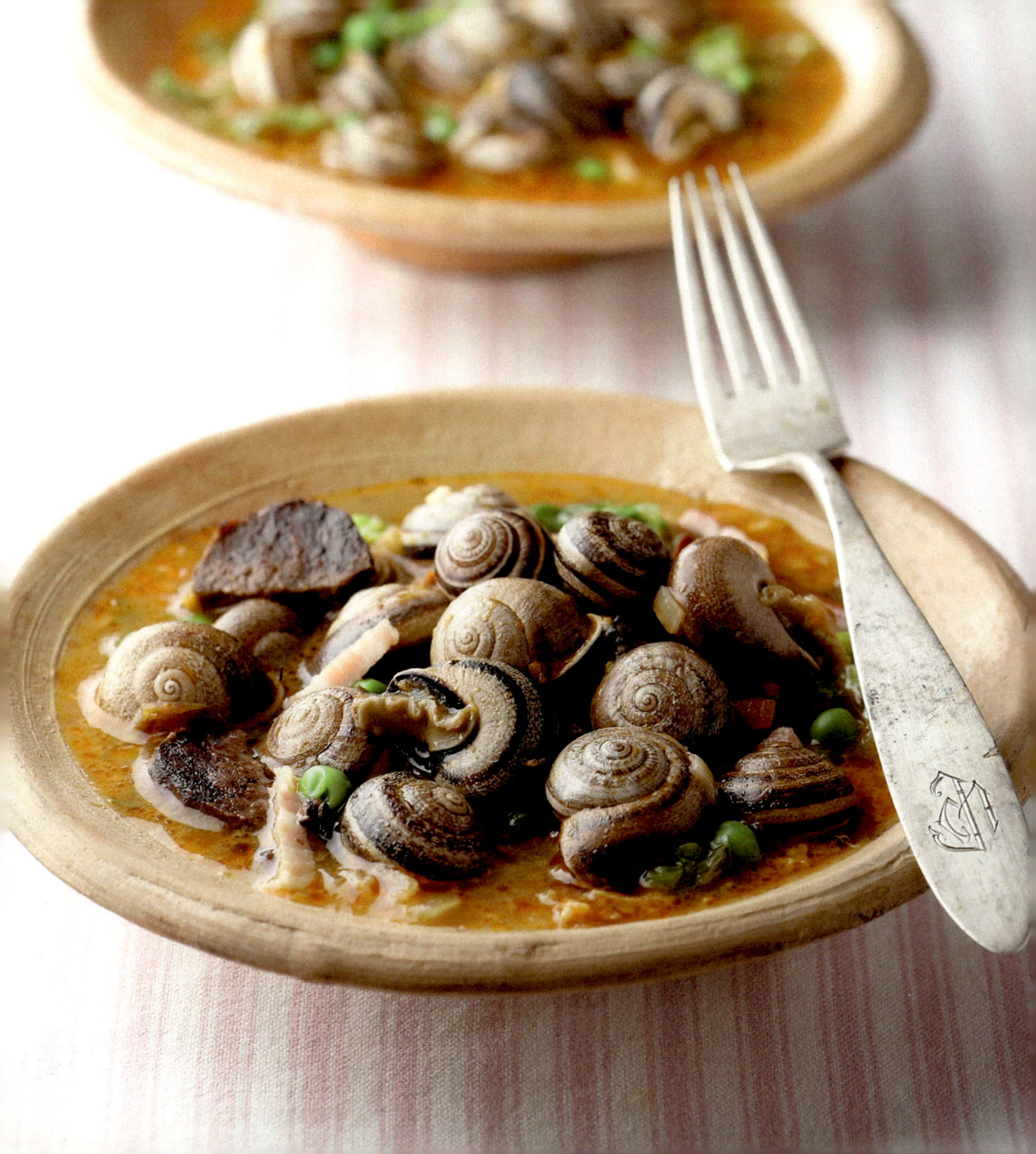

03

Dessert recipes

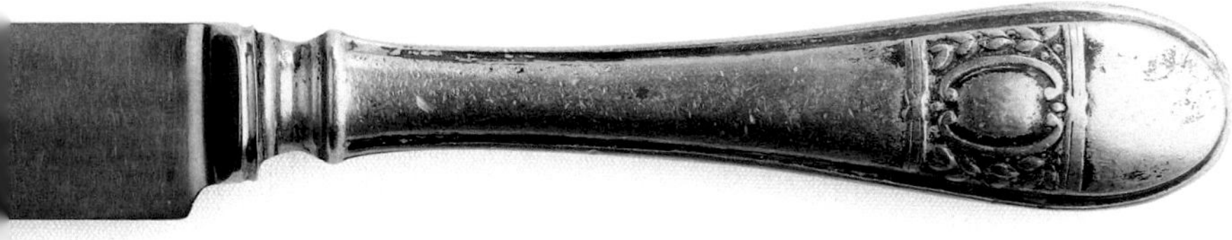

Flaó
Flaó

For 8 people

For the dough: * 350 g of flour * 1 glass of water * 3 spoonfuls of lard * 1 teaspoonful of aniseed * 1 teaspoonful of grated lemon

For the filling: * 400 g of fresh cheese or cottage cheese * 3 eggs * 200 g of sugar * 12 fresh mint leaves (*herba-sana*)

1. Place the flour in the form of a volcano and add the lard, grated lemon and aniseed. Knead until obtaining a consistent dough.
2. Spread the dough and line the base and walls of a lightly oiled detachable mould of some 22 cm diameter.
3. Chop the mint saving some leaves for decoration. Beat the eggs with the sugar. Crumble the cheese, add the mint and mix with the eggs until obtaining a uniform cream.
4. Fill the base of the cake with this cream, decorate the surface with the mint leaves and bake for 35 minutes at 180° C, until the surface is browned. Serve the *flaó* sprinkled with sugar.

There are many variants of this traditional tart of medieval origin. Some of these include aniseed seeds, sugar, eggs or oil in the dough of the base. In some cases the bottom is marked with a fork and the base baked prior to the rest for a few minutes.

Although today it is made all year round, traditionally the *flaó* was made at Easter, when eggs and fresh cheese were more plentiful.

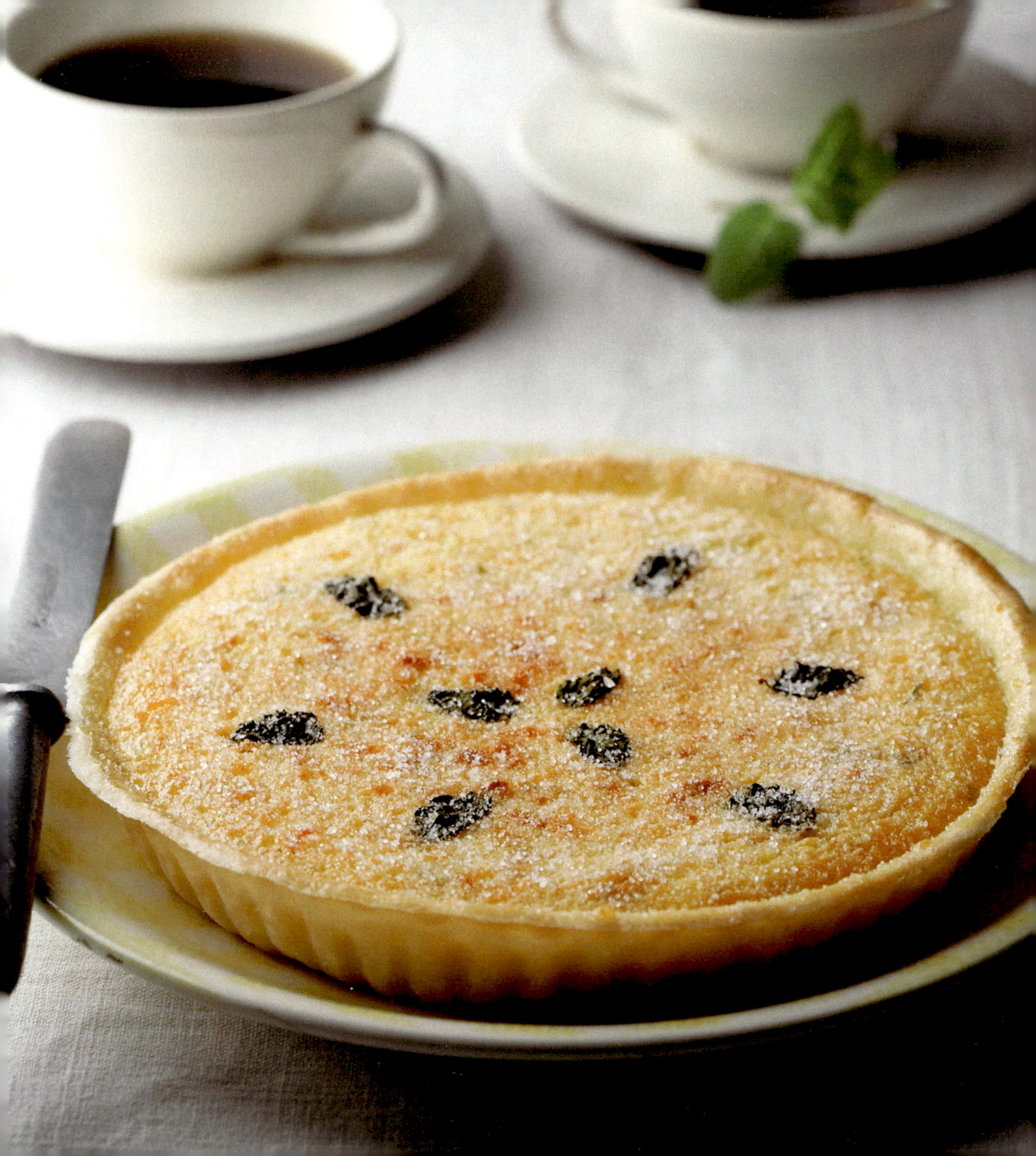

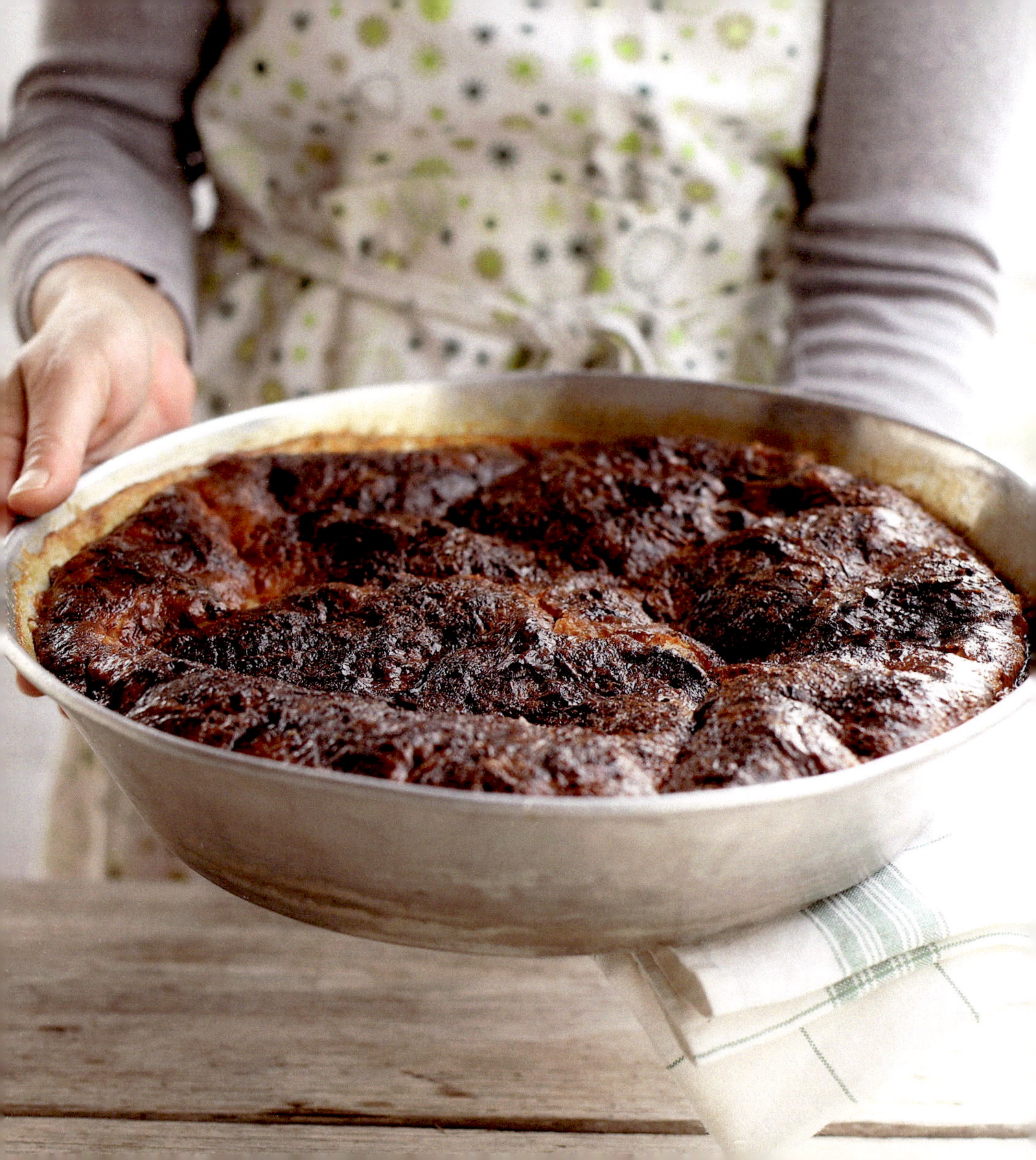

Greixonera
Greixonera

For 6 people

* 1 litre of milk * 6 *ensaïmades* pastries * 1 cinnamon stick * 1 lemon peel * 300 g of sugar * 1/2 glass of sweet aniseed * 8 eggs

1. Bring the milk to the boil with the lemon peel, sugar and cinnamon stick. Remove from the stove when it starts to boil up and leave to infuse covered, until it becomes tepid.
2. Remove the lemon peel and the cinnamon stick from the above preparation and mix it in a salad bowl with the beaten eggs, chopped *ensaïmades* and glass of aniseed.
3. Heat the sugar in a pan until it begins to form a caramel and pour it into the base of a lightly oiled ceramic casserole (*greixonera*). Pour the above mixture in and bake at 170° C for 45 minutes.

This popular recipe can also be used for other pastries such as croissants or simply for bread.
It can be served in the same casserole sprinkled, if you wish, with a mixture of sugar and ground cinnamon.

Macarrons de Sant Joan

Macaronis of *Sant Joan*

For 4 people

* 200 g of spiral pasta strips * 1 litre of milk * 1 cinnamon stick * 1 lemon peel * 2 spoonfuls of oil * 200 g of sugar * ground cinnamon

1. Bring the milk to the boil with the sugar, lemon peel and cinnamon stick in casserole. When the milk begins to rise, add the pasta strips and cook until they are just done and the liquid has thickened a little.
2. Leave to cool and serve the *macarrons* with the liquid in dessert bowls and sprinkled with ground cinnamon.

You can replace the milk with water or with a mixture of the two. If you wish, you can serve the macaronis with grated fresh cheese, sprinkled on top just before serving.
This recipe is typical of Formentera, where Saint John's night has always had a magical part associated with the festival and fertility.

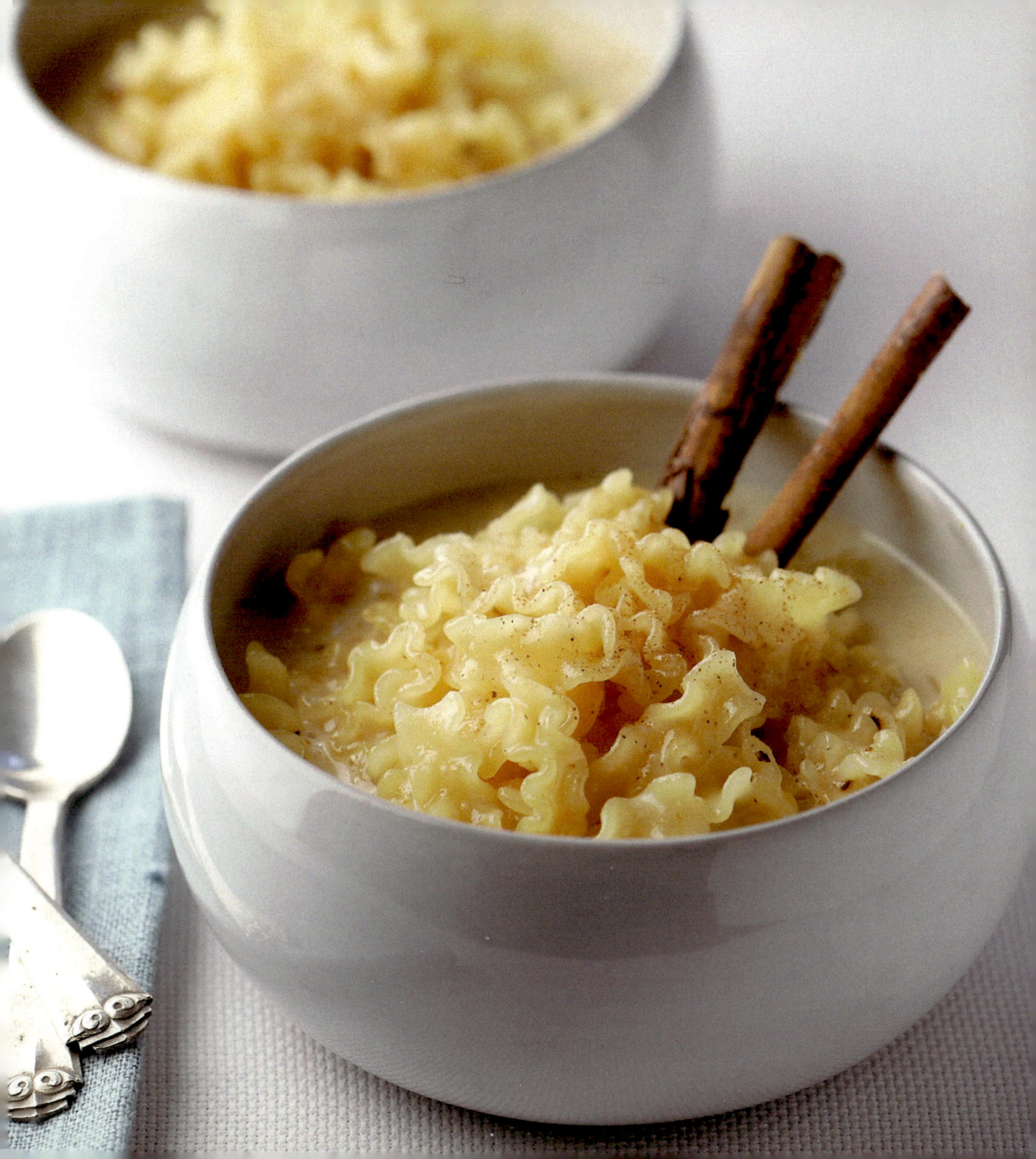

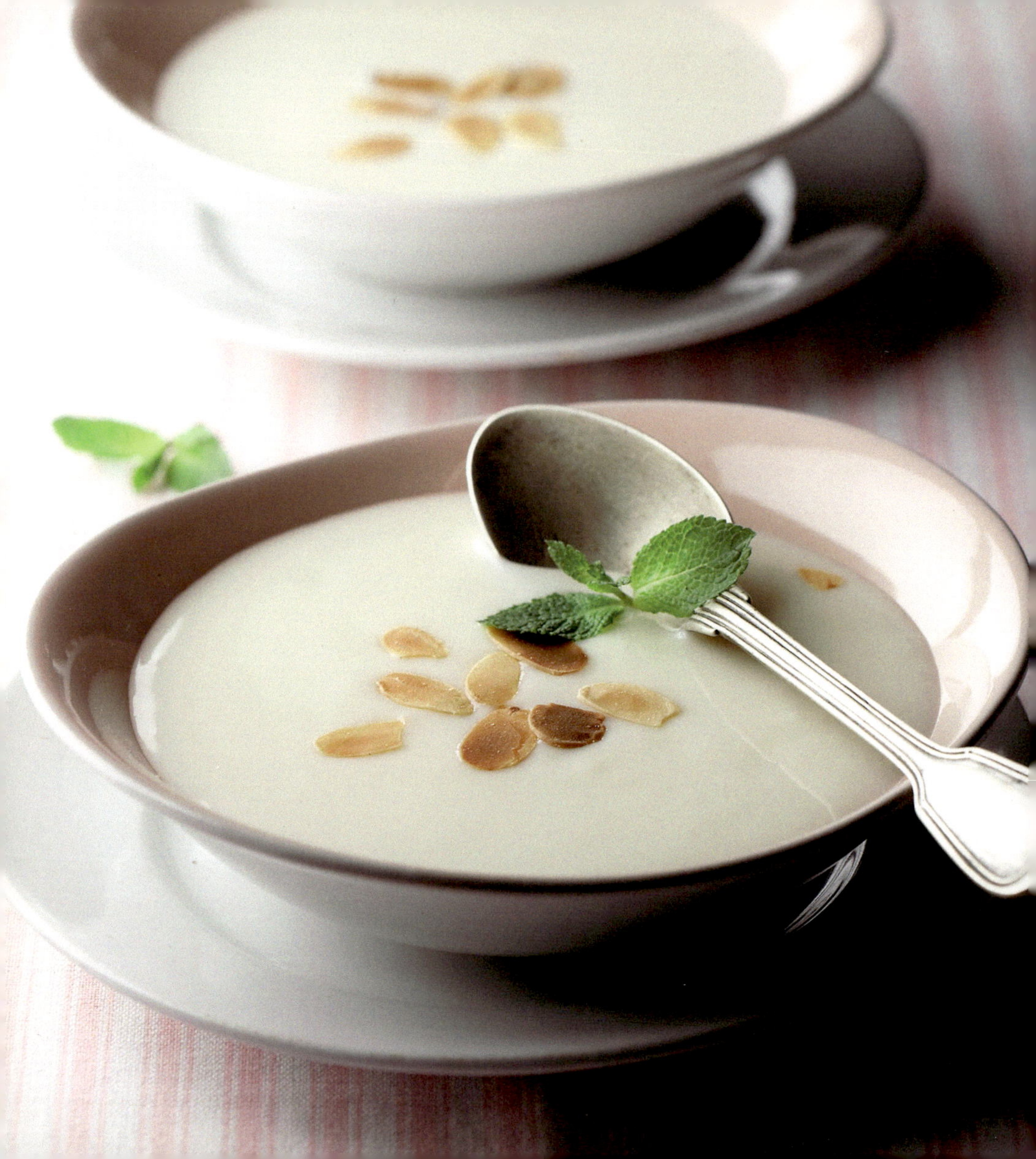

Menjar blanc
Menjar blanc

For 6 people

* 1 litre of milk * 50 g of cornflour * 20 g of potato starch * 8 drops of rose water * 1 egg yolk
* 50 g of sugar

1. Pour 5 cups of milk in a casserole and add the sugar. Bring to the boil and stir so that the sugar dissolves.
2. Mix the remaining cup of milk with the cornflour and starch. Add to the previous preparation, stir and cook the mixture on a low flame until it thickens, stirring continuously with a wooden spoon.
3. Remove the cream from the stove and add the previously beaten egg yolk. Lightly reheat on a very low flame, without letting it boil again. Remove from the stove.
4. Aromatise a bowl with the drops of rose water and pour the *menjar blanc* on top. Leave to cool and serve.

If you wish, you can serve it in individual bowls. For a different presentation you can set the cream with gelatine leaves. *Menjar blanc* is one of the oldest recipes of traditional Mediterranean cuisine and has many variants. Generally, it is made with almond milk thickened with starches. It can be aromatised with lemon peel and cinnamon.

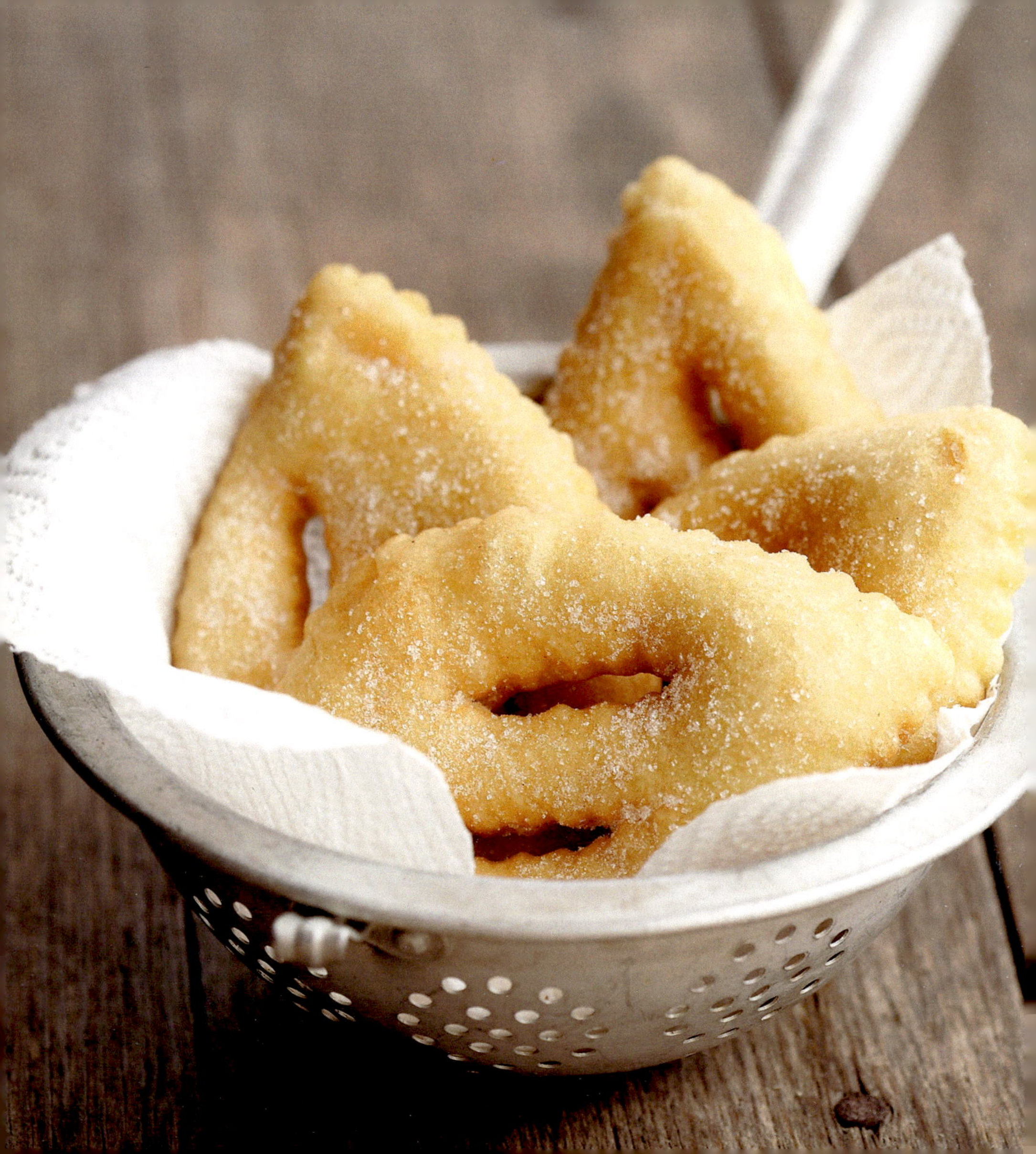

Orelletes
Orelletes

* 1/2 kg of flour * 150 g of sugar * 3 eggs * 1/2 cup of oil * 1 glass of aniseed * 1 spoonful of aniseed seeds * grated lemon peel * a pinch of salt * oil for frying * sugar for decorating

1. Beat the eggs with the sugar. Add the grated lemon, aniseed and aniseed seeds. Add the sieved flour and a pinch of salt, and work the mixture until achieving a consistent dough. Add a little more flour if the dough needs it.
2. Divide the dough into portions and roll it out flat on a worktop. Cut it with a toothed pastry cutter of some 15 cm diameter. With a smaller pastry cutter, cut small circles with the remaining dough. Cut them in half and place them over the *orelletes* to obtain the typical shape of an ear.
3. Heat a generous amount of olive oil in a pan and fry them in batches without letting them brown. Drain them on absorbent paper, coat them with sugar and leave them to cool.

There are many variants on this recipe, very popular in the Balearic Islands and other parts of the peninsula. In many cases the oil is replaced by lard, or the grated lemon by grated orange. Some add powdered yeast and let them rest so that they swell up when fried.
The *orelletes* from Sant Jordi de ses Salines are particularly popular.

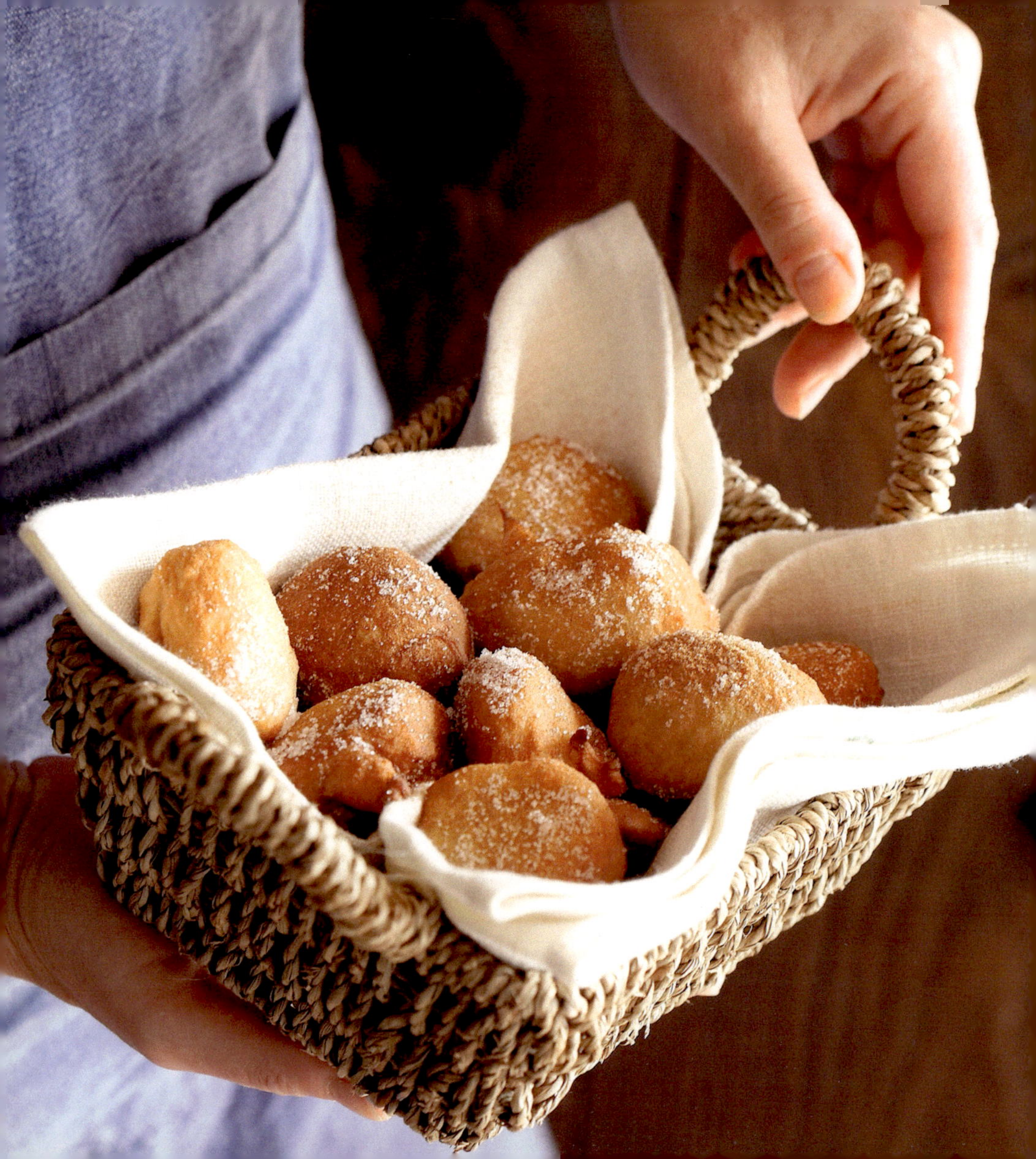

Pensats i fets de Formentera

Pensats i fets of Formentera

* 200 g of flour * 1 egg * 3 cups of milk * 50 g of sugar * a pinch of cinnamon * olive oil * sugar for decorating

1. Prepare a uniform dough beating the eggs with the sugar, milk and flour. Add a pinch of cinnamon and mix until everything is well mixed together.
2. Heat a generous amount of oil in a deep pan and fry the dough letting it drop in spoonfuls. Turn then over so that they are browned on both sides.
3. Drain the fritters on absorbent paper and though still hot coat them with sugar and a pinch of ground cinnamon. Leave them to cool before serving.

The traditional cuisine of Formentera is similar to that of Ibiza, with a total reliance on autochthonous products.
These fritters are very popular in festivals and family celebrations. They can be enriched with orange juice, mashed potato and other spices.

Salsa de Nadal
Christmas sauce

For 5 litres of stock

* 1 kg of peeled and ground almonds * 6 eggs * 300 g of sugar * 1 cup of honey * 1 teaspoonful of ground cinnamon * 2 cloves * salt

For the stock: * 500 g of chicken * 500 g of boiling chicken * a pinch of pepper * 8 threads of saffron * salt

1. Mix the ground almond with the eggs until obtaining a uniform mass.
2. Place all the ingredients of the stock in a large pot, cover with water, season with salt and boil for 50 minutes until obtaining 5 litres of tasty stock. Strain the stock through a colander or a fine canvas.
3. In a large casserole mix the stock with the almond mass and break it up with your fingers until it is all dissolved. Add the sugar, honey, cinnamon and cloves. Turn the stove on again and cook very slowly, stirring continuously, for one hour.
4. Serve the sauce nice and hot in mugs with pieces of *bescuit pagès*.

It is the typical Christmas dessert. A large amount of sauce is usually made so that it will last all over Christmas, and is brought to the boil every 3 or 4 days to avoid it going off.
The meats from the stock would be used traditionally to make the *sofrit pagès*.
In some cases, suckling pig, sausage and even *sobrassada* were also used to enrich the stock.
The custom is to clean the remains of the sauce in the cup with a little wine, which is then drunk.

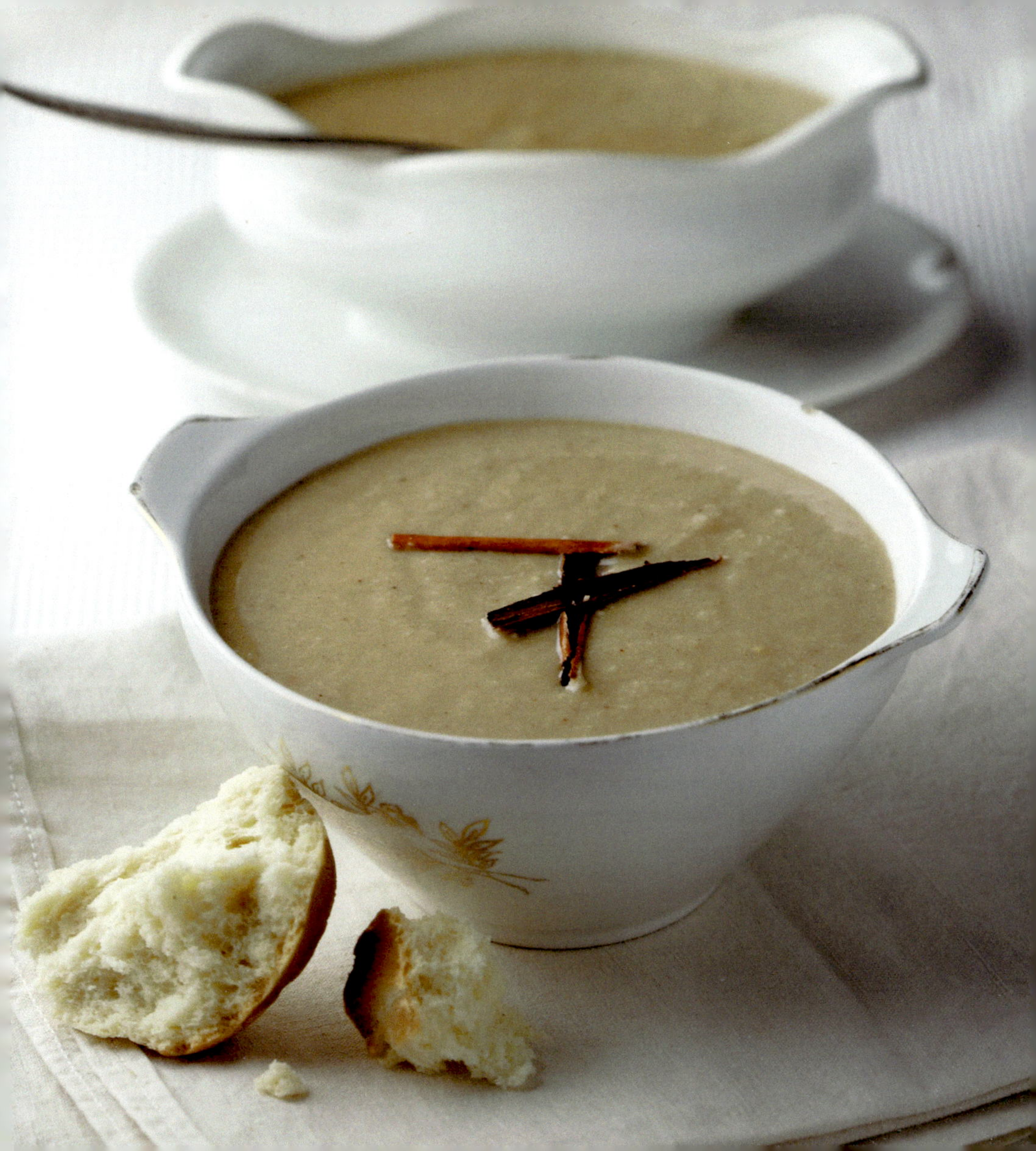

Bescuit pagès
Bescuit pagès

⁎ 500 g of flour ⁎ 250 ml of milk ⁎ one teaspoonful of aniseed seed ⁎ 1 small glass of aniseed ⁎ 100 g of lard ⁎ 2 eggs ⁎ 30 g of pressed yeast ⁎ 100 g of sugar ⁎ the peel from 1 lemon

1. Bring the milk to the boil with the lemon peel and the aniseed seeds. Remove from the stove when it starts to rise, cover and leave to cool.
2. Beat the eggs with the sugar until they change colour and have doubled their volume. Pour this mixture into a bowl (*llibrell*), add the sieved flour and small glass of aniseed and mix. Pre-heat the oven to 180° C.
3. When the milk has cooled, mix it with the yeast. Remove the lemon peel and add the milk to the previous preparation, carefully mixing until obtaining a uniform mass. Cover with a cloth and leave the mass to increase in volume for about 30 minutes.
4. Take portions of the mass and shape them into baguettes of bread of about 35 cm (*cócs*). Leave them to rest a few more minutes and bake at 180° C for 25-30 minutes. They can be serves sprinkled with aniseed and sugar to accompany the *salsa de Nadal*.

The *bescuit de pagès* is a kind of brioche or bread dough enriched with milk, lard and eggs that is made at Christmas for dipping into the irreplaceable *salsa de Nadal*.
Unlike in Ibiza, in Formentera they call them *cócs* to differentiate them from the *bescuits*, the bread baked twice which was used as provisions for sea crossings.

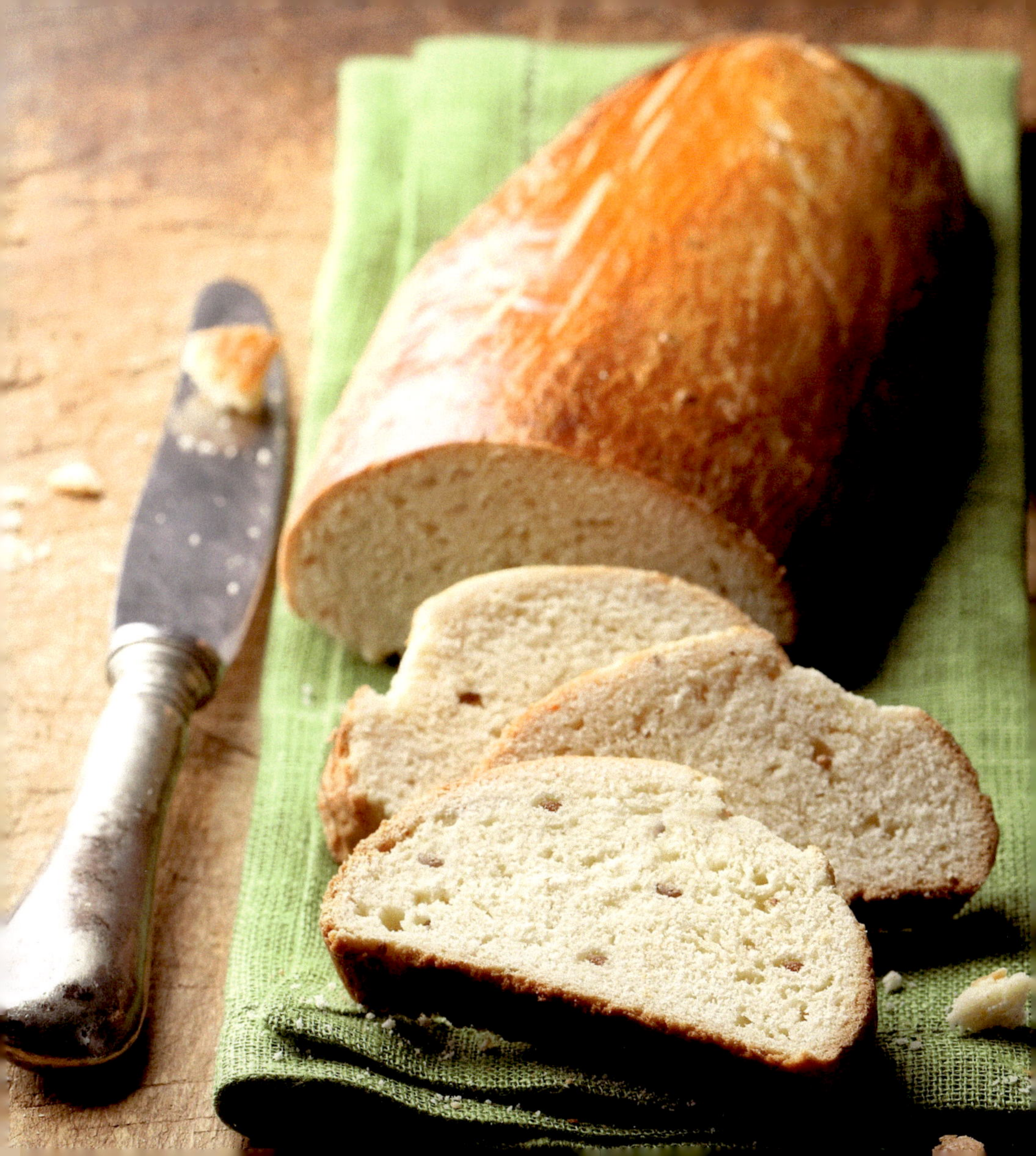

Glossary

Anfós. Grouper.

Aufàbia. Earthenware jar.

Bescuit. In Ibiza this is what they called the bread that was cooked twice so that it lost all its dampness and would last throughout the long sea crossings. It was given a squashed shape (*cócs*). The *bescuit de pagès* is a type of brioche that is made at Christmas to dip into the *salsa de Nadal*.

Botifarró. Cured meat made from pork, blood and spices.

Brossat. Cottage cheese.

Bullit. Stock or soup.

Burbaies. Popular way of referring to spiral strips of pasta.

Botifarra. Chopped pork sausage and generally mixed with blood and spices.

Canons. Popular term for macaronis.

Citrons. Small peppers or spicy chilli peppers.

Cócs. Bread rolls. In Formentera, this term is also used for the typical Christmas brioches.

Crostes. They are the pieces of dry bread (*bescuit*) that is used to make the *bòfegues* soups.

Flaó. Tart of medieval origin made from cottage cheese, eggs and chopped leaves of *herba-sana* (mint).

Freixura. Fried lamb's tripe.

Frita. Fried food.

Gató. Dogfish.

Gerret. Sardine. Very popular blue fish on the island.

Greixonera. Ceramic casserole dish. Many recipes are also called the same, both savoury and sweet, which are made in this type of recipient.

Guixes. Vetches.

Herba-sana. Mint.

Moltó. Lamb.

Moraduix. Marjorum.

Orelletes. Sweet fried pastry made from flour and eggs, generally aromatised with aniseed seeds, aniseed and grated lemon.

Palo. Typical liquor from the islands.

Patató. Small potatoes from the island.

Pebrassos. Mushroom from the *Lactarius* family. In English: milk mushrooms. In other places they are also called *escalatassangs* or *rovellons.*

Pinya de col. Cauliflower.

Porcella. Suckling pig.

Roja. Large-scaled scorpion fish.

Salpes. Giltheads. They were once a very popular fish, but today are rather disliked for the strong aroma of their belly section, due to their diet of algae.

Verdura. Campion. Wild edible plant (*Silene vulgaris*), autochthonous to the Mediterranean region. It is also called *restallones* or *gipsy grass*. Their flowers are popularly called "little rabbits".

Xulla. Bacon.

Bibliography

ARCHDUKE LOUIS SALVADOR OF AUSTRIA *Ibiza y Formentera (Las Baleares, Descritas por la palabra y el dibujo)*. J. J. de Olañeta, Editor. Third Edition. Palma, 2001.

CAPEL, J.C. *El banquete del mar*. R & B Ediciones. Donosti, 1995.

CASTELLÓ GUASCH, JOAN *Bon profit! El llibre de la cuina eivissenca*. Institut d'Estudis Eivissencs. Eivissa, 1993.

CATALÀ I ROCA, FRANCESC *Ibiza-Eivissa 1950*. Ediciones Gráficas Diseño. Ibiza, 2003.

CONSELLERIA D'AGRICULTURA I PESCA, GOVERN DE LES ILLES BALEARS *Les Illes a la Taula, I* and *II*. Palma, 2003.

CONSELL INSULAR D'EIVISSA I FORMENTERA *Enciclopèdia d'Eivissa i Formentera*. Vols. 1 to 10.

CONSELL INSULAR D'EIVISSA I FORMENTERA *La cuina d'Eivissa i Formentera*. Published by Mediterrània-Eivissa. Eivissa, 1991.

COSTA COSTA, MIQUEL *La cocina de Ibiza y Formentera*. Published by Mediterrània-Eivissa. 3rd edition. Ibiza. 2006.

DAVIDSON, A. *La cocina del Mar Mediterráneo*. Ed. Omega. Barcelona, 1996.

FÀBREGA, J. *El llibre de les herbes i les espècies*. Edicions de la Magrana. Barcelona, 1998.

FÀBREGA, J. *El llibre del peix*. Edicions de la Magrana. Barcelona, 1996.

FUNDACIÓ "SA NOSTRA", CAIXA BALEARS *Salines de les Balears*. Palma, 2005.

JUAN DE CORRAL, CATY *Cocina balear: Las cuatro estaciones*. Ed. Caja de Baleares "Sa Nostra", 1984.

JUAN DE CORRAL, CATY *Repostería balear*. Ed. Caja de Baleares "Sa Nostra", 1984.

LORMAN, JOSEP *Llibre de la Sal*. El Mundo-El Día de Baleares. Palma, 2001.

MILLO, L. *El libro del pescado*. R & B Ediciones. Donosti, 1982.

RIERA, F., OLIVER, J. TERRASSA, J. *Peixos de les Balears*. Conselleria d'Obres Públiques. Palma de Mallorca, 1995.

TORRES TORRES, M. *Antropologia d'Eivissa i Formentera*. Ed. Mediterrània-Eivissa. Eivissa, 1999.

TOUSSAINT-SAMAT, M. *Historia natural y moral de los alimentos*. Alianza Editorial. Madrid, 1991.

VALERO, VICENTE *Viajeros Contemporáneos. Ibiza, siglo XX*. Editorial Pre-Textos. Valencia, 2004.

Index of recipes

Acknowledgements

Eulària Marijuan, Toni Marí, Lluïsa, Guillermo (Sa Torre des Xebel·lins), Restaurant Els Pins, Joan Bonet (Sa Cova), Catalina (Cabrera), Catalina Riera, Jordi Peñaranda, Sandra Tarragó, Dani Redolat, Silvia Sánchez, Tia Maria, Joan, Daniel C. Witte (Sal de Ibiza), Joan (Moliner de la Mola), Joseph Maria Moreu, Juanito Riera, Ca n'Anneta, David (Peix sec Formentera), Cofradía de Pescadores de Formentera, Carlos Tur (Salinera Española), Companatge (ca'n Caus), Natalia Wilmanski (Atrezzo), Ana (Sargantana), Pura (Can Castelló).